Shooting a Revolution

Digital Barricades:
Interventions in Digital Culture and Politics

Series editors:
Professor Jodi Dean, Hobart and William Smith Colleges
Dr Joss Hands, Newcastle University
Professor Tim Jordan, University of Sussex

Also available:

Cyber-Proletariat:
Global Labour in the Digital Vortex
Nick Dyer-Witheford

Gadget Consciousness:
Collective Thought, Will and Action in the Age of Social Media
Joss Hands

Information Politics:
Liberation and Exploitation in the Digital Society
Tim Jordan

Unreal Objects:
Digital Materialities, Technoscientific Projects and Political Realities
Kate O'Riordan

Shooting a Revolution

Visual Media and Warfare in Syria

Donatella Della Ratta

First published 2018 by Pluto Press
345 Archway Road, London N6 5AA

www.plutobooks.com

Copyright © Donatella Della Ratta 2018

The right of Donatella Della Ratta to be identified as the author of this work
has been asserted by her in accordance with the Copyright, Designs and
Patents Act 1988.

British Library Cataloguing in Publication Data
A catalogue record for this book is available from the British Library

ISBN   978 0 7453 3715 9   Hardback
ISBN   978 0 7453 3714 2   Paperback
ISBN   978 1 7868 0186 9   PDF eBook
ISBN   978 1 7868 0211 8   Kindle eBook
ISBN   978 1 7868 0210 1   EPUB eBook

This book is printed on paper suitable for recycling and made from fully
managed and sustained forest sources. Logging, pulping and manufacturing
processes are expected to conform to the environmental standards of the
country of origin.

Every effort has been made to trace copyright holders and to obtain their
permission for the use of copyright material in this book. The publisher
apologises for any errors or omissions in this respect and would be grateful if
notified of any corrections that should be incorporated in future reprints or
editions.

Typeset by Stanford DTP Services, Northampton, England
Simultaneously printed in the United Kingdom and United States of America

Contents

List of Illustrations

Series Preface

Crisis and conflict open up opportunities for liberation. In the early twenty-first century, these moments are marked by struggles enacted over and across the boundaries of the virtual, the digital, the actual, and the real. Digital cultures and politics connect people even as they simultaneously place them under surveillance and allow their lives to be mined for advertising. This series aims to intervene in such cultural and political conjunctures. It will feature critical explorations of the new terrains and practices of resistance, producing critical and informed explorations of the possibilities for revolt and liberation.

Emerging research on digital cultures and politics investigates the effects of the widespread digitisation of increasing numbers of cultural objects, the new channels of communication swirling around us and the changing means of producing, remixing and distributing digital objects. This research tends to oscillate between agendas of hope, that make remarkable claims for increased participation, and agendas of fear, that assume expanded repression and commodification. To avoid the opposites of hope and fear, the books in this series aggregate around the idea of the barricade. As sources of enclosure as well as defences for liberated space, barricades are erected where struggles are fierce and the stakes are high. They are necessarily partisan divides, different politicizations and deployments of a common surface. In this sense, new media objects, their networked circuits and settings, as well as their material, informational, and biological carriers all act as digital barricades.

Jodi Dean, Joss Hands and Tim Jordan

Acknowledgements

This work sums up so many years of my personal and professional life that the list of people and networks to be thanked is a long one. Please bear with me, and my sincerest apologies if going back with my memory I have forgotten someone.

I wish to thank the University of Copenhagen, Professor Jakob Skovgaard-Petersen and colleagues and friends at TORS (Department of Cross-Cultural and Regional Studies) for the generous material and human support without which my PhD research on Syria would never ever have seen the light of day. I thank The Danish Institute in Damascus, its former director Hans Christian Korsholm Nielsen and his wife Sibba, its latest director Anders Hastrup, and all its staff. It was thanks to the Institute's welcoming atmosphere, to the people who lived and worked there, to the engaging discussions we used to have in the stunning courtyard of the most beautiful Damascene house, that it was possible for me to conduct part of the research that led to this book. It breaks my heart to think about it emptied of all of this, although I am told it has become a shelter for many internally displaced families in Syria.

I owe my appreciation to Ole Wæver and all the amazing researchers and staff at CRIC (Center for Resolution of International Conflicts), who, once Syria had become inaccessible to me, provided me with another shelter to think, discuss and develop my research further in the framework of my postdoctoral fellowship. I am grateful to Marwan M. Kraidy, Marina Krikorian and friends and colleagues at CARG (Center for Advanced Research in Global Communication) at The Annenberg School for Communication, where I've also had the chance, unfortunately too short for personal reasons, to spend a wonderful period as a Postdoctoral Fellow. My gratitude goes also to Lisa Wedeen and Michael C. Dawson at the University of Chicago for hosting me for a short fellowship at the Center for the Study of Race, Politics, and Culture, during which I had the chance to enjoy fruitful and passionate scholarly discussions.

There are no words to express how deep and life-changing my experience of working at Creative Commons has been. I met Joi Ito, at the time chairman of the organization, at a TV market in Cannes. I asked him how I might be involved in Creative Commons. He said: 'drop the champagne and join the community meetings'. Since that day, I have experienced unforgettable moments with the wonderful people working with the organization, from the headquarters in San Francisco to the wider community across the globe. It is because of Creative Commons that I have met the most wonderful Arab youths, women and men, techies, bloggers, activists, artists, educators, all passionate about sharing, all staunchly working to create a better future for the region. It is because of Creative Commons that I met Bassel Safadi, my beloved friend whom I have lost in the battle for knowledge, dignity and freedom. The memories I have shared with this fantastic human being, his crazy 'Fabricatorz' friend Jon Philips, and the Creative Commons' folks hanging out in the Middle East, travelling many kilometres by car, sometimes being stuck at shady borders and having to queue for hours while someone engaged in yoga exercises to avoid being overwhelmed by the local chaos, will always make me smile, despite what the Middle East has since become. I would like to express my infinite intellectual and professional gratitude to Joi Ito, and to Lawrence Lessig, the founder of Creative Commons, for having helped me gain insights into this global community of talented and inspiring human beings. But I would also like to thank them at a human level, as dear friends who have taught me important life lessons and constantly inspired me with their passion. This book offers a critical reflection on the values we have shared and believed in, which does not mean that these values were not genuine. The dark side of sharing and participatory cultures that Syria confronts us with should be taken as an incentive to push our reflection – and action – further, beyond the sad status quo that today's networks have set up and forced us into.

I can't forget the people who opened the doors of Syrian TV drama to me and helped me in pursuing my PhD studies. I am grateful to all the *musalsalat* workers – actors and actresses, directors, producers, advertisers, broadcasters, journalists, researchers – in Syria, and across the Arab region, who helped me navigate the complexity of this topic, granting me access to film locations, meeting rooms, parties, conferences and marketplaces. It is impossible to thank all of them but I want to remember here those I have bothered the most: Hassan Abbas, Najdat Anzour, Samer Baraqawi, Hikmet Daoud, Badih Fattouh, Laith Hajjo, Haytham Hakki, Fadi Ismail, Ibrahim al-Jabin, Khaled Khalifa, Adib Kheir (RIP), Iyad Krayem, Bassam and Mou'min al-Malla, Maher Mansour, Mohamed

Mansour, Najeeb Nseir, Ali Safar, Seif Eddine Sbei and Wafiq al-Zaiym (RIP).

I wish to thank the Syrian filmmakers Omar Amiralay (RIP), Nabil Maleh (RIP), Mohammad Malas and Osama Mohammed. And a new generation of Syrian filmmakers whose films have deeply inspired my scholarly reflection, particularly the work of: Ammar al-Beik, Sara Fattahi and Avo Kaprealian, the 'new wave' of Syria which I hope to see growing more and more. Thanks to Ali al-Atassi and his Bidayyat for giving a home to Syrian emerging talents in such troubled times. Thank you Orwa al-Mokdad: you have multiple talents, you are an amazing filmmaker and writer but, most of all, you are a dear friend, I will never forget our days at Aikilab with Bassel. Thank you Noura Ghazi Safadi: every time I see you I am humbled by your strength and passion for life, *habibti*.

I have great respect for the Syrian people who made me feel at home, opened the door of their culture to me, and shared with me their private lives, their concerns, their aspirations for the future. Thanks to Bernar, Nasser Dumairieh, Bassel A., Dahnun, Abed and all those I have lost track of because of the war. Thanks to Khaled Abdulwahed, Ziad Kalthoum, Zaher Omareen, Rafat al-Zakout and all those who have engaged with me in discussing their works. Thanks to those who have helped me and wish to stay anonymous. Some of them have lost their houses or jobs, some are in exile, others are in jail. I pay tribute to their courage and their humanity: thank you for the lessons you have taught me during these years, and that you still teach me every day.

Thanks to Enrico De Angelis, Mohamed Dibo, Yazan Badran, Katia al-Jbrail, Rula Ali, Waseem Hasan and all those who have worked with SyriaUntold over the years: I am proud to be part of a project that has managed to survive, after so many years and all the problems that have occurred, and happy that we are a family of humans, above all.

My scholarly work has been deeply enriched over the years by comments and feedback from, among many others, Kay Dickinson, Osama Esber, Malu Halasa, Marwan M. Kraidy, Anna Leander, Dina Matar, Thomas Poell, Philp Rizk, Naomi Sakr, Christa Salamandra, Jakob Skovgaard-Petersen, Rebecca Stein, Tiziana Terranova, Lisa Wedeen, Maxa Zoller; last but not least, David Weinberger and the greatly inspiring community at the Berkman Klein Center for Internet and Society at Harvard University. I owe a special thanks to Jodi Dean, who has thoroughly commented on this manuscript, and whose work has deeply inspired my reflection on the networks throughout the years.

This book would never have come to fruition without the passionate intellectual and friendly support of Geert Lovink. Our discussions via email, Skype and in greatly inspiring face to face meetings have not only provided me with theoretical insights to carry my work forward, but have also prevented me from descending into deep depression when friends were lost. Thanks for reminding me that hope should always be an aspiration, if not an inspiration.

Last but not least, I wish to thank all the 'families' who have surrounded me during the restless but amazingly enriching past years of travel: my Danish family (Helle, Anders, Albert, Jakob and Sille, Camilla, Marie S., Ole and Marie, Tia, Sune, Ehab, Lise, Charlotte, Michael and the IMS folks), my American family (Margo and Anthony, Alia, Hazami Hannah, Marwan, Nour, Omar, Lisa and Don, Osama and Maha, Khalil), my Italian family (my family of origin, my newly acquired academic family at John Cabot University in Rome, and all my friends, in particular Paola, Jonida, Marco S., Sara, Veronica, Gianluca C., Gianluca T., Alessia, Andrea, Laura, Kay, Francesca C., Maria G., Fouad, the 'Immagine Sparita' team, Chiara, and Clarita). Something which I cannot just express with a 'thank you' goes to Lorenzo, for loving me as I am. Without him, I could have never managed to sit down and write, and also, occasionally, smile, during the toughest days of the ongoing tragedy in Syria.

This book is dedicated to the loving memory of Mariapia Meloni, Bassel Safadi and Massimo Fichera, who have all left too early, too soon after the 'Spring'.

To the energy and passion of 2011. Nothing is lost, everything is transformed.

A Note on Transliteration

The transliteration method used in this study aims at combining accuracy with simplicity for those who have no knowledge of Arabic. It is primarily based on the system adopted by the *International Journal of Middle East Studies* (IJMES), except for those Arabic names that have widely recognized Anglicized variants, such as Gamal Abdel Nasser. Diacritical marks for long vowels and emphatic consonants have been omitted. Names of the people featured in this book (directors, actors, activists, etc.) appear according to the conventional way they present themselves, and not following the IJMES rules. The terrorist organization 'Islamic State of Iraq and the Levant' is referred to using its Arabic acronym in its Anglicized variant: 'Daesh'.

I wish to thank my friend Gennaro Gervasio from Università Roma Tre for his precious help in revising the Arabic transliteration.

Glossary

ana: I, first person pronoun

Daesh: Arabic acronym for 'al-Dawla al-islamiyya fi-'l-Iraq wal-Sham' (Islamic State of Iraq and the Levant, ISIL or ISIS)

fida'yyin (pl.): translated as 'freedom fighters' or 'guerrilla combatants', the term is widely used in the context of the Palestinian struggle against Israeli occupation

fitna: Quranic word evoking sectarian divisions

hara: neighbourhood

hurriyya: freedom

iftar: the first meal that breaks the fast after sunset during the Islamic month of Ramadan

karama: dignity

mujahid (sing.) *mujahidun/mujahidin* (pl.): fighter(s); widely used by terrorist groups such as Daesh to refer to their militants

mukhabarat: the Arabic term for 'intelligence agency' often has a negative connotation, hinting at a secret police that has absolute power and exercises arbitrary control over the life of citizens, regardless of the rule of law

musalsal (sing.) *musalsalat* (pl.): a TV series usually developed in 30 episodes of 30–45 minutes each

al-Qasr: the Palace, referring to Bashar al-Asad and his inner circle of seemingly reform-minded collaborators

shabbiha: an informal pro-regime militia made up of Alawites

sulta (sing.) *sultat* (pl.): power; here used mostly in its plural form to refer to the system of multiple, loosely connected powers that contribute to shaping Syria's regime

tanfis: literally 'letting off steam', referring here to a technique employed since Hafiz al-Asad's times, whereby seemingly progressive media and oppositional cultural production are used as tools for venting and conveying frustrations that might otherwise find a political expression

tanwir (noun) *tanwiri* (adj.): a process of enlightenment inspiring a modernist ideology of progress and development through mass education and edifying media products

al-watan: the nation, the homeland

wilayat (pl.): administrative provinces, here referring to the first-level administrative divisions through which Daesh is organized both on the ground and in its media units

Introduction

In Syria, every day, YouTubers film then die. Others kill then film.
(Osama Mohammed, co-director of *Ma'a al-fidda* ['Silvered Water: Syria's Self-Portrait'], 2014)

Never before has an age been so informed about itself, if being informed means having an image of objects that resembles them in a photographic sense … Never before has a period known so little about itself.
(Kracauer 2005: 58)

The shot opens with heavy shootings. We see buildings burning in the distance, smoke rising. More shootings, an ambulance siren, a live-chat message notification are all heard in the background. The camera moves slowly towards a group of armed men dressed in black, probably police or security forces. The male voice behind the camera screams 'peaceful, peaceful', while the sound of the shootings gets closer. 'No, no, I am peaceful, peaceful', the voice insists. More shootings. The camera shakes, yet the man does not leave or stop filming. 'The world must see!', he shouts. We hear another male voice in the background, worried, probably trying to get the man behind the camera out of there: 'Iyad, Iyad!' The man filming screams even louder, addressing the armed men: '*Shoot at me, shoot at me!* The world must see what is happening.'

This video was allegedly shot in Daraa, a city in southwestern Syria where a popular anti-regime uprising sparked in March 2011.[1] The anonymous filmer – Iyad? – embraces the camera to document the violence that unknown armed men are likely to inflict on his body, and no doubt on other disarmed bodies too. Yet the invisible man behind the camera would not move – like thousands of other anonymous citizens who have silently, fiercely, defiantly filmed the Syrian uprising. They would stand still, hiding behind the camera, shooting while being shot at, like in Iyad's video.

In March 2011 Syrian protesters found themselves in this unprecedented situation of being simultaneously victims and heroes. Victims, as they faced repression with bare hands, at the mercy of the armed killers' absolute will; heroes, as they bravely turned into first-person narrators of their own history, regaining agency through the self-documentation of the events they participated in, even when they took a violent, dangerous form. A defiant, extreme act of filming regardless, that pushed us as spectators to wonder why these anonymous filmers didn't throw their cameras on the floor and run away when facing death in the shape of a sniper, a militia man, or a police officer. Such a gesture should not be dismissed as the psychotic, narcissistic behaviour of few isolated individuals, but rather understood as a collective endeavour with a large-scale dimension.

The act of filming has become so inherently connected to Syria's post-2011 everyday life that it was appropriated by a wide spectrum of the country's citizenry, including its violent components. Security agents, armed groups, torturers, jihadis, all indifferently turned into image-makers, employing the camera to live-document their brutal acts, while also producing the most extreme and obscene forms of violence for the sake of the camera. Every day, everyone films and is filmed in Syria, a country where the visual form has been turned into a device to perform violence, and the quintessential tool to resist it.

The parallel, dramatically intertwined movements of *shooting* and *being shot at*, of filming and killing, of filming to kill and killing to film, lie at the core of this book. *Shooting* while *being shot at* is the gesture of capturing life events on camera while dying live in front of it and for the sake of it, so as to grant an extension to existence in the immortal form of witnessing and crystalizing the self in the historical document. Meanwhile, it is also the fascination for violence, the pursuit of an ideal visual form for its enactment on the ground. For *shooting* as in killing shares with *shooting* as in filming a concern for the aesthetic performance, a preoccupation with the (re)presentation of the act, a compulsive attraction to any visual format offering visibility to the violence, whether in the spontaneous form of shaky pixels generated in moments of anxiety and fear – like in Iyad's video – or in the orchestrated, cruel beauty of a static, surveillance-like shot properly fixed before the enactment of torture. Yet when filming disappears into everything and into the everydayness, becoming just another life activity among others, framing the question of the image around the aesthetic dichotomy between revolutionary, low-resolution, seemingly naive pixels and the self-declared objective form of 'caught-on-camera' torture videos risks diverting attention from the material conditions that allow these visual media to emerge, and from the power struggles they conceal.

Let us not be distracted, entrapped, mesmerized by the 'pixelated revolution'[2] or by the 'cinema of the murderer'.[3] For as Ernst Jünger noticed already in the aftermath of the First World War, the production of the visual in the context of warfare relates much more to labour than to a mere narration or aesthetic representation.[4] This is apparent, more than ever, in post-2011 Syria, where the parallel dynamics of *shooting* and *being shot at*, of filming and killing, of making images to preserve life and destroying life for the sake of the image, have invaded the domain of the ordinary and been converted into mundane forms of digital labour on networked communications technologies. The latter have added an unprecedented layer of complexity to the production of the visual and the violent in Syria, as the variety of immaterial labour – paid, unpaid, underpaid, volunteer – involved in generating, assembling and distributing content has fused with the plethora of material subjects – armed and peaceful, pro- and anti-regime, local, regional and international – engaged in the fight on the ground.

Never before in history have these dynamics of violence and visibility been so dramatically entangled, jointly captured and domesticated in the form of routine labour on the networks. Never before have forms of military conduct and forms of visual (re)presentation been equally rendered visible, shareable and 'likeable' for the sake of global circulation and consumption. Never before has the seemingly endless multiplication of media and its makers in the networked environment matched so astonishingly with the explosion and consequent disruption of subjects and meanings on the ground: a hyper-fragmentation of digital '*me*' versions of national belonging and identity that mixes up and confounds with the raw materiality of the armed conflict.

To be sure, reflecting on the material conditions in which visual media are generated as commodities in a time of conflict, and on the continuity between technologies of (re)presentation and mass mediation and the military apparatus of violence, is not new to the scholarship. Susan Sontag speculated on the inner violence concealed in the act of visual reproduction – conceived as an interference, an invasion – in the context of the Vietnam war.[5] Discussing the conflict in the 1990s in the former Yugoslavia, Thomas Keenan has hinted at the dimension of danger brought to surface by the sheer amount of visual production that emerged, generating confusion and a loss of authority, principles and meaning, causing inaction, indifference and indetermination as a result of 'the war of "live death"'.[6] In 1991, the Gulf War was so quintessentially mediated that it is hard for anyone to remember anything other than a pixelated screen with green missiles falling from the sky and hitting invisible targets, as in a video-game simulation – which led Baudrillard to state provocatively that the war never took place.[7] Conversely, the 2003 invasion of Iraq carried the highest degree of visuality, materializing the alleged triumph of the neo-colonial power in the iconic image of a US marine covering Saddam Hussein's statue with the American flag, or in the (in)famous imperial spectacles offered by the Abu Ghraib pictures, where orientalized bodies were co-opted into the rawest and most organic forms of violence, including sodomy and sexual abuse.[8]

Yet those conflicts – and the scholarly reflections they inspired – all lacked a networked dimension, since the participatory aspect[9] became a wide-scale popular feature of communications technologies only post-2003, after social networking platforms such as Facebook, Twitter and YouTube had been launched. In contrast, the non-violent Syrian uprising that turned into an armed conflict was born digital and networked from the very moment an unarmed activist used a smartphone camera to *shoot* while an armed man raised his gun to *shoot at him*. Suddenly, the performance of violence had become visible, shareable, reproducible, remixable, likeable.

This book maintains that is no longer possible to approach the question of image-making (*shooting*) or the question of violence (*being shot at*) in Syria – and more generally in contemporary warfare – without taking into consideration the technological and human infrastructure of the networked environment, where the 'visuality'[10] of the conflict gets produced and reproduced as labour. Syria is the first fully developed networked battleground in which the technological infrastructure supporting practices of uploading, sharing and remixing, together with the human network of individuals engaged in those practices, have become dramatically implicated in the production and reproduction of violence. The entanglement of visual regimes of representation and modes of media production with warfare and modes of destruction has exploited and prospered from the participatory dimension of networked communications technologies. The networks have granted the utmost visibility and shareability to the most extreme violence, finally merging the physical annihilation of places with their endless online regeneration, producing a sort of *onlife* which gets renewed every time content is manipulated, re-uploaded, re-posted and shared, as meanings are combined and recombined in different, clashing versions.

I call this process 'expansion'.[11] Expansion brings to the surface the dark side of peer-production, sharing economies, remixing and participation, suggesting that these networked practices, as well as enabling creativity and self-empowerment, can also multiply terror and fear. Expansion hints at the participatory dimension of violence that thrives on networked subjects who are both the anonymous, grassroots users celebrated by cultural convergence and remix cultures,[12] and the political and armed subjectivities active in the conflict – each probably overlapping with the other. The plethora of actors, local and international, military and civilian, peaceful and armed, involved in producing the conflict on the ground, is also the social workforce engaged (and exploited) in its reproduction on the networks, with military factions ultimately rendered into multiple forms of digital labour, and vice versa.

The explosion of personalized '*me*' media, enabled by platforms deemed quintessentially progressive by techno-utopias and digital democracy frameworks, has been matched by an explosion of violence and the expansion of warfare. Everybody seems to claim a right to create and re-manipulate on the networks, as much as the freedom to conquer, occupy and destroy on the ground. Everybody is an active maker, an empowered subject, at the level of both creation and destruction, contributing to reproducing that very destruction for the sake of networked circulation. *If it's dead, it spreads* – so Syria's networked environment seems to tragically suggest, in a bitter remix of Henry Jenkins' famous motto.[13]

The counter-movement to this process of expansion, yet directly following from it, is the fragmentation of media – and, in parallel, of civil society. The latter has been even more disruptive in Syria as it emerged from a context where, for decades, the authoritarian power had carefully crafted messages aimed at providing citizens with a shared idea of national identity and belonging. At the core of this mediated process of nation-building was the popular form of *musalsalat* (TV series), used since Bashar al-Asad's seizure of power – by elite cultural producers employing what I call 'the whisper strategy'[14] – to engineer seemingly reformist content directed at educating the public on issues of gender, religion, political rights and citizenship. Networked communications technologies have contributed to disrupting and undoing these concepts constructed through TV drama, dispersing the elite-sanctioned idea of nationhood into a plethora of '*me*' versions of the country's identity and future which parallels, at a media level, the clashing (armed) subjectivities active in the making of conflict. However phony the once-shared idea of the nation was, it no longer exists in Syria, neither in the media nor on the ground.

As media production accelerates – with more remixes, more sharing platforms, and the accumulation of layers in a permanent mode of circulation – so does war also accelerate and degenerate, involving more actors and interests at local, regional and global levels, expanding in time and space with no end apparently in sight. The mediated mimics the military, and vice versa. In the networked environment, media messages circulate rather than communicate, embracing a status of 'constant emulsion':[15] a permanent, entropic, circular movement that dramatically mirrors the ceaseless bombings, sieges, chemical attacks and humanitarian crises that have unfolded in Syria since 2011. We are far from the abstract media spectacles offered to international publics during the 1991 Gulf conflict: the 'perfect' war, marked by a precise beginning and end, carefully orchestrated and performed for the sake of media (re) production and (re)presentation.

The Syrian conflict hints at a new mode of warfare and visibility marked by a sort of 'neverendingness', which is also a quintessential feature of the networked environment. The war is stretched in a multi-layered time continuum that appears endless, its space dimension exploding and expanding in a way that perfectly mimics networked processes lacking a centralized organization, a hierarchy or a sense of order. Syria no longer exists as a coherent geographical entity; at the time of writing the regime controls certain areas, while rebel factions, as well as the Kurdish YPG, oversee fragmented pockets of territory across the country. Meanwhile, Syria's space continuum has stretched and over-expanded in the virtual, global-embracing entity of Daesh's caliphate, which occasionally finds a material existence on the ground – as previously happened in Raqqa.

Regardless of its alleged physical elimination by the international anti-terrorism coalition force, the self-proclaimed 'Islamic State' remains alive and well in the networked environment. Daesh seems to have fully understood the nature of networked communications technologies, as it has succeeded in creating aesthetically compelling networked forms and formats of violence and, at the same time, novel ways of enacting violence on the ground for the sake of media reproducibility, peer-to-peer sharing and viral redistribution on the networks. Despite proprietary web 2.0

platforms and governments jointly engaging in policing Daesh-made media, the terrorist group has managed to resurrect itself in the domain of the open web, turning the internet pioneers' libertarian fantasies of openness and accessibility into nightmares about the viral redistribution of terror spectacles.

That's the tragedy of the digital commons. Paradoxically, and sadly, contemporary forms of networked terrorism have come to materialize the dreams of the 'commons' in their indifference to copyright and rejection of individual recognition, embodying the quintessential idea of collective ownership. 'The artist is absorbed, the madman in the street is absorbed and processed and incorporated ... Only the terrorist stands outside', Don DeLillo once wrote.[16] Today Daesh embodies the anonymous, grassroots, amateur, web 2.0 terrorist as '*auteur*'.[17]

Conversely, user-generated digital commons have dramatically evolved into commodities, as Syrian activists, who once filmed as a collective 'we',[18] now have to face the loss of control and ownership over their own creations. The keepers of the Syrian image are today's Silicon Valley corporate platforms who have set the legal framework for sharing and distributing over the networks, and who get the ultimate say on the circulation of Syrian visual production and on its definitive disappearance – as several cases of content removal on social networking sites have sadly demonstrated in recent years. Yet the image-keepers are also those activists who became image-makers during the outbreak of the uprising; with the unfolding of the armed conflict and the fading away of the revolutionary possibility, they have claimed back their authorship and ownership, recognizing that Syria's visual production has turned into a market good highly sought-after by international NGOs, journalists, TV networks, film festivals and the global art market.

In the routine labour of *shooting* and *being shot at*, this process of commodification, and the logics of exploitation it entails, have moved far beyond images to invest social beings who have become fully image-defined and image-determined. Contemporary Syria seems to have materialized Debord's prophecy of the 'spectacle' becoming 'a social relationship between people that is mediated by images'.[19] In the networked environment of hashtags and emojis, retweets, selfies, 'stories' and streaks, participants are hyper-mediated, eager to be circulated, re-posted, tagged and liked, even when death and violence are the content to be rendered into a form of spectacle now collaborative and peer-produced.[20]

The Syrian image is a quintessentially 'networked image'.²¹ In the non-stop sharing and manipulation over the networks, the production of the visual has moved away from the activists' original attempts to generate 'evidence-images'²² that would hold the regime accountable for the violence and the violations of human rights. Rather than meaning, circulation is in fact what creates value on the networks. Images either circulate or die. They have to be copied, downloaded, re-uploaded, manipulated, redistributed, no matter what information they carry. Those that are not distributed in the networked circuits of drive and affection are condemned to permanent extinction. The a-social, the anti-social, has to disappear from the networks.

This new form of 'sociality' of the image bluntly surfaces from Syria's rubble. It will likely remain a permanent, vital feature of conflicts to come, a curse of future networked forms of warfare – where 'networked' implies the mere circulation of data, regardless of meaning and *in spite of* it. Syria's networked images are not interested in bearing witness or conveying a truth value or a moral position. They no longer aim at representing, mirroring or interpreting the real. They *make* the real, a *new real*. They are affirmative and world-making, the offspring of remix and participatory cultures where everyone and anyone can create and manipulate meaning, spreading it quickly with a clever use of hashtags and other 'social' tools. Networked images distance themselves from fake news, as truthfulness or falseness no longer hold as values, parameters, or ways of assessing the visual.

This emerging mode of the visual is taking over the language of representation. Images become a process rather than a content: dynamic entities, moving around, ever changing, filled with a sort of ready-to-explode detonation energy. Disconnected from the thing represented, liberated from the slavery of representation, they are free to express all possibilities and to allow new connections to be made and unmade. In this endless combinatorial possibility, where their fascinating yet annihilating beauty lies, images have abandoned any preference, organization or order, and, ultimately, have given up on signification. Deleuze called this visual mode 'langue III',²³ seeing it rising in connection with television. Yet it is with networked communications technologies that it takes the most complete and perfect form.

In the process of making the image as something disconnected from the object, filtered of individual features in order to become common and reproducible, the individual is dried up, turned into 'the exhausted'.²⁴

Exhaustion is about combining all sets of variables and possibilities, playing with them, trying them out infinitely. It's the network logic of endless circulation, the fantasy of abundance offered by Instagram and Snapchat filters, the McLuhanian fascination for the media whatever it mediates. Make the image, then die. Shoot, then be shot. Syria, in its terrifying yet compelling enmeshment between violence and visibility across the networks, is Deleuze's 'exhausted'.

Syrian human beings are not spared the cruelty of this process that turns the visual and the violent into two inevitable components of contemporary networks. Willing or unwilling, victims or perpetrators, displaced or evacuated, Syrians are irremediably cogs in the labour chain granting 'vitality' to the image through its circulation.[25] The sociality of networked images not only invests their human makers, but actually expands them, multiplies them, dispersing them into a wider spectrum of entities all equally responsible in giving *onlife*. Algorithms, interfaces, bots, AIs and other non-human subjectivities have the same agency as their human counterparts – if not more – in making and keeping the networked image alive.

The parallel movements of *shooting*, whether as filming or as killing, dissolve meaning into a plethora of individual and fragmented forms and formats, mere occurrences of divided and hyper-mediated selves that do not have enough strength to embrace any consistent, political, social, collective shape, nor to propose any solution to the conflict. The latter seems caught in the same mechanism of unceasing circulation that defines its quintessential 'mediator', the networks. The conflict should never end, but only circulate, reaching peaks, stopping abruptly and then re-starting again, in the endless sequence of attacks, bombings, sieges, evacuations, displacements, starvations and deportations that we have all sadly become accustomed to. We are all condemned not only to watch this endless sequence, as we did with previous wars, but also to share it, remix it, hashtag and archive it, upload and download it, 'like' or attach an emoji to it.

The perpetual state of acceleration in which networked media find themselves, matching the escalation of the conflict and the proliferation of armed forces and political interests on the ground, is revelatory of dynamics that are not exclusive to Syria. More broadly, they mark the ways in which the enactment of violence has been structurally transformed in the presence of participatory media that make everything and everyone visible, archivable, likeable. Yet I do not wish Syria to be taken merely as an empirical case study employed to support a theory of violence and visibility in the age of the networks. It was, in fact, through living in Damascus for some years (2008–11), witnessing the March uprising unfolding, watching friends of different socio-economic and religious backgrounds becoming improvised image-makers, and seeing some of them sacrifice their comfortable lives for the revolutionary cause, that I started developing these theoretical questions. It is also thanks to my professional experience in the field of digital activism, both as Arab world community manager for Creative Commons and as co-founder of the web repository SyriaUntold, that I was able to place these reflections within the broader debate on networked communications technologies and political mobilization.

Fundamental to this discussion is Syria's pre-networked media environment, heavily characterized by the attunement between the makers of edgy, taboo-breaking television and Bashar al-Asad's idea of reformism. The president's rise to power in the early 2000s was marked by a parallel rise in popularity of Syrian TV drama, which was highly sought-after on the Pan Arab, Gulf-backed media market. Quite surprisingly at a first glance, these TV series openly discussed taboo issues such as religion, gender relations, government officials' abuse of power, and even corruption, in a country that had been under authoritarian rule for decades. This was, however, absolutely coherent with Bashar al-Asad's seemingly reformist project, launched when succeeding his father Hafiz with the promise of implementing reforms, on the condition that they followed a gradual process managed by enlightened minorities. Throughout the 2000s, al-Asad's regime and Syrian TV drama enjoyed their golden age, the country's political and cultural elites firmly aligned on an idea of *tanwir* (enlightenment) adapted to neoliberal times. *Tanwir* was conceived as a project to make the country progress and indoctrinate Syrian citizens on how to think about personal and civic freedoms, so as to shelve political reforms in favour of social and market-oriented ones.

The book photographs these two key moments in Syria's contemporary history: the pre-networked environment profoundly marked by the TV drama industry, the *tanwir* ideology, the elective affinities between political and cultural elites; and the ongoing post-2011 phase, where this carefully engineered idea of nationhood and identity has crumbled following the collapse of meaning facilitated by the mutual interaction between a disruptive political event (the uprising turned armed conflict) and a disruptive medium (networked communications technologies), both in perpetual acceleration mode. To make this shift visible, the book offers a series of anecdotes collected first-hand during my fieldwork up to 2011, and then through ethnography conducted online or in neighbouring countries after Syria had become inaccessible to me.

A better word to describe these incipits, used to frame the main theoretical questions in each chapter, would be 'snapshots'. They portray: the filming of a TV fiction on rebellion at the very moment when people are demanding freedom on the ground (Chapter 1); watching the uprising unfolding in a Ramadan TV series (Chapter 2); attempting to make a documentary about the war and the refugee crisis (Chapter 3); witnessing a meme spreading in the streets of Damascus and on the virtual alleys of the web (Chapter 4); kick-starting digital activism in Syria (Chapter 5); rediscovering an archive of civil disobedience practices from 2011 (Chapter 6); comparing user-generated videos made by armed militants and peaceful protesters (Chapter 7); reflecting on a documentary film that will never see the light of day (Chapter 8).

Snapshots have two key features that capture the condition in which I find myself while trying to make sense of these fragments of lived experiences in book form. Firstly, they are casual photographs made typically by an amateur with a small handheld camera. An 'amateur' is someone who loves engaging in an activity for pleasure, rather than for professional reasons or financial benefits. The Syrians who committed to shooting as a life activity back to 2011 were amateurs, as are the anonymous users who gave a new push to creativity, and new meanings to meaning, through the practice of remix.[26] Amateurs are key characters in my account of the transformation of violence and warfare at the time of the networks.

Secondly, snapshots are impressions or views of something brief or transitory: a snapshot of life *back then*; in this case, back at the time when the revolutionary moment was still unfolding and full of promise, before being shot at and silenced. I do not wish to make predictions about Syria's future, or conduct geopolitical analyses of the latest developments in the Arab region. Rather, I offer these views from Syria's recent past as an entry into the present moment. How and why did we get to this point in Syria? How did we move from the over-celebrated 'Arab Spring', globally praised for the courage, dignity and resilience of its protesters, to the biggest humanitarian and refugee crisis of our time? How did the US and Europe shift from declaring Bashar al-Asad's regime illegitimate and unable to bring Syrians together, into forming a de facto alliance with him in order to fight Daesh as the most urgent international priority, finally endorsing the Syrian president's narrative of a country targeted by a foreign conspiracy and terrorist plots?

This is not a sanitized book on Syria. I have approached the country as a long-time analyst of Arabic-speaking media, and as an ethnographer who conducted several years of fieldwork exploring the connections between the local TV drama industry, the authoritarian power, and the wealthy Gulf market. At the same time, I undertake the difficult task of writing about a country which I deeply love and which is experiencing a moment of utmost distress, as an activist and a committed human being who has lived there and empathized with people whom I witnessed first-hand giving their lives to shape a courageous and peaceful protest movement. I do not wish to conceal the deep emotional bond that I feel regarding Syria and its people; indeed, it is precisely because of this bond that I have developed the theoretical reflections offered in this book into a broader discussion on the transformation of contemporary conflicts in the age of networked visual culture, while also, hopefully, helping to frame a more informed debate on the current situation in Syria.

In 2011 there was a peaceful uprising in Syria which was later dragged into a brutal proxy war. In 2017, at least a part of this conflict – the one named 'war against terrorism' – was officially declared ended. Daesh was removed from Palmyra and Raqqa, Aleppo was 'cleansed' of the rebels, and Bashar al-Asad, together with his Russian and Iranian allies, called it a day. Should we call this a victory and let it pass into history? At the time of writing, several areas of the country still lie in the hands of armed rebels of different factions; others, like al-Ghouta, are being subject to the most brutal starvation and extermination of their civilian population with the excuse of cleansing them of terrorism. Meanwhile, although Daesh has physically evacuated Raqqa, the capital of the so-called caliphate, its small-scale terror attacks are ongoing in Europe and the US, and videos are continuously released to feed the organization's propaganda machine, many of them featuring children and reminding us of the terror that will likely haunt future generations in unexpected and unpredictable forms. Syrians are displaced everywhere, both within the borders of the country, and scattered across the planet, mostly in Europe and the Middle East but also in Canada, South America and Asia. Syria's once vibrant, incredibly smart and talented youth – if not dead like my friend Bassel Safadi, who has been an inspirational source of this book, or imprisoned like thousands of disappeared people – now sit in refugee centres, waiting to sort out papers in order to be sent somewhere, someday, by somebody who probably knows very little of their story, language or culture. Many of these young people are depressed – a reaction to the exaltation generated by the glorious moment of change they seized on in 2011 and that seems now irremediably lost. Some have committed suicide. Others are resiliently building a new life, learning a language, making art and films, or starting a new business.

In offering these snapshots of Syria's recent past both as guides to the crucial turning points post-2011 and in order to illuminate and inspire future reflections, I wish to bring with me Antonio Gramsci's lesson: intellectual work should be grounded in a project that requires active political commitment, recognizing 'the ethical imperative to bear witness to collective suffering and to provide a referent for translating such a recognition into social engagement'.[27] The revolution has been *shot*, yet the *shooting* is not over, as history will write the final scene. Snapshots are antidotes to oblivion and violence because, ultimately, 'forgetting extermination is part of extermination'.[28]

SNAPSHOT #1

Tanwir is the ideology of development that has traditionally informed the relation between political and cultural elites in Syria. With Bashar al-Asad's rise to power at the beginning of the 2000s, the new president's seemingly reformist programme found its quintessential media form in *musalsalat*, with their aspiration to make society progress through thought-provoking content. Al-Asad's political project and the drama makers' cultural project converged on the *tanwir*-inspired belief that reforms should be both gradually implemented and carefully orchestrated by enlightened minorities.

Reformism took the shape of individually centred initiatives, replacing institutions with volatile, arbitrary endeavours connecting the reform-minded option to al-Asad and his indulgence as an 'enlightened' leader. Moving away from its modernist version, shaped around social commitment, and fully entering the neoliberal atmosphere, *tanwir*, which once served the goal of building the common good, was ultimately used to disrupt it and to strengthen the belief that reforms were to be implemented only if the president's political persona was preserved. Syrian TV drama makers fully embraced *tanwir* in its neoliberal version, and endorsed al-Asad's political plan by packaging ideas of freedom and citizenship in the commodity form of seemingly progressive *musalsalat*, failing to acknowledge the grassroots demands that emerged with the 15 March 2011 uprising, as the following story suggests.

1
Making Media, Making the Nation: Syria's *Tanwir* in Neoliberal Times

When freedom knocked at the door, and it was just a TV series

It was sometime in April 2011, a glorious Damascus spring morning. Not that I was fully aware of the warm jasmine-scented air wafting through the open window as I sat at home, huddled over my laptop, obsessively following my Twitter timeline and trying to make sense of what was going on in the country. I was concerned how events would affect friends and acquaintances, not to mention my PhD research into Syrian *musalsalat*, the highly popular 30-part TV drama series that traditionally entertained audiences throughout the Arab world during the holy month of Ramadan.

The phone rang. It was a well-known director and good friend. 'Come and celebrate!' 'Celebrate what?' I asked, hesitantly. For over a month, images of street demonstrations and other signs of protests in the poor, run-down outskirts of Damascus and in parts of rural Syria had spread across the internet and forced their way into the consciousness of those enjoying the frenzy of consumerism offered by the elegant cafés, gleaming shopping malls and boutique hotels of the residential areas and the city centre where I also used to live. The well-heeled denizens of central Damascus kept repeating their reassuring mantra: 'It won't last', 'it' being the unrest that had been shaking the suburbs of the capital and a few other cities since 15 March 2011, filling the streets with calls for 'freedom' (*hurriyya*) and 'dignity' (*karama*). At first ignoring the street protests, Syrian official media began to refer to them as 'the crisis' (*al-azma*) or 'the events' (*al-ahdath*). In a sort of unspoken gentlemen's agreement, neither Syrian TV nor the wealthy elites ever used the word 'uprising' (*intifada*) or 'revolution' (*thawra*) to describe the growing unrest.

My director friend – famous for producing edifying TV dramas focusing on taboo-breaking issues with the aim of dragging Syrian society into the present and eventually 'curing it of its own backwardness'[1] – wanted to celebrate the end of filming on his new *musalsal*. I shut down the computer, got ready and took a cab to the location in the countryside around Damascus. On the way the car was stopped at a checkpoint. I was nervous: this had never happened to me before, but the ruthlessness of *mukhabarat*, the Syrian intelligence service, was legendary. The security officer just checked my papers, broke the tension by making a joke about Italian football – my emergency exit in several tough situations in the Middle East – and then waved us on.

The location where the crew had been filming was right outside the city, but was not a typical rundown suburb like those in which the protests were escalating – Duma, Harasta, Jobar in the area of Eastern al-Ghouta. It was just a small green area of calm next to a stream, the silence broken by the trill of birdsong. One of the characters in the TV drama, a teenage girl fleeing the injustices of the city where the fictional narrative was set, was supposed to be hiding in this peaceful place. In a previous scene, seized by a fit of adolescent rage, she had scribbled slogans and doodles in large crayons on a wall near the stream. The director was about to shoot a close-up of the writing on the wall, while all around the cast and crew were merrily roasting meat and preparing other food for a celebratory barbecue. The atmosphere was festive. Everyone was enjoying the spring weather, thinking about how much money they had earned and how they were going to spend it, or making plans for their future and that of their families.

As I glanced at the wall I saw the slightly faded Arabic characters that formed the word 'freedom' (*hurriyya*). Then I silently ran my eyes over the whole sentence the young protagonist had written in pink: 'we want … freedom' (*bidna … hurriyya*). Possibly guessing what I was thinking, the director, who was making the final preparations for the close-up, suddenly said out loud, in a kind of solemn, almost prophetic way, as if he were talking from a sacred place: 'What those marching in the street are asking for *is not* freedom. Freedom is something you practise every day; something you obtain gradually. Unfortunately, our society isn't ready for it yet.' Then he swung round to his crew and shouted 'Action!', while I sat down and kept my mouth shut.

The close-up of the word 'freedom' written on the wall lasted less than 20 seconds. Then the director declared a wrap and everyone cheered: the party could finally begin.

*   *   *

After several years of fieldwork on Syrian TV drama, and countless hours of passionate discussions over coffee and cigarettes with its socially engaged makers, this episode struck me as an epiphany, as if it were the first time I fully realized that all those debates about citizenship, gender, religious freedom and the like were, in fact, merely Television. If it were not so, how then was it possible that one of the most prominent, provocative and smart Syrian directors, shooting a TV drama revolving around the quest for freedom of the Syrian youth, had not even stopped for a minute to think about what was happening in the streets in terms of a genuine, homegrown movement? Why was he so quick to dismiss it as a foreign conspiracy rather than a grassroots phenomenon? Why, after decades of pedagogical TV series like those he had himself produced in the belief that they would contribute to society's progress, was he absolutely convinced that the Syrian people were not ready for freedom *yet*?

My director friend's reaction hints at a widespread attitude among the wider community of Syrian TV drama producers. They describe it using the Arabic word *tanwir*,[2] which indicates a morally edifying process connected to the firm belief that Syrian society has to be healed of its alleged social backwardness (*takhalluf ijtima'i*)[3] in order to progress and develop. This process, in their view, cannot be initiated by the people, but has to be gradual, engineered and managed from the top down by an enlightened minority uniquely capable of guiding the country towards progress and development. In order to lead this 'enlightening' process, Syrian *musalsalat* inspired by the *tanwir* ideology have adapted all sorts of taboo subjects for the TV screen: from religious extremism to gender discrimination and sexual violence, from terrorism to corruption and the abuse of power among state officials.[4] They have provided their audiences with ideas on how to be a good citizen, what constitutes proper religious behaviour, and how to think about tolerance, piety, gender and freedom. They have debated everything that could possibly be deemed taboo by a largely conservative-oriented society, including highly sensitive political issues such as the ubiquitous presence of the *mukhabarat* in citizens' daily lives, and other topics unlikely to be publicly discussed by any other media in any other context, not only in Syria but in the wider Arab region.[5]

One could legitimately ask why an enduring authoritarian regime in a country that has been firmly ruled by the same family for more than 40 years, and that appears so resistant to change, would not only allow but actively encourage such seemingly progressive media content to be produced and publicly broadcast. At the same time, one might also wonder why these cultural producers would dare to raise such taboo-breaking topics without fearing sanctions or imprisonment. That the Syrian regime decided not to prevent TV drama from discussing these sensitive subjects in the public sphere – including directly political issues connected to its own authoritarian character – certainly seems paradoxical at a first glance. Yet, after coming to power following the death of his father in 2000, President Bashar al-Asad had always staunchly supported Syrian TV drama by hosting public hearings and debates, and by praising cultural producers for their courage in breaking social and political taboos.[6] For more than a decade, the Syrian president had met with actors, directors, producers and writers to discuss how to move society forward through a process of gradual reform that media and culture would help politics to implement. In the 'era Bashar' (Perthes 2004: 110), political power and cultural producers seemed to be in tune regarding *tanwir*, with a unified vision of Syria's need for a top-down, elite-engineered path towards careful reform.

The rise of tanwir *and of the nation state: packaging reformism into 'enlightened' TV drama*

Tanwir as a political ideology informing cultural production did not emerge with Bashar al-Asad. The belief in media and culture as key factors in shaping the nation's identity was originally conceived by former Egyptian president Gamal Abdel Nasser when building the post-colonial state, after overthrowing the monarchy and ending British occupation of Egypt in 1952.[7] A few years later, the charismatic president became the leader of the United Arab Republic (UAR), a political union between Egypt and Syria which lasted only briefly (1958–61). Yet Nasser's fascinating ideological blend of modernist values, progress and mass indoctrination had a long-term impact on Syrian political elites, cultural producers and in particular the nascent TV drama industry. Strongly influenced by their Egyptian peers, Syrian drama makers saw it as the quintessential tool to build shared ideas of nationhood and identity, and help develop and educate the wider population. 'Discourses of enlightenment' (Abu-Lughod 2005: 43) forged a solid bond between state powers and the elite of cultural producers, and served to shape a common view of how to make the nation progress.

Yet it was only after 1963, when the socialist-inspired Baʻath party seized power in a coup, and especially after Hafiz al-Asad took leadership of the party and of the country,[8] that Syrian cultural producers were finally offered a robust ideological platform as the basis for an agreement with the emerging regime over a shared commitment in the name of progress, development and modernism. The Syrian elites' view of culture as a potential catalyst for social change and national progress was in alignment with the Baʻath party's desire to centralize all cultural practices under a government-controlled apparatus.[9] As film critic Rasha Salti has pointed out: 'The immediate impetus for the establishment of the institution came from the demands of a politicized intelligentsia and groups of artists who expected their state to foster artistic production. Their aspirations and expectations were organically embedded in the prevailing ideological mindset of the Baʻath Arab Socialist Party that had seized power that year' (Salti 2006: 4).

Finally, *tanwir* was shaped as a regime-backed cultural ideology and materialized into state-sponsored cultural production. During Hafiz al-Asad's presidency (1970–2000) this bond was fully institutionalized. If its immediate advantage consisted in freeing cultural producers from the imperatives and constraints of the market, at the same time it created an interdependence that subjected them to negotiations and compromises with various components of the regime apparatus, whether government officials or secret services.[10] Nevertheless, as miriam cooke has noted, this was a mutual interdependence: 'The state that controlled them and sometimes silenced them also needed them' (cooke 2007: 4). A two-way mechanism has regulated the relationship between Syrian cultural producers and state powers since the beginning of the Hafiz al-Asad era, where one needs the other, while at the same time being constrained by the other: 'Just as culture needs the state for support and distribution, so the state needs culture to legitimate and extend its power' (cooke 2007: 29). This bond has kept state powers and cultural producers in a permanent state of mutual dependence, which has pushed the latter to fight for wider margins of freedom, and shaped a generation of intellectuals torn between the desire to criticize the regime and the obligation to compromise with it. Cooke (2007) calls it 'commissioned criticism', i.e. a condition in which even the work of intellectuals who see themselves as engaged in a critique of the regime is appropriated by the latter as a political strategy, and eventually turned into official propaganda.

Syrian TV drama producers are no exception to this pattern. The *musalsalat* released under Hafiz al-Asad were all aligned to the Ba'ath party's developmentalist rhetoric and used to promote social progress in the country, dealing with issues of Syrian daily life in a rather daring way, in line with the beliefs of the common ideology of *tanwir*.[11] *Al-Wasit* ('The Mediator'), a TV series directed by Haytham Hakki and produced by state television in 1978,[12] offers a compelling case study on this matter. The *musalsal* touched upon several critical issues related to the transformation of Syria from an agricultural to an industrial society, and was so bitterly criticized by the Union of Peasants that the minister of information in person had to defend the show in front of the Syrian parliament. Obviously, the series had touched a nerve in a conservative society that the elite of cultural producers was trying to shake up and push towards economic, social and cultural progress. The official conclusion was that 'the censoring power of society is sometimes bigger than any government censorship', as Fuad Ballat, General Manager of Syrian Television at the time, publicly declared.[13]

Haytham Hakki's alignment with Syrian TV's modernist values – and the Ba'ath Party's ideology – parallels the case of Fathiyya al 'Assal, a feminist *musalsalat* writer whose progressive politics were perfectly in tune with President Nasser's modernism. A general attitude of 'knowing what is good for society' (Abu-Lughod 2005: 42) – together with a slight disdain for its alleged primitiveness – has united Egyptian and Syrian cultural producers and pushed them to commit to the state's seemingly progressive ideology. As anthropologist Lila Abu-Lughod – author of the first comprehensive study of the role of TV fiction in the process of nation-building in Egypt – has noted in discussing the cultural producers' alignment with the regime's ideology:

> those in authority ... are there to ensure social justice, to help those in need and generally to improve society ... And it is this message, with its moral framework, that is probably the most powerful means through which television contributes to the hegemony of the state and the bourgeoisie, despite the claims to oppositionality or social criticism of so many of the finest writers and directors. (Abu-Lughod 2005: 91)

In the Syrian case, this ideological alignment also came as a natural result of the process that nurtured the formation of a domestic TV drama production sector. Unlike Egypt, Syrian state TV had neither the financial means to develop its own *musalsalat* production line, nor a domestic market large enough to absorb the costs of manufacturing TV fiction. To solve these structural problems the private sector was encouraged to grow within certain guidelines carefully designed by the regime. The main criteria was to encourage state TV employees – people like Haytham Hakki – to start their own production companies without leaving their public sector jobs.[14] State TV would allow them to use its studios and equipment to produce their own *musalsalat* for sale to the Gulf market, on one condition: that it could keep one copy of the final product to be aired free of charge on the domestic channel. This way it managed to retain talented employees, while encouraging the growth of an informal yet carefully managed private sector without the need to invest state resources.

Thus, the birth of private production in the TV drama field was the result of the state's need to acquire a national product for its media outlets and to become more competitive on a promising regional media market that was just beginning to expand.[15] At the same time, by engineering it from the top, political powers could better exercise their influence and control. On their side, talented state employees had the chance to develop their own businesses and invest in the rapidly growing and wealthy Gulf market, which enjoyed a healthy flow of capital thanks to increasing oil revenues. This process took shape at a moment in which Syrian cultural producers, whether formally affiliated to the Ba'ath or not, were engaged in spreading the values of *tanwir*, perfectly in tune with political powers.[16] Moreover, many TV directors and scriptwriters from the first generation of Syrian drama makers were given the chance to enjoy government-sponsored scholarships to study in the former Soviet Union or Eastern bloc nations. Here, they became acquainted not only with the 'aesthetics' (Salamandra 2011: 284) of Soviet cinema's social realism – which would later become a distinctive trait of Syrian TV drama[17] – but also with its ideology of serving the development of the nation and bringing progress to the masses.

Throughout the 1970s and 1980s, *musalsalat* enjoyed the benefits of being a cultural project jointly supported by both state powers and private producers. As a result of this shared support, domestic audiences (and the Gulf channels that had started to acquire and also invest directly in Syrian TV drama) enjoyed quality products tackling sensitive topics related to contemporary civil society in Syria.[18] Domestically, the result was to encourage a public debate around such issues, within the safe context of a fictional product that apparently had no connection with real events.[19] The state powers, however, were not formally involved in these discussions – a strategy to avoid taking full responsibility for failing to provide practical solutions to the social problems (unemployment, corruption, gender issues, etc.) depicted in the fictional universe of the *tanwir*-inspired *musalsalat*.

Even in the context of an apparently harmonious agreement with the ruling powers, Syrian cultural producers enjoyed a limited range of freedom and self-expression. The fact that many *musalsalat* – or parts of them – were censored or prevented from being aired by state media proves that, despite the shared ideological ground, drama makers were still forced to negotiate and compromise. Even when TV drama was directly produced by state media or by people who had an official role in the political power structure, the final product still had to be submitted to censorship, which could lead to it being removed from the schedule if deemed too sensitive.

Riad Nasaan Agha – political advisor to Hafiz al-Asad until his death in 2000 and a former minister of culture under Bashar al-Asad – once told me a revealing story about how this relationship between political powers and cultural producers was understood under Hafiz al-Asad. Having enjoyed a career as a *musalsalat* writer in parallel with his political position, in 1987 Nasaan Agha wrote *Al-Sawar* ('Bracelet'), a TV series which, in its author's words, told the story 'of a decent man who is pushed into corruption because it is impossible to resist the existing corrupt system'.[20] Surprisingly, after having produced it, Syrian TV decided not to broadcast the show because of its political sensitiveness. One day, seeing that Nasaan Agha was rather down, President Hafiz al-Asad asked him about *Al-Sawar*. Nasaan Agha replied that the *musalsal* had just been blocked by censorship at Syrian TV. 'Hafiz al-Asad shrugged, and that was it. He did not propose to intervene in order to get the *musalsal* on air. He did absolutely *nothing*.'[21]

Under Hafiz al-Asad, institutions (*mu'assasat*) still seemed to prevail over personal interventions in regulating media and cultural production and distribution. State power in its highest expression – the president himself – did not seem to attempt to heavily influence the administrators' decisions on what TV drama should be aired; apparently, it did not want to interfere with the working of the institutional process. The same emphasis on institutions and institutional process can also be observed in the management of the cinema sector. Here the balance of power between officials at the Ministry of Culture and employees of the National Cinema Organization (*Mu'assasa al-'amma li-l-sinama*) on the one hand, and the secret services on the other, tended to favour the former.[22] This process was facilitated by intermediaries who moved between political powers and cultural producers, knew how to navigate the system, and could find inventive ways to smooth the negotiation process without the security services' interference.[23] Yet this balance was soon to shift as a result of a joint process of 'dismantlement of the institutional framework' (Boëx 2011: 123) and the implementation of market reforms. Beginning in the early 1990s, this process eventually led to the emergence of a class of cultural investors and businessmen of a completely different character to the old generation of *tanwir* supporters.

Selective liberalization and the 'new class'

At the beginning of the 1990s, Syria initiated a process of formal withdrawal of the state from the national economy's key businesses. While seemingly opening to market pluralism, this strategy rather aimed at legitimating 'the private sector's compromised role' (Haddad 1999), and at giving it an institutional place in the country's economy. Informal networks associating state powers and business communities had in fact existed in Syria for decades.[24] Already in the 1970s an emerging class of a commercial bourgeoisie – often referred to as *al-tabaqa al-jadida* ('the new class', Perthes: 1991) – started consolidating from 'the special exemptions, monopolies, or quasi-monopolies in certain economic fields' (Perthes 1992: 225) that were de facto granted by state powers to a limited number of individuals who acted as middlemen and agents between companies and the government.[25] These businessmen would buy licences to commercialize products on behalf of foreign companies, such as car manufacturers, long before they were officially allowed to enter the Syrian market. Then the state would pass a law to institutionalize the situation and make the intermediary business legal.[26]

A similar development took place in the domain of audio-visual production, where private ventures were officially banned until the launch of investment Law No. 10 in 1991, which aimed at formalizing an arrangement that already existed in shady, unofficial forms. By allowing private TV companies to officially operate inside Syria, state powers apparently granted them a certain degree of autonomy and a legal status to overcome the arbitrariness of the previous situation, where a sort of private sector operated de facto and was even incubated by state television, albeit lacking an institutional form. Law No. 10 was part of a broader political strategy, defined by political scientist Steven Heydemann (1993: 88) as 'selective liberalization', by virtue of which state powers would formally disappear from the national economy's key sectors, but would retain the arbitrary power of selecting companies and businessmen to benefit from the opening, and use it as political leverage.

This move not only implied the rise of informal profits boosted by corruption practices, and less public accountability in terms of services that were no longer provided by the state; more importantly, it broadened and strengthened the regime's political base: something that would be of strategic importance two decades later, with the outbreak of the 2011 uprising. If one wonders why, several years into the present conflict, some of the wealthiest businessmen in Syria are still supporting Bashar al-Asad, one key reason can be found precisely in this selective liberalization process initiated by his father Hafiz back in the 1990s. Granting privileges and economic concessions to a selected class of people,[27] in order to secure a political payback and broaden the regime's support base, was a strategy successfully tested by the late Syrian president during the Muslim Brotherhood's revolt and the massacre at Hama in 1982.[28] This 'military-merchant complex' (Rabil 2003: 125) built by Hafiz al-Asad is something his son Bashar can still rely on, even after many years of unrest.[29]

The logic of selective liberalization, with its implications for the crafting of new forms of political consensus based on comfortable compromises rather than coercion, impacted on TV drama as well. On the surface, the state had almost withdrawn from TV drama production, directly producing only a limited number of *musalsalat*.[30] In practice, political powers continued to influence Syrian drama by forging alliances with businessmen who were partly related to the regime through kinship or other business connections, and were ready to act as its proxies. In its turn, the 'new class' entered the television business both as a way to secure profit and prestige, and to consolidate a greater political leverage[31] with the regime, in order to expand other economic interests, from real estate to banking. Driven by these motivations, the entrepreneurs behind the production companies allowed to operate after the 1991 law entirely lacked the commitment to *tanwir* that had characterized the first generation of drama makers – who were also the first de facto private producers – and their commitment to progressing society through edifying media.

A compelling insight into this new generation, and their entanglements with the powers that be, is provided by the fate of Sham International (*al-Sham al-duwaliyya*), a private company launched in the early 1990s by Jihad Khaddam, son of the former deputy prime minister Abdul Halim Khaddam. As Turki Shabahana – vice-president of the Saudi owned Rotana group and consultant to the MBC group, one of the top Pan Arab networks and among the wealthiest buyers of *musalsalat* – has remarked: 'Khaddam was the son of the deputy prime minister, he was a man within the *sulta* [power] and this counts a lot when you want to set a business in Syria, or in the Arab world in general.'[32]

The fact that the success of these ventures depends not so much on the market as on political alliances makes them extremely volatile and exposed to the vagaries of the prevailing political agenda. Sham International sheds light on this pattern: after several acclaimed TV productions,[33] and a history of successful business in Syria and in the wider Arab region, the company was abruptly shut down by the Syrian authorities in December 2005. Having once been a prominent member of Hafiz al-Asad's old guard, Abdul Halim Khaddam had resigned as Syria's vice-president in June 2005. His influence among Bashar al-Asad's closest collaborators had declined, and his close ties to Rafik Hariri – once a political asset – had turned into a liability after the former Lebanese PM's assassination in February the same year.[34] In a TV interview on al-Arabiya television aired from his exile in Paris on 30 December 2005, the former deputy prime minister accused Bashar al-Asad of being directly involved in Hariri's murder. That very same day, Sham International, his son's enterprise, was shut down and all its assets seized.[35] Whether Jihad Khaddam was aware of the imminent decision or not, Sham International's case clearly shows that political alliances and leverage with state powers count much more than any profit-making strategy. Despite being commercially successful and enjoying a reputation for professionalism, the company could not survive the volatile shifts in domestic and regional political alliances.

Other members of the new class were much luckier than Jihad Khaddam, managing to preserve and even expand their business ventures under Bashar al-Asad, in return providing a solid support base to the regime after 2011. One of the most prominent in this category is Mohamed Hamsho, a former member of the Syrian parliament and a successful businessman, linked particularly to Bashar al-Asad's brother Mahir,[36] commander-in-chief of the Fourth Armoured Division, the core of the country's security forces. In 1999 Hamsho founded Syrian Art Production International (*Suriya al-duwaliyya li-l-intaj al-fanni*, SAPI), a TV company that over the years was able to strike lucrative deals with top Pan Arab channels and produce many successful *musalsalat*.[37] In 2007, after having eliminated several competitors for the assignment of a commercial TV channel licence,[38] he launched Addounia TV, formally owned by a consortium of six Syrian entrepreneurs. However, editorial and executive decisions were reported to lie firmly in Hamsho's hands.[39]

Hamsho's market share in Syria is considerable, since Addounia TV has no commercial competitor, the only other Syrian media player being the state broadcaster. Moreover, the state-owned Arab Advertising Organization (AAO) regulates the Syrian advertising market on political rather than commercial principles, preventing any Syrian company from buying advertising slots in what are deemed opposition channels, even if operating from abroad, like the Dubai-based Orient TV.[40] This has given Hamsho's Addounia a monopoly on commercial broadcasting in Syria. His influence, however, is not only manifest at a domestic level: for many years Hamsho has been working in the intermediation business with Gulf ventures, gaining a certain regional leverage, particularly in the UAE. Here his company Hamsho Communications was able to strike an exclusive distribution deal with Thuraya, an Emirati company that provides satellite mobile communications (Albawaba 2001). This agreement provided to be very strategic when the Syrian uprising broke out in March 2011, as the activists were mostly using Thuraya phones to feed international channels with news and live testimonies from the ground and, at the same time, avoid being identified by the Syrian secret services. The fact that such a powerful businessman and pro-regime supporter was the exclusive agent of Thuraya for the Arab region (Badran 2006) greatly helped the Syrian government to track these communications and identify activists (Harkin et al. 2012: 15).

Addounia TV also proved to be a faithful ally to Bashar al-Asad in the war on the airwaves that has matched the conflict on the ground since 2011. Immediately after the first street protests, in fact, the channel started building and spreading Bashar al-Asad's narrative of a foreign conspiracy against Syria, and acted as an aggressive co-optation machine on behalf of the regime. To quote just one episode involving some of the most prominent members of the Syrian TV drama industry, in May 2011 the channel hosted a debate on the artists' engagement in 'the events' (*al-ahdath*)[41] happening in the country. A few days before the show, in fact, a group of 400 artists, including several drama makers,[42] had issued a communiqué, known as 'the milk statement' (*bayan al-halib*), denouncing a 'food embargo' (*al-hisar al-ghadh'i*, Syria News 2011) imposed on Daraa after the Syrian army had entered the rebel city in response to the ongoing unrest. The signatories called upon the Syrian Ministry of Health or the Syrian Red Crescent to supervise a humanitarian mission to the southern city in order to deliver milk, baby food and medicines for children in need.

The 'milk statement' immediately generated a spiral of verbal violence against the artists who had signed it, which later turned into threats to prevent them from working in Syrian TV drama. A counter-statement, known as 'the companies' statement' (*bayan al-sharikat*), was released on 5 May by *musalsalat* director and producer Najdat Anzour, and signed by prominent Syrian production companies, including Hashmo's SAPI.[43] The new communiqué endorsed the regime's narrative of the Daraa events being fabricated by fake eyewitnesses and activists connected to foreign circles. The day after, in a tense atmosphere, Addounia TV called upon prominent drama makers[44] to discuss the 'exemplary position' (*al-mawqif al-mithali*) that Syrian artists had to adopt vis-à-vis the crisis, implicitly suggesting that they should stand firmly by the leadership in order to avoid precipitating the country into chaos. The talk show made apparent the extent to which Syrian drama makers were deeply enmeshed with the country's political powers, signalling their obligation to pay back for the support granted to their TV works, which had helped them build careers and prestige.

The 'milk statement' story is just one of many that could be told to shed light on the key role played by the new class of entrepreneurs in supporting the political powers who, in turn, allowed them to grow and prosper in both Syria and the wider Arab region. Hamsho's Addounia TV is revelatory of how a media outlet that prospered from its owner's liaisons with the regime later proved to be a powerful propaganda device for boosting the official rhetoric in a time of crisis, anxiety and unrest. The smiling face of Kinana Allouche, a prominent Addounia reporter, happily taking a selfie in Aleppo with corpses in the background (Rampen 2016), saluting the braveness of the Syrian army in defeating what the official rhetoric has always described as 'armed gangs' or 'foreign infiltrators', is one of the most troubling visual examples of how far the propaganda war has gone in Syria.

From state institutions to personal interventions:
upgrading tanwir *in neoliberal times*

If the collusion between political powers and the new class of entrepreneurs is motivated by the networks of mutual benefits put into place by the selective liberalization process, one might wonder what happened to Syrian drama makers and the commitment to *tanwir* that had inspired their works. At a time when people were hitting the streets risking their lives to demand reforms and civil rights, these cultural producers, once engaged in a battle for education and social progress through committed media, now denied society the very possibility of demanding change. Like my director friend whose story I narrated at the beginning of this chapter, shooting a drama about a fictional quest for freedom while ignoring the *real* quest for freedom agitating the country.

Undoubtedly, fear and anxiety about losing material benefits and a privileged status might have motivated the decision of these drama makers, even those who had initially signed the 'milk statement', to later take an active pro-regime stance, or at least to stay silent. Yet there is something more, in my view, than just a reasonable distress in their attitude to the Syrian leadership. For Bashar al-Asad's political project and Syrian TV's cultural project were deeply intertwined in the ideology of *tanwir*. It is no coincidence that Bashar al-Asad's first decade in power (2000–10) coincided with the golden age of Syrian *musalsalat*. It was as if media and culture on the one hand, and politics on the other, had converged on a harmonic vision of society and the way to move it forward. The entanglement between the Syrian president and the drama makers was so powerful that the latter were perceived in the wider Arab region as government representatives, being part of official state visits and behaving like ambassadors embodying the very idea of Bashar al-Asad's reformism.

To understand this quasi-magical bond we have to go back to the very first moments of Bashar al-Asad's rise to power. After Hafiz al-Asad's death in June 2000, Syria entered a brief period of intense public debate over political and social reforms, a period commonly known as the 'Damascus Spring'.[45] During quasi-public meetings, hosted by members of the cultural elite, many topics related to empowering civil society were debated in the hope that the new president would usher in a new season of openness and personal freedom.[46] Bashar al-Asad was considered a reform-minded leader: he had lived all his life far from politics and the military, his only formal title in Syria being President of the Syrian Computer Society.[47] He had studied ophthalmology in the UK, where he had met his British-born wife Asma Akhras, a former JP Morgan executive and daughter of a London-based Sunni cardiologist from Homs. The presidential couple were young, well-educated and had been raised at a distance from politics. On paper, this was the premise for a new season of reforms and a move towards greater freedom, both at the level of the national economy and in regard to civil liberties and rights.

Bashar al-Asad's first quarter was marked by this atmosphere of trust and hope, in which civil society forums (*muntadayat al-mujtama' al-madani*) were opened not only in Damascus but across the country, to discuss a wide range of issues related to citizenship and its role as the pillar of a modern society in place of patronage relationships, tribal or religious affiliations. In this climate of excitement and political exper-imentation prominent members of Syrian civil society – including TV drama makers – issued the so-called 'Statement of the 1000', a decla-ration advocating for 'liberty, equality and justice' (George 2003: 44) that clearly attacked the Ba'ath party's authoritarian rule and openly demanded a multi-party system.[48] A few weeks later, the crackdown on the Damascus Spring began, and many of its more active members were arrested – such as the economist 'Arif Dalila, and Riad Seif, a businessman and independent parliamentary representative who had been involved in initiating the public forums movement. Many deemed the clampdown a victory for the 'old guard' – the hardliners guided by Vice-President Abdul Halim Khaddam – over the newly appointed 'politically relevant elite' of the young president (Perthes 2004: 90). The latter was still too weak to impose his modernizing, reform-minded agenda (George 2003: 47) – or so went the mantra that all those who put their trust in Bashar al-Asad repeated throughout his first decade.

Ten years later, in response to another reform movement – this time shaped by grassroots street protests rather than by cultural elites – the Syrian President explained that his project had to be temporarily shelved, as a result of the situation Syria was now in. In the first public speech given after the outbreak of the March 2011 uprising, Bashar al-Asad gave an assessment of what had been achieved,[49] concluding that, due to US interference in the region after 9/11 and the outbreak of violent conflict in Afghanistan and Iraq, Syria's 'priorities' had to be adjusted and the reform process had to be sacrificed, for 'the top priority became Syria's stability' (al-Asad 2011a) – and so it has been since.

In the Syrian regime's political jargon, 'stability' means granting more power to the security apparatus. This resonates with the bitter reflections of TV director Haytham Hakki, one of the most enthusiastic supporters of the reform movement initiated in 2000: 'Starting from the repression of the Damascus Spring, the control of the security services over every single aspect of life – which seemed to have been put on hold at least for a short period – was fully revived.'[50] Once it became clear that the reform project had been shelved, many Syrian drama makers decided nonetheless to stand firmly by the president and his circle, wanting to support the narrative that more time was needed to implement the changes since Hafiz al-Asad's old guard was still too influential. In reality, a void had opened up in the *tanwir* project in which the drama makers had so strongly believed, as the political powers that could have turned the media's aspirations for change into real reforms were clearly no longer interested in supporting it.

At a time when a combination of neoliberal market reforms and the growing influence of the security apparatus had started to dismantle state institutions and undermine their symbolic power, official support for progressive, *tanwir*-inspired media projects was unlikely to be secured. In this political atmosphere, Bashar al-Asad continued to promote his public image as an enlightened leader committed to reform but surrounded by an old apparatus responsible for delaying its implementation. He offered his personal support to the drama makers, emphasizing his commitment to *tanwir*, which allowed him and his circle of advisors to publicly differentiate themselves from other powers within the regime structure that were resistant to change and had opted to prioritize security. Gatherings and hearings hosted periodically throughout the 2000s served Bashar al-Asad's goal of publicly reiterating his personal engagement in a reformist agenda. These meetings with actors, directors and producers were aimed at informing the Syrian public that both sides were still involved in the project of producing *tanwir*-inspired TV drama as the perfect vehicle for the struggle 'to heal social backwardness' – as the president himself reportedly affirmed during a hearing in 2004.[51]

This publicly sealed alliance carried advantages for both sides. On the one hand, drama makers needed to reaffirm their commitment to *tanwir* as something unique, something upon which to forge a new bond with power in a time when the pressure of neoliberal markets had overtaken the old state-driven mission towards mass education and enlightenment.[52] On the other hand, Bashar al-Asad had to prove that his reform process would not be stopped, but only temporarily put on hold, in times of crisis – during the Damascus Spring as much as in the 2011 uprising. He therefore encouraged the drama makers' hope of getting the *tanwir* message back on track, and promised they would always have official backing within the Syrian regime – at least from one of its multiple sides, the seemingly reform minded. When disputes occurred with the security apparatus seeking to stop *tanwir*-inspired media, the president's personal interventions became an increasingly institutionalized way of solving the problem, finally allowing the content to pass through censorship, and be aired and debated in the public sphere.

Bashar al-Asad's behaviour reinforced the drama makers' belief that the reformist project was alive and well, embodied by the president's personal engagement with protecting their freedom to tackle socially sensitive issues. This, in turn, strengthened his public persona as an enlightened leader determined to battle with the most backward elements of his own regime in order to drive the country forward, slowly but surely. A new bond was created between the president and the drama makers, free of the oppositional behaviour that had characterized the relation of the previous generation of cultural producers to Hafiz al-Asad.[53] With Syria evolving from an authoritarian country into a fully-fledged 'neoliberal autocracy' (Wedeen 2013: 843), power had dramatically changed its way of acting, disciplining and seducing; it had found a more attractive means of co-option and inducing compliance.

For Bashar al-Asad's Syria has a completely different face than his father's. Urban legends, or perhaps Ba'ath party spin doctors, conveyed an image of Hafiz al-Asad as a sober leader, inspired by the socialist rhetoric of equality and austerity, who suffered from food shortages as much as his people,[54] in a country that was being held back by international sanctions and its lack of attractiveness to foreign investors. In Bashar al-Asad's Syria of the 2000s, the studied casualness and 'cunning understatement'[55] of the new president's British-born spouse Asma had deliberately replaced Ba'athist austerity, feeding international media with the idea of a modern, reform-minded, down-to-earth leadership, equally at ease engaging in reform talks at the Élysée Palace on Bastille Day, or beguiling Hollywood celebrities Brad Pitt and Angelina Jolie with the wonders of Old Damascus.[56] This magazine-cover image of the new leadership was in harmony with a brand new impression of Syria that was in the making, in the local and international media as much as on the ground. In the second half of the 2000s, trendy new cafés and restaurants had popped up across the larger Syrian cities, offering free wi-fi connections and beverages with exotic names such as *latte*, together with the traditional tea and narghile. People started visiting modern shopping malls as often as they trawled the crowded old souks to buy gifts for Muslim and Christian religious holidays, or for imported festivities such as Valentine's Day and Halloween. English-language publications like *Forward Magazine* encouraged entrepreneurship and initiative, and private radio stations aired feel-good programmes such as *Ana suri* ('I am Syrian'), advising listeners on 'how to be a modern, responsible citizen; how to be the solution and not the problem'.[57] The culture of glamour and gossip burst out of the pages of women's magazine *Layalina*, while advertising billboards advised young Syrian girls to get married, not to comply with religious traditions, but because 'he's got a house' (*'ayndu beit*).

The idea of *tanwir* has had to fit into this new way of political and economic thinking, where individual and market freedoms have replaced the belief in a common social good. The once privileged relation forged between cultural producers and state institutions had been disrupted by

Figure 1.1   Advertising billboard in Damascus, late 2010. 'He's got a house' (photo: Donatella Della Ratta).

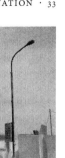

Figure 1.2   Construction site of a new housing and working complex in the area of Baramke station, Damascus, late 2010. 'Together we build' (photo: Donatella Della Ratta).

the process of selective liberalization, dismantling the public framework and replacing it with private initiatives in all domains of life, including media and culture. *Tanwir* also had to readapt to the changed scenario in order to survive as a political and cultural ideology. With the shrinking of state-centred initiatives, it took the form of an individually centred action, replacing institutional forms with the arbitrary decisions of an enlightened leader. This upgraded version of *tanwir* in the context of neoliberalism was completely void of the political engagement and social objectives of its first, modernist type. Paradoxically, having served to construct and strengthen ideas of nationhood, *tanwir* now helps disrupt the latter, emphasizing the cult of personality over the common good, and implying that reforms can only happen if the president's political persona is safeguarded – a belief that seems to have survived until today, several years into the uprising at the time of writing. *Tanwir* in neoliberal times takes the commodity form of cutting-edge TV drama confronting taboo-breaking themes, such as the teenage rebellion of my director friend's *musalsal*, packaging freedom for the sake of market consumption while failing to acknowledge the agency of those demanding that very freedom in the streets of Syria.

SNAPSHOT #2

The vicissitudes of *Fawq al-Saqf* – a 2011 *musalsal* focusing on the uprising and suggesting that dialogue is the only way to avoid chaos and instability – shed light on the structure of the Syrian regime as a set of loosely connected powers that, according to their agendas and priorities, might opt to oppose each other's messages in the public space. The seemingly progressive content of such *tanwir*-inspired media is agreed upon by way of what I call the 'whisper strategy': a sophisticated communication mechanism through which the president and the drama makers manage to fine-tune messages to indoctrinate the Syrian public about what makes good citizens, and how to think about religion, gender, human rights, freedom, and, eventually, the protest movement unfolding in the streets.

The whisper strategy also involves Gulf-backed Pan Arab broadcasters to whom Syrian *musalsalat* are sold, showing the extent to which there is no conflict between the commodity logic of the market and the Syrian elites' reformist *tanwir*-based national project; not even when, in the polarized climate post-2011, Gulf powers have positioned themselves as staunch opponents of Bashar al-Asad.

Yet inside the country the reformist option has to be shelved. With the parallel growth of the protest movement and of its violent crackdown, a security-driven solution has taken over and left no room for dialogue, not even at the surface level of seemingly progressive *musalsalat*, as the fate of *Fawq al-Saqf* shows.

2

The Whisper Strategy

Fawq al-Saqf: *The revolution will (only) be televised*

In the oppressive heat of the summer of 2011, I remember sitting at home in front of the TV screen, trying to catch up with the latest Ramadan *musalsalat*, yet absent-minded and filled with frustration. The start of the Muslim holy month that year was marked by violence: the Syrian government had just sent the army to the city of Hama as part of a nationwide crackdown on the street protests that was dubbed by some 'the Ramadan Massacre' (*Washington Post* 2011). I felt that this was going to be the beginning of the end of the peaceful uprising whose exciting blossoming I had witnessed with my own amazed eyes that same year in the streets of Damascus, a few meters away from where I used to live. No more street parades and shouts of *hurriyya, karama* – the slogans chanted in the squares of Syria that resonated in the virtual alleys of the internet thanks to the user-generated footage uploaded by Syrian activists. Instead, sounds of gunfire were going to be heard more and more, in the country as well as on the web, silencing the joyous chants of *silmiyya, silmiyya* ('peaceful, peaceful').

My gloomy thoughts were interrupted by precisely these familiar rallying cries of the street protests: a crowd was chanting *hurriyya, hurriyya* from my TV screen, a guy who looked like a government official standing nearby. I held my breath as, horrified, I thought: now he's gonna shoot at them. I closed my eyes to avoid watching a scene that was sadly all too well-known in Syria. Then I heard him saying: 'Maybe I should have ... but precaution cannot stave off destiny.' His voice brought me back to reality, as it sounded so strangely soft, so familiar. He was a *musalsalat* actor, and the scene was just from a Ramadan TV series. Yet it was surreal, to say the least, to realize that the logo of the Syrian Satellite channel was there on the screen. Until that moment, state-owned media had never screened any such evidence of peaceful demonstrations in Syria, nor admitted that they had ever taken place in the country.

As I watched the last scene of the *musalsal*, featuring a desolate landscape of ruthless destruction (the default image that comes to mind when thinking about Syria, though it was not at the time), I decided I should learn more about this strange TV object, and so started investigating. The TV series was called *Fawq al-Saqf* ('Above the Ceiling'), and was produced by a government-sponsored media unit. Each episode, made up of two or three sketches of around 15–20 minutes each, was filled with dark humour and biting satire, following the narrative and visual style of *Buq'at al-daw* ('Spotlight'), a TV series that symbolically recalled the atmosphere of openness in the early days of the Damascus Spring in 2001.[1] Not by chance, and precisely to make a connection to a period permeated with the promise of reform, selected writers from *Buq'at al-daw* were hired to work on *Fawq al-Saqf*. The choice of the director for the series was apparently also the result of careful, strategic consideration: Samer Baraqawi was deemed a talented representative of the younger generation, someone not directly aligned with the regime's positions. All these elements seemed to suggest that, through the medium of a progressive Ramadan show, the political powers wanted to send a message of openness demonstrating their willingness to start a dialogue on the issues raised by the ongoing street protests. *Fawq al-Saqf* apparently criticized, or at least problematized, the security apparatus' violent intervention in the peaceful demonstrations and its continuous abuse of power; it seemed far from being a propaganda broadcast, crafted only to promote the regime's position vis-à-vis the political unrest.

The Syrian public, however, was by now well aware of the media tactics used by political powers to show a reformist face, and had become familiar with *tanfis* ('letting off steam'), a technique used in media and cultural production since the Hafiz al-Asad era 'to vent frustrations and displace or relieve tensions that otherwise might find expression in political action'.[2] *Fawq al-Saqf* could have been a quintessential operation of *tanfis* orchestrated by state-owned media, a masterpiece of 'commissioned criticism' – 'an official and paradoxical project to create a democratic façade' (cooke 2007: 72) by crafting a seemingly critical media product to demonstrate openness and an inclination towards reform. Yet I was not fully convinced by this argument:

Had it served the purpose of *tanfis* or commissioned criticism, the *musalsal* would at least have been promoted and advertised over the

Syrian official media network to attract the public's attention. By contrast, the official Syrian TV daily show *Drama 2011* – which helps viewers navigate the crowded Ramadan drama schedules – would not even mention it. No promos of the *musalsal* were ever aired on state-owned TV channels and, unlike other *musalsalat*, the serial was never re-scheduled after its first broadcast. (Della Ratta 2015a: 66–7).

This was already odd, but then something even odder happened: the show was abruptly cancelled before the end of Ramadan, with no official reason given. It simply disappeared from the TV screens in silence, as it had made its debut. Nobody seemed willing to talk about it, and all the prominent drama makers I approached for information just shrugged and said they had never heard of it.

Only later – once I'd left Syria – did I realize what *Fawq al-Saqf* was really about, and why people in the drama industry pretended not to have heard of it. It was not a badly promoted operation of *tanfis* or commissioned criticism. It was not even a *musalsal. Fawq al-Saqf* was revelatory of the power dynamics inherent in the structure of the Syrian regime, composed of multiple powers (*sultat*) that are only loosely connected – the state and its government apparatus, the different branches of *mukhabarat*, the religious authorities, and the Palace, *al-Qasr*, a word used to hint at the president and his inner circle of col-laborators. Sometimes they fail to communicate, or are unwilling to, and therefore ignore or miscommunicate messages, creating confusion and ambivalence. 'The various opportunities for communication and mis-communication suggest that alliances between one *sulta* and another in Syria's power structure are not stable and can shift and recombine' (Della Ratta 2015a: 55–6). In the end, *Fawq al-Saqf* was a hot potato not because of its content, but because of the network of power relations it brought to the surface and finally unveiled. The *sultat* within the regime structure can, and do, put forward very different messages and agendas that are likely to clash with one another in the public space of TV drama, exactly as they did with *Fawq al-Saqf*.

The TV series was produced and broadcast at a very peculiar moment in Syria's history, agitated as the country was by the first street protest movement in decades to publicly question the seemingly untouchable power structure of the al-Asad regime. It was a moment in which the different *sultat* were pursuing contrasting political agendas, and it was still unclear which might prevail: whether the reform-minded, seemingly supported by the Palace with its emphasis on national dialogue, or the security-minded, promoted by the more hawkish elements of the regime.[3] *Fawq al-Saqf* can be used to shed light on the political dynamics of this particular moment of uncertainty vis-à-vis which kind of path – a security solution or a political solution – was to be taken to resolve the crisis. More generally, the series is revelatory of the quintessential power dynamics and struggles that mark the political infrastructure of the Syrian regime, and of its loose and ambivalent nature. It is not yet another TV show; it is a living example of *tanwir* that, in a particularly heated political context such as the uprising, finally revealed its function; namely, to serve as ideological support for media projects crafted with the goal of promoting change that, in the end, is merely cosmetic and realized only in the realm of television fiction.

Fawq al-Saqf is the brainchild of the president's inner circle, made by seemingly reformist political elites. The idea of a *musalsal* that would resolve 'what is happening in the streets in an artistic way'[4] reportedly grew out of a proposal made by Sami Moubayed during a meeting held at the presidential palace in spring 2011.[5] At the time, Moubayed was close to Buthaina Shaaban, Bashar al-Asad's media advisor, who first addressed the crisis in a public speech calling for dialogue and national reconciliation (BBC News 2011); they both embodied the reformist agenda of the Palace and its diplomatic face. Apparently, the initial pitch for *Fawq al-Saqf* was filled with hopes of crafting a media product that would promote a 'third view' on the unrest, one which would 'not embrace the regime's or the street's view. Something that the regime would not feel as a provocation when watching, nor the street would be angered at or encouraged to demonstrate after its broadcast.'[6]

Using the compelling satire and dark humour that were the signature of Syrian TV drama, the *musalsal* would criticize both sides, advocating for a middle ground, a dialogue-based solution to the crisis for the sake of national unity. This dialogue, however,

is to be conducted solely under the regime's auspices, driven by political and cultural elites; its margins are to be fixed strictly from the top down. The idea is transposed to the title of the *musalsal – Above the Ceiling –* which sets the standards of the dialogue at the highest level possible,[7] reproducing a metaphor often repeated in Bashar al-Asad's public speeches to suggest the great degree of freedom that Syrian media allegedly enjoys. (Della Ratta 2015a: 68).

Not by chance, the original title – *Al-Sha'ab yurid...* ('The People Want...') – had to be changed (Halabi 2011), probably because it was deemed too close to the anti-regime slogan chanted throughout the Arab world during street demonstrations. Opting for the metaphor of the ceiling – used by Bashar al-Asad in his public speeches to hint at the platform under which the entire nation (*watan*) should come together[8] – was no doubt a safer choice and a tacit disclosure of which side, regardless of its declared search for a third view, the *musalsal* had implicitly taken.

This harmonious coincidence of interests between the Palace and enlightened drama makers did not prevent the *musalsal* from becoming a contentious issue in the power struggle between different *sultat*, demonstrating the extent to which competing political projects may eventually collide with each other in Syria. The TV show's very troubled production made these clashes apparent. For example, despite the idea of the *musalsal* having been approved at Palace level, each edited episode had to be given the go-ahead by a viewing committee within Syrian state media (*lajnat al-mushahada*), which ended up rejecting many episodes.[9] The *musalsal* finally premiered during Ramadan only at the very last minute, and just because the Palace itself was reported to have directly intervened to authorize its broadcast.[10] Yet protests and complaints from 'different parties' (*mukhtalif al-atraf*) did not stop, and phone calls were reportedly made from 'other official sides' (*jihat rasmiyya ukhra*) – i.e. the secret services – to put pressure on state television to cancel the series.[11] No wonder the state media had never advertised it, nor sold it to any other station after the Ramadan season, which would be common practice in the Arab TV drama industry.

Fawq al-Saqf disappeared abruptly from the Ramadan TV schedule. During an interview, Ma'an Haider, the Director General of Syrian TV, promised to reschedule it once all the episodes were ready to air, blaming the non-completion of the series as the main reason for it coming to a halt (Halabi 2011). 'The reaction of the Palace was silence, which basically meant agreement to interrupting the broadcast', Mahir Azzam declared.[12] This silence reveals both the nature of the so-called reformist side of the regime represented by Bashar al-Asad's inner circle, and how quickly the power balance within the Syrian regime can shift, especially in a time of emergency:

It is very likely that, once the unrest started in 2011, the *tanwiri* project, jointly backed by the Palace and by the elite of drama makers, had to succumb to the security plan pushed by the intelligence and the more hawkish sides of the Syrian regime. It might also have been, however, that the Palace itself decided to put the *tanwiri* project on hold in order to help the other *sultat* implement the security plan, judged as a priority in a time of unrest. (Della Ratta 2015a: 70).

During that same spring-summer 2011, other media projects planned along the same conceptual lines as *Fawq al-Saqf* suffered a similar fate.[13] At the time, Damascus Spring activist and prominent filmmaker Nabil Maleh was also in talks with Buthaina Shaaban on setting up a satellite TV channel dedicated to national dialogue. The channel would have hosted open debates on key political issues, and given the floor to anti-regime figures to express their point of view. 'After getting the green light from Bashar al-Asad in person, Shaaban should have got back to me with a list of steps needed to quickly implement the TV channel idea, which the president in person had mentioned as part of a wider reform package in his first televised speech after the events unfolded', Nabil Maleh reported. 'But Buthaina Shaaban never got back to me. She disappeared and, only a few days later, we heard the president's speech promoting a completely different message from the reformist one we were all expecting.'[14] Journalist and former host with Syrian TV Ibrahim al-Jabin was also reportedly asked by state media to plan a talk show whose task would have been to simulate a parliament and discuss controversial laws and decrees regarding the country's social and political life in an apparently free and open-minded fashion.[15] He declined and immediately flew to Dubai, later seeking political asylum in Europe. This media proxy of the parliament has never seen the light of day.

In most cases these ideas were never pursued, or, as with projects like *Fawq al-Saqf*, were halted soon after their launch. The likely reason is that, already in the early months of the uprising, the security-minded project had become more popular within the Syrian regime power structure than the reformist one. The *sultat* – including the Palace – had probably decided to opt for it in order to preserve their political influence. In any case, all these ideas – from the *musalsal* to the virtual parliament – were far from being truly reformist in any real sense, being nothing other than media projects.

Under Bashar al-Asad, media and culture personalities have been charged with political tasks and have acted as state proxies on several occasions; including in 2011, when Syrian TV actors and directors visited areas of unrest – such as Duma (a Damascus suburb) or Daraa – to listen to the protesters' demands and try to negotiate a way out of the crisis. As a prominent Syrian TV producer remarked at the time: 'The fact that TV actors and directors went to negotiate with protesters in Duma or Daraa on behalf of the state is an indication of the weakness of the state itself. It means that there are no organizations to do the job. It signals the lack of institutions – rather than just individual efforts – appointed to propose any political solution.'[16] Which resonates with the words of another prominent dramatist: 'It is a sign of how empty and illusionary our politics are that actors now play politicians in real life' (Sands 2011).

Blurring the lines between politics and the media, especially *tanwir*-inspired TV drama, and assigning the latter a prominent role in his reformist strategy, is exactly what Bashar al-Asad has been advocating for in the past decade. Talking to *The Wall Street Journal*, just two months before the uprising broke out, the Syrian president declared: 'The first thing you have to learn is how to conduct dialogue and how to make it productive. So, we started having dialogue in Syria through the media' (*Wall Street Journal* 2011). In this very conversation in which he emphasized the role of the media in leading the national dialogue aimed at opening up Syrian society, al-Asad expressed his confidence that Syria would not follow the same path of other Arab countries touched by the political unrest of the so-called Arab Spring. 'We have more difficult circumstances than most of the Arab countries but', he underlined, 'in spite of that Syria is stable. Why? Because you have to be very closely linked to the beliefs of the people. This is the core issue.' However, less than two months after this interview was released, people filled the streets of Syria calling for more rights and dignity, proving that the situation on the ground was quite different from what Bashar al-Asad – and *tanwir*-inspired media – had imagined.

The whisper strategy

The vicissitudes behind the rise and fall of *Fawq al-Saqf* brought into bold relief the complicated and loosely connected network of power that characterizes the infrastructure of the Syrian regime. Although there was to be no happy ending for the TV series, its genesis at least – that spring

2011 at the Palace, when a member of the enlightened elite suggested addressing the crisis through *tanwir*-inspired media – reveals a virtuous circle of communication linking cultural producers to the seemingly reform-minded *sulta*. What I call the 'whisper strategy' (Della Ratta 2012c, 2015a; Esber 2014) refers to this communication mechanism, through which the parties manage to 'discuss and agree upon issues deemed worthy and suitable to disseminate through media outlets' (Della Ratta 2015a: 53). The metaphor of the whisper captures the soft, gentle, non-coercive form of communication between cultural producers and political powers: a bilateral, circulatory dynamic through which both sides express their needs and address the necessity of tackling certain issues using *tanwir*-inspired media.

Whispers are not top-down orders imposed from one side on the other. The *sulta* does not, in a mandatory and coercive way, demand that the drama makers produce certain kind of media, or use their TV series to deal with specific issues that political powers deem strategic at a determined time. And the cultural producers have their own agency, being able to bring up in their conversations with the Palace topics considered relevant and strategic for themselves and for their own agendas.[17] They whisper back to power as much as power whispers to them.[18] To this extent, the whisper bears a resemblance to Michel Foucault's 'strategy without a subject'. Here the needs of both parties mutually converge to define a strategy that is clearly identified and identifiable; unlike the 'subject' of the strategy itself, as, in Foucault's reading of power, the latter is shaped by heterogeneous elements in an ongoing 'interplay of shifts of positions and modifications of functions' (Foucault 1977: 202, 204, 195).

The whisper strategy expresses the strategic necessities of both sides, although neither of them can claim full ownership or control of the whispers. On the one hand, Bashar al-Asad needs to preserve his reformist credentials in front of the Syrian public to differentiate himself from other *sultat*. Since his rise to power the Syrian president has emphasized the role that reforms would play in his political strategy. Although not much has been achieved on this front[19] – as al-Asad himself admitted in his March 2011 speech, blaming external circumstances for the slowness in implementing reforms (al-Asad 2011a) – the president needs to maintain his image as a reformist, both domestically and internationally. The regime's reformist façade is a successful strategic move at a PR level; particularly abroad, as it seems that al-Asad has managed (so far) to convince international diplomacy that a political solution to the crisis can still be brokered if he is kept in power.

On the other hand, what is at stake from the perspective of Syrian drama makers is their centrality within the cultural production process, which they partially lost with the rise of the new class of producers in the 1990s. Furthermore, after their public involvement in the Damascus Spring in 2000, they were accused of being 'hateful' and 'wanting to lead Syria back to the period of foreign occupation or military coups' (Perthes 2004: 104). There is thus a clear need for them to regain some support from the *sulta* for their reformist agenda as a homegrown national project, as if what temporarily cannot be achieved at a political level could be at least executed at a media and culture level.

It is here that the president's and the drama makers' needs finally converge in the ideological discourse of *tanwir*, which helps maintain the unity and specificity of both sides, and serves as a common ground to inspire their public actions and practices. The whispering never happens underground; on the contrary, the alliance between the president and the drama makers needs to be continuously highlighted, reaffirmed, and promoted in the public space, hence whispers always happen in public or quasi-public venues. Since his rise to power in 2000, the Syrian president has regularly held informal meetings or more formal hearings at the Palace with the drama makers. By discussing the cultural politics of Syrian *musalsalat* with writers, directors, producers and actors, Bashar al-Asad has made official the strategic importance of the drama industry in shaping the nation's future,[20] at the same time reaffirming his own commitment to *tanwir* and to the reformist agenda.

The cartoonist Ali Farzat – who in the wake of the Damascus Spring was granted authorization to set up *al-Dumari* (The Lamplighter), the first satirical newspaper in Syria – has reported on his personal meetings with the president, in which the latter encouraged him to start the paper, apparently suggesting that he uses it as a tool to break political taboos and attack members of the Syrian Parliament. Ironically, less than a decade after being encouraged to break taboos, it was instead Ali Farzat's hands that were broken. Reportedly carried out by Syrian security forces (Ali 2011), this was likely the punishment for having criticized Bashar al-Asad at a time of unrest, during which the president would have preferred the full and uncontested support of the cultural elite. Precisely because of this need, the whispers never stopped, not even at the start of the uprising; on the contrary, the unrest made it even more urgent to publicly reaffirm the full agreement between cultural and political elites on the strategy to lead the country out of the crisis.

As an example, in May 2011, a few days after the violent polemics that followed the 'milk statement' signed by several drama makers, the president called for a meeting at the Palace. The gathering, attended by the promoter of the media companies' counter-statement, director Najdat Anzour, together with actors Mustapha Khani, Jihad Saad, Zuhair Ramadan and many prominent representatives of Syrian TV drama, was clearly aimed at reaffirming Bashar al-Asad's personal support, and that of his reform-minded entourage, for the *musalsalat* industry. After the polemics and the polarization generated by the publication of the various statements, the gathering served to signal to artists that the entire drama sector needed to continue to stand by the president and his gradual path towards reform.

These meetings have been widely documented by Syrian media (Muhanna 2011), conveying to the audience the idea that the president and domestic cultural elites share the same progressive vision in the name of the national interest.[21] On these occasions whispers are exchanged about 'which politics and policies should find their way into *musalsalat* and be re-injected into the public sphere in the form of narrative fiction' (Della Ratta 2015a: 58). As journalist Taysir Khalat has underlined: 'There is no need to give orders, everything happens through a circulation of ideas.'[22] For Hani al-'Ashi, a producer of several successful series for his AJ company, decisions about what topic to transpose into the fictional universe of a *musalsal* are always taken in 'harmony' with the 'public mood'.[23] In Ramadan 2010 he attributed his decision to craft a TV series about a woman who chooses, against all the odds, to keep the disabled child she is pregnant with, to precisely this sort of sensitivity to the general atmosphere,[24] as if integrating and accepting disadvantaged children were a top priority discussion within Syrian society.

In reality, looking more closely at the circulation of ideas between the Palace, the drama makers and the media, an advocacy campaign for the rights of disabled children had been initiated by first lady Asma al-Asad in 2005, and was later intensified with the Special Olympic Games for the disabled hosted by Syria in September 2010 (DP News Sana 2010b). Not by chance, that very same year, *Wara' al-Shams* ('Behind the Sun') was broadcast during Ramadan, spreading its message of tolerance and acceptance towards the less fortunate. Alaa, the disabled boy who played the leading role in the TV fiction, was photographed with the first lady during the Special Olympics and featured on the front cover of the October issue of *Forward Magazine*, a publication promoting the idea of a liberal, progressive Syria under al-Asad's leadership. At the time, the magazine's editor-in-chief was Sami Moubayed, who first conceived the idea of *Fawq al-Saqf*: another clear signal that Syrian political and cultural elites are aligned to the same message of *tanwir*, the circulation of which happens through whispers sent out in the public space by both sides, in the form of different media formats, from news items to the fictional storylines of *musalsalat*.[25]

This triggers a dynamic by which issues deemed relevant do not need to be directly commissioned or imposed by the *sultat*, as they are circulated and encouraged through whispers.[26]

> The whisper strategy is an oral dynamic, where nothing happens in a formal, written, obligatory way: everything works informally, phrased as subtle hints. As to suggest the importance of oral communication in the making of cultural production, TV drama writer Najib Nusair [Najeeb Nseir] once stated: 'Syria is the country of phone calls'. This image well resonates with the oral, informal, unofficial character of the 'whispers'. (Della Ratta 2015a: 59).

This seemingly virtuous circle of communication between the reformist side of the *sultat* and the cultural producers is often interrupted by the interference of other elements that are also part of the power structure in Syria and yet pursue completely different priorities and agendas, as observed in the case of *Fawq al-Saqf*. Foucault's idea of power as a 'more or less coordinated', and sometimes 'ill-coordinated' (Foucault 1977: 199) cluster of relations, once again throws light on the way in which Syrian *sultat* interact and eventually clash, ensuring the failure of the objectives set through the whisper strategy. The *sotto voce* conversations in which priorities are negotiated and commonalities established can be hindered or blocked, intentionally or unintentionally, by other components of the *sultat*.

The history of these power struggles can be traced through the vicissitudes of *tanwir*-inspired TV drama produced during Bashar al-Asad's first decade: from the first season of the darkly satirical, cutting-edge comedy *Buq'at al-daw* ('Spotlight', 2001) to *Ghazlan fi Ghabat al-Dha'ab* ('Gazelles in a Forest of Wolves', 2006), *Laysa Saraban* ('It's Not a Mirage', 2008), *Ma malakat aymanukum* ('Those Whom Your Right Hand

Possesses', 2010) and *Chiffon* ('Chiffon', 2011).[27] This history seems to suggest a recurrent pattern in the pre-uprising era, in which clashes between security-minded and reform-minded *sultat* in the field of cultural production were always resolved in favour of the latter.

A particularly cogent example is offered by the first season of *Buq'at al-daw*, the *musalsal* that came to symbolize the reforms promised by the young Bashar al-Asad, and the dreams of freedom and openness of the Damascus Spring. Dealing with sensitive issues, such as corruption and the secret services' abuse of Syrian citizens, the satirical series enjoyed a smooth production process, probably because, as the director Laith Hajjo once remarked, 'People thought the show had a green light [from the authorities] because of the producer[28] ... In fact, the producer didn't really know what we were up to. We kept telling the censors that, look, the president said X, so we're following that policy' (Dick 2007: 8). With the start of the broadcast problems arose, and *Buq'at al-daw* was partly censored by Syrian TV. It was only thanks to the direct intervention of the Palace that the *musalsal* passed through the censorship and was finally aired.[29] Even after the president's personal intervention, clashes between *sultat* continued during the broadcast: apparently, former vice-president Abdul Halim Khaddam – whose son's company Sham International was a direct competitor to Mohamed Hamsho, the producer of *Buq'at al-daw*[30] – was furious at a sketch highlighting corruption and discouraging foreign investment in Syria (Dick 2007: 19). Despite the ongoing fights and reported interferences, however, *Buq'at al-daw* managed to stay on air.

In the end, the Damascus Spring was sacrificed but *Buq'at al-daw* wasn't: a smart move by the Palace to reiterate – at least in the media field – its reformist message and preserve its progressive facade by airing edgy, taboo-breaking TV drama thanks to the president's personal intervention. In this way *tanwir*-inspired *musalsalat* became structurally tied to Bashar al-Asad's political project: they became its acclaimed media face, and the face of his reformism. When other, more hawkish sides of the *sultat* attempted to sabotage these seemingly progressive media – or perhaps just pretended to, to give the regime the opportunity to show its reformist features in public – the president was immediately ready to reaffirm his politics by personally intervening in favour of the censored TV drama. The promise of reform remained intimately associated with al-Asad's persona: 'a more sophisticated way for [him] to earn reformist credentials without being obliged to hand over responsibility to institutions that would have to find structural, rather than personal ways to implement reforms' (Della Ratta 2015a: 71).

The fate of *Fawq al-Saqf* and other seemingly progressive TV dramas produced in 2011 (Della Ratta 2015a: 73–5) signalled that, in the post-uprising atmosphere, priorities had shifted towards a security-driven solution to the crisis that admitted no room for reformism – not even at a media level. Bashar al-Asad's non-intervention on behalf of the *musalsalat* in 2011 might suggest a weakness on the reformist side of the *sultat*, or simply imply that reforms can be quickly shelved when other more urgent priorities, such as the regime's own survival, are at stake.

Bab al-hara: *Whispering in the ears of the market*

Tanwir-inspired TV drama is not just a product of Syrian domestic politics in which the mutual needs and shared priorities of political and cultural elites have to be negotiated and accommodated. The whispers need to have an international dimension as well, or at least not contradict the commodity logic that Syrian *musalsalat* fully embrace on the Pan Arab market. Historically, Syria developed a domestic drama production sector in order to cater to a regional, fast-growing Pan Arab market consisting of hundreds of free-to-air channels controlled by a few wealthy Gulf-backed networks,[31] such as the Dubai-based and Saudi-owned MBC Group.[32] Throughout the 1990s, when these networks started operating,[33] the demand for TV drama rose, particularly during Ramadan – the Muslim holy month being the most crucial period in terms of viewership, advertising spending[34] and market competitiveness.[35] Due to their production quality and moderate market price,[36] Syrian TV series were sought-after by Gulf buyers, becoming an established component in the top Pan Arab channels' schedules, rivalling the Egyptians when it came to dominating drama slots during Ramadan.[37]

Structurally speaking, Syrian TV drama – an avowedly national asset – cannot survive without the financial support of the Pan Arab market and its Gulf-backed top players. One might legitimately ask how such a national, so markedly Syrian project came to have a Pan Arab dimension, enjoying prestige and market success regionally. Beside their competitive advantage in terms of price, why did these *musalsalat*, so strongly characterized by local storylines, characters, settings, dialects – and politics – attract the interest of a very different part of the Arab world, i.e. the Gulf? Moreover, if they result from whispers between one side of the

Figure 2.1   With the actors on the filming location for the *musalsal Bab al-hara*, May 2010 (photo: Donatella Della Ratta).

sultat and the drama makers, why would these private, commercially driven broadcasters – which are also expressions of Gulf state powers – support a political project negotiated between Syrian elites? Is it that the whisper strategy also works in a Pan Arab context? Is the politics of Syrian drama – the ongoing accommodation between political and cultural elites – ever at odds with the politics of the Pan Arab market?

Being at the same time a national project and a highly sought-after commodity with regional appeal, *Bab al-hara* ('The Gate of the Neighbourhood', 2006–17) – probably the most famous multi-season *musalsal* ever broadcast on a Pan Arab channel[38] – provides a powerful insight into the dynamic at work between Syrian political and cultural elites on the one hand, and Pan Arab capital on the other, offering a pattern that can be read into the relation between market and politics across the Arab region. After premiering on MBC during Ramadan 2006, the TV series immediately conquered the entire Arab world.[39] Millions of viewers followed the vicissitudes of the *musalsal* protagonists – coffee-shop owners, barbers, fruit sellers and bakers – in an imagined *hara* (neighbourhood) in the Old City of Damascus, in a time frame falling somewhere between the collapse of the Ottoman empire and the French occupation of Syria. Originally conceived as a two-part series,

Bab al-hara – first directed by Bassam al-Malla and produced by AJ's Hani al-'Ashi – romanticizes the lifestyle and traditions of the Damascene neighbourhood, inspiring a feeling of 'nostalgia for the past'[40] aimed at reminding the 'new generations in Syria of its noble values'.[41] Although it mentions historical events, such as the British occupation of Palestine and the consequent popular revolt, the *musalsal* mostly works as a sort of handbook of traditional life in this imagined Old Damascus, providing viewers with an idea of how people used to live, marry and raise children, and following 'the logic of a grandmother's bedtime story'.[42]

This fairy-tale atmosphere has changed dramatically since season 3. As a consequence of the incredible success of the first two seasons, in fact, MBC decided to commission three more,[43] although this had not been originally planned by the show's Syrian producers. The Pan Arab group also acquired exclusive rights to commercialize the *musalsal*, sell it to other stations, manage the merchandising, and deal with all operations concerning marketing and derivative products.[44] At the same time as *Bab al-hara* was turning into the perfect commodity for the Pan Arab market, its content became more and more politicized, introducing the leading theme of the *hara*'s resistance against the French occupation of Syria, and legitimizing the local armed struggle against foreigners – something which seemed to hint at the US-led invasion of Iraq in 2003, or at Israel's attack on Gaza in 2008–9.

This politicization of the series, rather than being a result of the Pan Arab group's interference in its storyline and editorial policy,[45] actually happened '*in spite of* MBC', as an expert on Pan Arab advertising has stressed.[46] It seems, in fact, that the Syrian producers – who had to find three extra seasons' worth of stories and characters than they had initially planned for – decided to draw inspiration from regional politics in order to give Arab audiences what they believed they wanted. This was emphasized by Kamal al-Murra, the *musalsal*'s writer:

Politics is a very important part of any Arab citizen's daily life, even if he is far from expressing this through political participation. What happens in Palestine is our daily bread. These topics are not perceived as artificial or far from life, but as real issues. That's why our audience likes them. Anyone who writes drama is a part of this Arab society, so he chooses topics known to be close to his people's interests ... There is no TV drama outside of politics.[47]

These words resonate with Syrian TV drama critic Mohamed Mansour's remark that 'the political message in *Bab al-hara* has overcome everything else, not because it was required by MBC. It is rather the audience who requires it; or, better, what its authors think the audience wants.'[48]

It is likely that the perspective of an increasing Pan Arab success, with the related prestige and material benefits, and the belief that Arab viewers would be sympathetic towards stories and characters inspired by current events, pushed *Bab al-hara*'s producers to turn the bedtime stories of the first two seasons into something closer to a war bulletin. Images of revolt and armed struggle featured throughout the newly commissioned three seasons.[49] The struggle of the Palestinian people against the British, which had been just a background theme in the previous parts, turned into the fierce armed resistance of the Syrians against French colonial rule, a dominant thread from season 3 on. Suddenly, *Bab al-hara* had shifted towards the explicit celebration of revolt against the oppressor, connecting resistance with religion and showing how it should be performed as a divine task. Throughout the newly commissioned seasons, religious expressions and practices pinpointed peak moments of resistance and heroism against the foreign occupier.

Figure 2.2   A set of *a musalsal* in the city centre of Damascus, 2010 (photo: Donatella Della Ratta).

The religion portrayed in the *musalsal* as intimately connected to the national resistance movement is Sunni Islam; something that is at least problematic in the eyes of the Syrian *sultat*. On the one hand, the equivalence between resistance and Islam plays down the multi-confessional dimension of the country, diminishing any contribution made by minorities to forming Syria's identity and shaping an idea of the nation. On the other hand, the emphasis on a Sunni movement against foreign occupation suggests, albeit involuntarily, a sectarian reading of Syrian history in favour of Sunni resistance, and symbolically questions the country's leadership. The idea of a religiously and ethnically mixed society is, in fact, at the basis of the 'Syrian exception' (Donati 2009); the protection of minorities has been turned by the al-Asad family – themselves members of a religious minority, the Alawites – into an argument for justifying their decades-long rule.[50] Preserving religious diversity in the country has been turned into a badge of identity and a political strategy in al-Asad's Syria. It became a key element of the regime's rhetoric, and its centrality was always emphasized in public discourse.[51]

Surprisingly, the Syrian exception was initially not reflected in *Bab al-hara*. Yet, considering the fairy-tale-like atmosphere of the first two seasons, that was not so problematic as it was in the following seasons, in which the newly introduced logic of 'time and space' (*makan wa zaman*)[52] suddenly presented the problem of historical validity in relation to the events narrated. 'The troubles began when *Bab al-hara* stopped being about stories and started to be about history', Syrian TV critic Maher Mansour remarked.[53] There was now too much at stake for Syrian *sultat*, since the *musalsal* was strategic both as a catalyst for the country's tourism revenues and as a diplomatic PR tool. *Bab al-hara* had become, in fact, a sort of political ambassador for Syria, to the point that its actors often accompanied Syrian officials during diplomatic visits (Black 2009), and were received as representatives of the Syrian government (Ma'an News Agency 2009).

At this point, the Palace whispered to try to work out a solution to the discrepancy between the mono-dimensional, Sunni-led country portrayed in *Bab al-hara*, and al-Asad's Syria, marketed as a mosaic of cultures and religions[54] in which leadership should be held by a minority elite group in order to protect other minorities and allegedly defend their cultural and religious assets. When a Christian woman – Umm Joseph, played by veteran Syrian actress Mona Wassef – was introduced as a leading character in season 4, this was likely the result of whispers between the *sultat* and the Syrian producers, and was intended to restore a multi-religious order to the *hara* and compensate for the Sunni-inspired rhetoric of resistance overplayed in season 3 (2008).

The latter had in fact generated polemics and discontent among elite groups vis-à-vis a TV series that had become the official face of Syria in the Arab world. Bashar al-Asad's literary advisor Colette Khoury, a prominent Christian novelist and staunch supporter of the president's reformist project,[55] had openly attacked the drama for its religious mono-dimensionality. She publicly declared that 'the *Bab al-hara* TV series is beautiful, but it's not Damascus', adding: 'I expressed my opinion on television, and they reported it to the minister' (Kusa 2008). Bashar al-Asad was reported to have intervened in person, aiming at injecting 'religious diversity'[56] into the TV series; while his wife Asma apparently gave *Bab al-hara*'s director her personal advice on how to conclude season 5 (Ain News 2010). As for the series' producers, none of them has ever officially admitted the president's intervention in favour of multi-religiosity, but the writer Kamal al-Murra has acknowledged that introducing the character of Umm Joseph resulted from 'constructive criticism that has made us think'.[57]

During Ramadan 2009, exactly one year after Colette Khoury's open criticism of *Bab al-hara*, Umm Joseph made her TV debut as one of the leading characters of season 4. A few months later, Mona Wassef was honoured by Bashar al-Asad in person with a prestigious award for 'the important role of the Syrian drama in embracing the national and Pan Arab principles and presenting Syrian culture and heritage' (Cham Press 2009). In a perfect feedback loop, Syrian media stressed that during the meeting 'the President also highlighted the remarkable contribution of drama in finding solutions to social and daily life issues' (Cham Press 2009). Closing the circle of whispers, Wassef was chosen to play Umm Joseph: as the daughter of a Damascene Kurd, she was herself part of a minority within the Syrian cultural prism, the perfect incarnation of Bashar al-Asad's unity-in-diversity vision. Moreover, Wassef has always been a staunch supporter of the president, to the extent that she publicly renounced paying a visit to her only son, Ammar Abdelhamid, a prominent opponent of the al-Asad regime, who had been obliged to leave Syria for the US in 2005. At the time she decided, against all the odds, to stay in the country and stand by its leadership, a decision she has respected even following the outbreak of the 2011 uprising. This controversial choice – that of a mother renouncing the love of her son for the love of her country – had consolidated her public image as an icon of patriotism and national unity, making her an even stronger tool in the hands of al-Asad's PR strategy. Given all this, it is no wonder that during Ramadan 2009 she was turned into a powerful marketing instrument to embody the message that the Palace had whispered to *Bab al-hara*'s producers. Once again, the Syrian political and cultural elites seemed to be heading in the same direction. There was no fight, no controversy, no disagreement between them; on the contrary, the gentle suggestion of the whisper was immediately incorporated by the drama makers into a brand-new media message.

To be sure, the dynamic of the whisper is not only about harmony and affinity between the *sultat* and the cultural producers. After the outbreak of the 2011 uprising, open dissent and criticism came to mean exile, even for those members of the cultural elite who had previously supported the president and his project of *tanwir*. Samer al-Masri, who played the successful character Abu Shehab until season 3, has only recently spoken about the TV series in public. Following a long silence after he left Syria in 2011, the actor declared in an interview with al-Arabiya that the *musalsal* expressed a 'political agenda', being written in 'the corridors of the Syrian government' in order to convey 'messages to the Arab world'.[58] This is what whispers are meant for: circulating messages between like-minded Syrian elites to inject them into media that will be commodified and consumed on the Pan Arab market.

The paradoxes of the whisper

Why would a private, Pan Arab venture like MBC accept, or at least not oppose, the interference of the Syrian *sultat* in one of its most successful media properties? How was the whisper negotiated at the time between Syrian domestic politics and the Saudi-owned Pan Arab network, and consequently adjusted to the cultural logic of the latter? For the representation of the Christian religion in Saudi-owned media is problematic to say the least. As an example, during Ramadan 2010 an episode of the renowned Saudi comedy *Tash ma Tash*[59] dared to tackle the issue of Arab Christians,[60] generating polemics and troubles for MBC, including the issue of *fatwas* by religious scholars. Despite the family-oriented brief of MBC1[61] – the flagship channel that broadcasts Ramadan-exclusive hits like *Bab al-hara* and *Tash ma Tash* – the controversies and threats have also brought MBC high audience ratings, media attention and a reputation for being a modern, taboo-breaking TV network.

Similarly, purely marketing calculations might have been behind the channel's decision to accept a female Christian hero in one of its flagship programmes during the Muslim holy month. The group's move to commodify the character of Umm Joseph, making her an official icon of *Bab al-hara* 4's merchandising, seems to confirm its centrality in the *musalsal* and MBC's support for this choice and its implications.[62] In the end, the depiction of Christianity in *Bab al-hara* is not at odds with the editorial line of a TV network backed by Saudi Arabia, a country which, as caretaker of the Muslim religion and its holy places, is highly problematic in terms of granting visibility to religious diversity. Yet Umm Joseph is never portrayed as a threat to the markedly Islamic environment of the *musalsal*. Her Christianity is not antithetical to Islam; rather, her faith is presented as a sub-cultural nuance within the wider spectrum of religious pluralism in a multi-confessional but united Syria.[63] Muslims and Christians are finally joined in the struggle against foreign invasion, colonialism and oppression. 'Injustice is not a matter of religion, or country, or identity'[64] –is Umm Joseph's solemn remark when her nephew, a Christian fighter from Palestine, dies trying to help his Damascene friends in a clash with the French. Later, when her nephew's Muslim friend is martyred, she takes part in the Islamic ritual to honour him. Here Christian morality has been adapted to fit a universal rhetoric of national resistance and unity in the name of the *hara*, which turns into a metaphor for an entire country fighting for freedom and independence from foreign occupation. In *Bab al-hara*'s moral universe, forgiveness exists among Syrian citizens, whether Muslims or Christians, if it helps the national cause against the occupiers; but no forgiveness is granted to the latter and their collaborators.[65]

In the end, with the appearance of Umm Joseph, *Bab al-hara* turned resistance into a national duty that everybody should perform – Muslims and Christians, men and women – beyond any religious or gender differences. This reinforcement of unity-in-diversity is key to Bashar al-Asad's political and media discourse, and to the officially sponsored idea of a Syrian mosaic of cultures. In line with this political project, the religious differences of Old Damascus have faded away and disappeared. Reduced to just a cultural nuance, an 'ethical system' (Christmann 1996), Christianity in the *hara* has been wiped clean of any historical detail or references to practices of worship. This process takes a visual form on the cover of season 4's attractively packaged official DVD box: here Umm Joseph wears a dark veil, with no cross or any other symbol to signify her religion. In the eyes of the MBC marketing department, Umm Joseph seems to be just another character with the same visual features as the *hara's* Muslim women. She is a marketing novelty, yet conveying a sort of familiarity the viewers are accustomed to; in the end, *Bab al-hara's* aestheticizing of religion 'as costume history' also invests Islam, turning it into a 'charmingly antiquated practice' (Salamandra 2010: 282, 4).

Both religious faiths thus become part of a vague anti-colonial and anti-imperial critique, where resistance to foreign occupation is portrayed as something belonging to an idyllic past, part of a bygone tradition. Religion and resistance melt together into a vague nostalgia for the past that waters down any potentially contentious element. This commodified, nostalgic image of the past not only serves MBC's strategy of crafting a product suitable for sale across the Pan Arab market; it also works in line with the Syrian *sultat's* attempt to turn Damascus' Old City into 'a politically neutered museum, a playground for new middle class money spenders' (Salamandra 2004: 135), regardless of their religious or sectarian identities. Local politics and the regional market's exigencies finally converge in accommodating values and messages in Syria's most famous Pan Arab TV series.

Bab al-hara shows how the whisper strategy can work at a regional, Pan Arab level, as well as it functions in regulating domestic cultural politics. The *musalsal* in fact sheds light on a pattern that regulates the multilateral relations between Syrian *sultat*, drama makers and Gulf capital; i.e. a pattern of accommodation and convergence of interests. This model is so rooted in the cultural politics of the Arab region that it seems to have survived (so far) even the post-2011 political crisis between the Syrian regime and those Gulf states – especially Saudi Arabia – that are openly supporting the opposition to Bashar al-Asad. Despite the ongoing problems with filming in a war-torn country,[66] *Bab al-hara* is still being produced in Damascus and regularly broadcast on MBC.[67] Even if it clearly reflects the political agenda of the Syrian *sultat* – as recently observed in a TV interview with one of the show's most famous actors[68] – this seems not to be an issue for the Saudi-owned network.

Even at a regional level, the strategic needs conveyed through the whispers tend to converge rather than clash. On the one hand, Gulf capital is key to ensuring the sustainability of Syrian TV drama; not only on the Pan Arab market, but also domestically. On the other hand,

Pan Arab TV networks need quality product to feed their schedules, especially during Ramadan: given the scarcity of Gulf drama productions, they are obliged to purchase products from Egypt and Syria, the top *musalsalat* producers in the region.[69] Even in times of political crisis – such as in 2011, when rumours circulated of an alleged embargo against Syrian TV drama[70] led by Saudi Arabia and Qatar, who openly supported the anti-regime uprising – there has been no evidence of the Gulf-owned channels stopping purchasing Syrian *musalsalat*.[71]

This is a clear sign that market exigencies and local politics are not at odds in the Arab region, despite the ongoing power struggles, and that the whisper strategy still functions not only as a specifically Syrian mechanism, but as a pattern in the broader geopolitical dynamics at a Pan Arab media level. In light of the alternating fortunes of *Fawq al-Saqf*, however, one should always bear in mind that the balance between multiple powers may shift, such that the whispers can be abruptly subverted whenever urgent priorities or issues of regime survival are at stake.

SNAPSHOT #3

Syrian *musalsalat* dealing with issues such as sectarian chaos, jihadism, forced exile and the refugee crisis are what I call 'real-time drama': *tanwir*-inspired media focusing on the implications of the conflict while the latter is unfolding, and committed to facilitating national dialogue and a political solution to the crisis. These attempts highlight the failure of *tanwir* to serve as a catalyst in rebuilding a post-uprising national, collective, unifying project through progressive media, and to act as a Habermasian platform that would establish a dialogue between the factions involved in the conflict and help overcome sectarian divisions.

Tanwir's final collapse in post-2011 real-time drama is to be attributed to its profound resonance with Bashar al-Asad's political project conceived as a top-down engineered and minority-led process of change. Belief in that process – upon which an entire generation of drama makers has been brought up – seems to have survived even in those who have opted for open opposition to Syria's ruling powers, and who live and work in exile. Paradoxically, the same scheme of the pre-uprising *tanwir*-inspired content is repeated in post-2011 real-time drama, where individuals within the regime structure, or the Syrian people at large, are blamed for dragging the country into hell. This patronizing approach and the reluctance to hold the president accountable have dissolved *tanwir*-inspired media for reconciliation into vague appeals to a generic patriotism and phony forms of humanitarianism that fail to address the political and material causes behind the conflict, or to explore and criticize the inner power structure of the al-Asad family.

3
The Death of *Tanwir* in Real-Time Drama

Ethnographies of real-time drama

In February 2015 I embarked on a new project with a filmmaker friend. Since it had become impossible for me to return to Syria for fieldwork, my research interest in Syrian cultural production shifted towards Lebanon, where the majority of the domestic drama industry had relocated due to the instability and insecurity in their native country. That winter, as I was about to leave for Beirut to catch up with Syrian drama makers and their works-in-progress for the holy month due to start in mid-June, a filmmaker friend asked whether she could join me. A veteran and award-winning documentary director, she had a masters in anthropology and shared my scholarly interest for TV fiction as a privileged site shaping national politics and identities. At the time, she was thinking of making a film about the Syrian conflict as seen through the lenses of TV drama and the way in which the *tanwir*-inspired drama makers were transposing sensitive issues related to the events in their country into edgy *musalsalat* addressed to a Pan Arab audience.

Among the topics in the pipeline for Syrian drama in Ramadan 2015, one that had immediately caught my interest was the refugee crisis. That year the UN refugee agency UNHCR had estimated the total number of Syrian refugees to amount to 4,013,000 people distributed between Turkey, Lebanon, Iraq, Egypt and other parts of North Africa. Rami Hanna, an esteemed Syrian actor and director, was working on a *musalsal* project dealing precisely with the issue of displaced Syrians, which was a hot potato not only for the hosting countries. Just one year earlier, in a speech given after the first multi-candidate presidential elections were held and won by Bashar al-Asad with an overwhelming majority, the Syrian president had made clear that those who left the country 'as traitors, agents or corrupt individuals are of little concern; the country has been cleansed of those individuals and they no longer have a place or status among Syrians' (al-Asad 2014).

Producing a Ramadan TV drama depicting refugees as including not only those who had sided with the uprising, but also people who were displaced despite being al-Asad's supporters, was a courageous move for a Syrian TV drama maker. In an effort to tackle national reconciliation and serve as a platform for dialogue in accordance with *tanwir* ideology, *Ghadan Naltaqi* ('We Will Meet Tomorrow', 2015) featured the story of two young men: an idealistic poet supporting the uprising, and his conservative brother, who sides with the regime more for fear of the country being dragged into chaos than out of any strong conviction. Despite their contrasting political positions, they both end up in a refugee camp in Lebanon, where they fall in love with the same woman, Wardeh, a beautiful displaced Syrian who earns her living cleaning the corpses of deceased fellow citizens, preparing them for the Islamic burial regardless of their political faith. National unity and reconciliation are evoked by the very title of the *musalsal*, *Ghadan Naltaqi*, which recalls a famous TV show from Hafiz al-Asad's times. As writer Iyad Abu-Shamat has remarked: 'We all used to follow the program, although not everybody liked it. It was a TV event putting together people from different ages, religions, and social classes. It made us feel united, even if it was just a fake unity celebrated in front of TV screens.'[1]

Besides its provocative and timely subject, however, it was the *musalsal* production process that had most captured my scholarly attention.

Figure 3.1 Actor Maxim Khalil on the set of the *musalsal Ghadan Naltaqi* ('We Will Meet Tomorrow'), Beirut 2015 (photo: Donatella Della Ratta).

The two brothers were played by two prominent Syrian actors, Maxim Khalil and Abdel Moneim Amayri, themselves with conflicting political positions, the former being a supporter of the uprising living in exile, and the latter a staunch pro-regime artist still residing inside Syria. In stark contrast with their political beliefs, the director had asked Khalil to play the pro-regime brother, while Amayri was given the role of the pro-opposition poet – probably in an effort to produce a TV show that would act as a living site of reconciliation and dialogue among media professionals with opposite visions concerning the future of their country.

This was not unprecedented in contemporary Syrian *musalsalat*. There is a clear pattern in the efforts of Syrian TV drama produced after 2011 to perform two operations simultaneously: 'to act as a text attempting to make sense of a conflict that is still unfolding, and to do so in a context in which its cultural producers – from the artistic cast to the technical crew – are all involved, as citizens of a war-torn country, in the events that they are trying to describe through their serialized television product' (Della Ratta 2014a: 3). This genre – which I call 'real-time drama' – has tackled all sorts of timely and sensitive issues, from the outbreak of the uprising to the rise of Daesh and other armed militias and terror organizations. Contemporary real-time drama is located in a tradition of social realism (Salamandra 2010) that has always distinguished Syrian *musalsalat* and helped differentiate them from Egyptian melodrama for the contemporaneity of their topics and their visual style of filming (Della Ratta 2014a). What is really unprecedented in post-2011 real-time drama, though, is that its makers have to act as both observers and participants, witnesses and storytellers of events touching them in the first person. In such a peculiar – and precarious – situation, Syrian cultural producers have to adopt 'multiple strategies of survival ... both surviving as *players in a market* where they have to sell their product as a commodity and surviving as *citizens of a country* undergoing a civil war' (Della Ratta 2014a: 4).

In light of these considerations, the filming of *Ghadan Naltaqi* was an ideal site of scholarly reflection on how cultural production and the power struggles behind it – both at a domestic level between Syrian *sultat* and drama makers, and in their mutual relationship with the Gulf-backed Pan Arab market – were shifting and recombining as a consequence of the unrest in Syria and of its impact on the broader Arab region. The question was whether the mechanism of the whisper and the dynamic of accommodation between regional market and local politics were still holding, years after the uprising; and how Syrian cultural producers were coping with producing TV fiction that was required to act simultaneously as a national reconciliation platform, and as a commodity to be consumed by Pan Arab audiences.

After arranging the trip with the director and the scriptwriter, and having secured the authorization for my friend to film a short promo that could serve as a pitch for a longer documentary to be shot the following year, we left for Beirut full of hope and curiosity. When we got to the filming location – an abandoned school a few kilometres from the Lebanese capital – we were struck by its simplicity, but also by its effectiveness in evoking the desolation of a refugee camp. Everything on the location was essential, from the clothes of the actors and extras, to the props and the lighting. In stark contrast with the unpretentiousness and simplicity of the set, people seemed quite ambivalent and there was a palpable tension among them. After years of ethnographic work in Syrian TV drama, I knew most of the actors and the filming crews in the local industry, and they were very familiar with my presence on set. Yet this time their way of welcoming me signalled that something was inherently different from our days in Syria, including the period when the uprising had started.

After a long day of filming and chatting with people we sat in our hotel the next day, waiting for the director's call to give us the green light and go back to the location. That green light never came; instead, the embarrassed director tried to explain on the phone that unexpected problems had occurred with the production and we were not allowed to visit the location again. Not even without the camera, he cautiously added. Only after reaching out to the producer, who was traveling out of Lebanon, did I realize that he had nothing against our presence on set. We were frustrated but couldn't do anything other than comply with the director's wishes, guessing that probably the actors and the crew, rather than the producer, had been bothered by our presence. So the trip came to an abrupt end.

The following year my friend and I went back to Lebanon. A long time before flying to Beirut we had contacted the Syrian director Hatem Ali, who was about to shoot the second part of a *musalsal* version of 'The Godfather' (*al 'Arrab*), the saga of a mafia family in Syria that bore more than a similarity with the al-Asad clan. He had given us his word that we could spend as much time as we wanted on set, and had full permission to film the entire making of the TV series. 'The Godfather' presented us with a situation similar to *Ghadan Naltaqi*, being a live site of contention between media professionals with very different political views, and having to serve both as a national project of *tanwir* in troubled times for Syria, and as a commodity to be consumed during the crowded Ramadan TV season.

Despite all our cautious advance arrangements, our adventure ended exactly as it had done with *Ghadan Naltaqi*. After a late phone call and some embarrassed excuses, we finally learned that we were not allowed to go back to 'The Godfather' set, a random 'issue with the production' being the only reason given for this unexpected news. On the one day that we were able to spend on location I saw Syrian youths coming from Damascus and the surrounding areas to earn a small amount of money

Figure 3.2   Director Hatem Ali on the set of the *musalsal al 'Arrab* ('The Godfather'), Beirut, 2016 (photo: Donatella Della Ratta).

that would barely allow them to make a living in a country with less and less business, and more and more inflation. In the breaks between filming, they did not hesitate to tell stories of destruction, violence and abuse of power, some of them inquiring if there was a way to get a visa to Europe, even illegally. One boy in his twenties, with the saddest eyes I have ever seen, came up to me and asked where the biggest forest was – 'perhaps in Germany?' – as he did not want to live among humans any longer – 'I want to see animals only. I am sure they do less harm.'

That was the first time in years I had heard somebody openly blaming Bashar al-Asad for the destruction brought upon Syria. Suddenly I realized that, perhaps, the production team had been equally bothered by my friend's camera and by my understanding of Syrian dialect. They wanted us to listen to 'The Godfather' story, not to those stories coming from the devastated heart of their homeland.

Don't shoot the leader, shoot the people!

It is no coincidence that two prominent Syrian directors, both of whom had publicly sided with the popular uprising and were openly committed to using their TV works as platforms for *tanwir* in troubled times, adopted the same attitude when problems occurred on location. On the one hand, they agreed to make their filming process – and, consequently, the controversies it would very likely generate among artists and crew with such different political views – transparent and open to external observers, being proud to produce progressive media supposed to facilitate national dialogue on issues that had dramatically divided the country. On the other hand, however, with an elitist attitude typical of *tanwir*-inspired media, they wished to manage the outcome, and were afraid that an uncontrolled reaction – like that of the young boy openly blaming the Syrian president – might emerge and be registered by external observers.

At first glance, this behaviour appears ambivalent and odd. Why would enlightened cultural producers, living in exile and in favour of the uprising, be worried that anti-regime sentiments might be expressed during a TV production presenting itself as a progressive platform for dialogue, in which clashing opinions are supposed to be aired, exchanged and, eventually, reconciled for the sake of national unity? Contrary to initial appearances, Syrian real-time drama crafted in the post-uprising years by oppositional cultural producers seems to be still enmeshed in mechanisms of fine-tuning with domestic and regional powers – whether the Syrian *sultat* or the Pan Arab market. It is as if, even when living abroad and taking an open pro-uprising position, Syrian drama makers still feel the charming influence of the whispers from the Palace; as if they want to hold the regime accountable for the violence devastating the country, but not its president.

A prominent *musalsal* from 2013, *Wilada min al-khasira* ('Birth from the Waist') part three,[2] rendered this feeling in a compelling real-time drama storyline. The TV series – whose previous seasons in 2011 and 2012 had focused on corruption in the country and the miserable lives of people in suburban, haphazard neighbourhoods – narrates the events that led a peaceful protest movement for dignity and justice to degenerate into armed riots and, eventually, into a fully-fledged civil war, as a consequence of the violent intervention of the *mukhabarat* and the hawkish side of the regime. In a telling sequence we see protestors negotiating with a government official, who finally agrees to meet the demands of the citizens.[3] However, as soon as they come out of the ministerial building, the protesters are violently harassed and arrested by the secret police. The government official eventually disappears into thin air, together with the promise of establishing a dialogue with the protestors, reminding us of the impossibility (or unwillingness) of the reform-minded side of the *sultat* to control and win over the more security-minded forces of the regime.

Throughout the entire *musalsal* we see pictures of Bashar al-Asad in government buildings and police stations, in a realism-oriented style which is the signature of Syrian TV drama. Yet the word *ra'is* (president) and his actual name are never directly mentioned, the only exception being when the president issues an amnesty for people who have been indiscriminately arrested – which Bashar al-Asad did in fact issue in May and June 2011, as a symbolic act to show openness and willingness to establish a dialogue (al-Jazeera 2011a). However – in the TV series as in real life – only ordinary criminals were released, while the civil rights movement activists remained in jail; the Palace never monitored the enforcement of the amnesty and did not oppose this de facto situation. When asked directly whether he held just one side of the regime responsible for the escalation of violence in the country, Samer Radwan, the author of the *musalsal*, politely answered that '*Wilada* has a patriotic perspective on the situation … Not everybody is guilty, not everybody is *shabbiha* [an informal pro-Asad militia]. I want to send a human message to both sides.'[4]

In fact, despite being an opponent of the Syrian regime who was briefly arrested during the filming of *Wilada*, Radwan publicly declared his intention of having Syrian professionals with diverging political beliefs work together in the *musalsal* 'to show that "dialogue and cohabitation" were still possible in Syria' (Della Ratta 2014a: 11). His idea that *Wilada* might act as a sort of Habermasian platform for rational, deliberative dialogue among Syrians with different affiliations underlines to what extent Syrian TV drama – whether 'oppositional' or 'pro-regime', whether manufactured inside the country or abroad – is still very much imbued with the values of *tanwir* that, for decades, have linked Syria's political and cultural elites on a common ideological ground.

With its firm belief in enlightening the masses, Syrian TV drama has addressed the most sensitive issues, including the abuses of power perpetrated by the *mukhabarat*. Yet the critiques offered by these seemingly progressive media never directly touched the leadership, as the telling example of *tanwir*-inspired drama denouncing corruption has clearly demonstrated for more than a decade. Throughout the 2000s, in fact, several Syrian *musalsalat* focused on the vexed question of corruption in the country. Not surprisingly, in a perfect whispering circle between the drama makers and the political elites, this was a trend topic when the young president seized power in 2000, focusing his PR efforts to establish the legitimacy and morality of the new leadership precisely on 'the fight against corruption' (*mukafahat al-fasad*).[5] This emphasis on corruption as one of the worst evils in Syrian society has long been ingrained in Bashar al-Asad's public discourse.[6] Later, when more urgent issues challenged the leadership – such as the escalation of the civil war and the rise of violent extremist groups on the ground – the president's narrative still stressed the centrality of this struggle in ensuring the progress of Syrian society: 'Let us make fighting corruption our priority in the next period, in state institutions and across society as a whole; let's make it a priority not only for state officials, but also for every individual' (al-Asad 2014).

Even if other priorities have emerged, the emphasis on corruption is not surprising: in the Syrian leader's public discourse, as much as in *tanwir*-inspired media, it has long been portrayed as the country's endemic disease, the most urgent problem to solve and the most difficult to eradicate. Paradoxically, the 'need for corruption' (*darurat-al-fasad*)[7] has become a political strategy to preserve the moral persona of the Syrian president. Corruption should not be completely eradicated, as the leader requires it in order to claim his supreme moral authority in fighting it. It must be constantly identified as a core problem, and the public always reminded of its urgency and seriousness, while at the same time no attempt should ever be made to completely eradicate it.

Blaming individuals for corruption, even those in the upper echelons of the political system, is an inherent part of this strategy that aims at preserving the regime and, at the same time, facilitating its reorganization with the removal of specific people whose presence might be deemed, at some point, inconvenient for the survival of the ruling *sultat*. This has happened several times throughout decades of al-Asad rule; charging individuals with corruption and abuse of power has ended up being the most effective way to get rid of inconvenient members of the regime, and to legitimize their removal in the eyes of public opinion. *Tanwir*-inspired TV drama, crafted by cultural elites perfectly in tune with the politics of the Palace, has helped strengthen this logic. For more than a decade, TV series have targeted and denounced corruption within Syrian society, yet none of this seemingly progressive social drama has been able to suggest a way of reforming the system, apart from simply removing or punishing those individuals who have compromised themselves.

TV drama dealing critically with corruption issues existed under Hafiz al-Asad's rule,[8] but the topic has never been as emphasized as in the Bashar al-Asad era, during which the Palace has used the socially and politically engaged *musalsalat* as evidence of its own openness, transparency and willingness to reform.[9] Corrupt figures portrayed in TV series – like the main character in *Ghazlan fi Ghabat al-Dha'ab* ('Gazelles in a Forest of Wolves', 2006), who bears more than a passing resemblance to Mahmoud al-Zoubi, a former Syrian prime minister accused of corruption who later committed suicide,[10] or like the protagonist of *La'nat al-thin* ('The Curse of the Mud', 2010), who seems to hint at former vice-president, Abdul Halim Khaddam, a 'hawk' from Hafiz al-Asad's old guard who sought asylum in Paris in 2005[11] – are the best demonstration of how 'the fight against corruption' campaign travelled from Bashar al-Asad's public speeches to the fictional universe of *musalsalat*, in a perfect circle of whispers between political and cultural elites. In the end, the series concludes that corruption is naturally intertwined with all political structures, even at a high level – yet never at the highest, as it does not touch the leader whose role is to embody the fight against the system's malfunctions.

The leader's good intentions to reform a rotten system were emphasized in another *musalsal* from Bashar al-Asad's first decade, *Buq'at al-daw* ('Spotlight'), which became a media symbol of the openness and commitment to change initially manifested by the young president. *Hawamish* ('Margins'), a short sketch from the 2003 season, features a top official telling his staff that freedom of expression has to be encouraged. 'The official gives the orders but at each stage subordinates gradually alter the directive and cast increasing abuse on journalists and writers who have been voicing the criticism' (Dick 2007: 13). Here the satire does not touch the highest level of the system, that of the enlightened leader ready to commit himself to change; rather, low-ranking elements are to blame for their inability – or unwillingness – to keep up with the reforms promoted by the leadership. Similar to the metaphor of the roof spread across the media spectrum from Bashar al-Asad's televised speeches to the fictional universe of TV series like *Fawq al-Saqf*,[12] *Hawamish* also conveys the impression of a society that, thanks to an enlightened leadership, enjoys a wide degree of freedom which citizens are not ready to reach for and grasp. For these media it is rather Syrian society that bears responsibility for perpetrating the evils of the system, while the leadership appears always open to drive change. As in the words of Laith Hajjo, who directed the first season of *Buq'at al-daw* and several successful *tanwir*-inspired *musalsalat*: 'more than political control, religious and social control are our real problems and the cause of social backwardness ... drama can help solve this'.

Individuals are to be continuously reminded that they are responsible for generating a corrupt system and keeping it alive; as partners in its dysfunction they guarantee its survival. *Al-sirr* ('The Secret'), another episode from *Buq'at al-daw* season 7, provides an exemplary representation of this political strategy. The satirical sketch features Syrian officials and representatives of foreign countries who are eager to learn Syria's secret concerning its economy. The proud officials explain that the secret lies in the 'added value', an informal extra fee that every citizen has to pay in order to get services that otherwise the state would not provide. Through comedy the *musalsal* reminds Syrians that they are all part of the corrupt system and complicit with it.[13] Every citizen is a gear in the rotten mechanism, as the system's survival is intertwined with personal survival. This is how Syrian citizens are constantly made aware that they are culpable for the perpetuation of social diseases that enlightened TV drama is ready to unveil and denounce.

Preserving elective affinities between Syrian political and cultural elites

The paternalistic and elitist approach of Syrian *musalsalat*, their inclination to hold society accountable for its alleged backwardness, and their reluctance to blame the leadership, seem to have survived the post-uprising period and the split within the drama industry between those who chose to support the regime and those who sided with the protest movement. The latter, although living in exile and producing TV drama outside Syria, still appear to be entrapped in the president's political rhetoric to the extent that none of their products dares to openly criticize his persona. Rather, they prefer to blame rotten individuals within the system, or society at large, for having pushed a peaceful uprising into a brutal civil war in which citizens appear to have sold the country for their personal interests instead of fighting to defend the national interest – as several real-time dramas, from *Wilada min al-khasira* to *Ghadan Naltaqi*, seem to argue. Once again, this narrative resonates with the president's official rhetoric: 'national corruption ... creates people who sell their homeland and the blood of its children to the highest bidder' (al-Asad 2014).

There may be other reasons for this behaviour, rather than simply the attunement between the Palace and the drama makers that still seems to be operational, despite exile and the political divergences that have emerged. Some cultural producers have become bolder in expressing open criticism of the al-Asad family since the uprising.[14] Because such public expressions of dissent can have serious repercussions for families or friends still living inside Syria, many artists have resorted to anonymity or using pen-names – something that is less likely with industrial, serialized products such as *musalsalat*. The silent censorship mechanism of the regional market has also played a role in preventing Syrian drama makers from attacking the country's leadership through their real-time dramas. Hatem Ali is a Syrian filmmaker with high leverage on the regional scene, who managed to get a *musalsal* commissioned by Sheikh al-Maktoum, the emir of Dubai (Gulf News 2010). When asked why his TV remake of 'The Godfather' set in contemporary Syria never openly mentions the al-Asad family, he explains that 'the Gulf would not buy a product explicitly criticising a ruler and his family. It might seem odd, as Gulf countries and the Syrian regime have contrasting political positions at the moment. This is a non-written rule in Arab media. The market simply does not acquire such products.'[15] Comparisons between the al-Asad family and the mafia clan portrayed by 'The Godfather' can be gently implied, but everything must remain generic and indirect, otherwise the product would risk not being acquired by any of the top Gulf-owned Pan Arab players, or be censored later when it aired.[16]

Ali's argument shows that, even in the heated post-2011 atmosphere, and despite the political disputes between Gulf monarchies and the Syrian ruling family, the regional market and local politics are not at odds; on the contrary, they follow a pattern of mutual accommodation. As Qatar TV director-general Mohamed Abdulrahman al-Kuwari has made clear, Gulf buyers generally follow a sort of 'good neighbour policy',[17] even if not directly influenced by the Syrian *sultat*. They do not want to stir up controversy or provoke the Syrian powers on issues that could be deemed sensitive at a local level; they prefer to be accommodating rather than confrontational.[18]

Fears and anxiety over the security of loved ones back home, together with the reluctance of the regional market to accept explicit criticism in Ramadan TV fiction, are two valid reasons for the soft attitude of cultural producers towards the Syrian leadership. Even in exile, the producers are, after all, still citizens of Syria and professionals who have to survive in a highly competitive media landscape. Nevertheless, the elective affinities between Syrian cultural and political elites still seem to bind them together, even in a fragmented drama industry where harsh controversies, fights and splits have strongly manifested since 2011. Immediately after the outbreak of the uprising, in fact, Syria's once united TV production sector started to fall apart. After fighting through Facebook posts, public statements and communiques, several professionals began to officially 'defect' from the national TV drama industry and go into exile – mostly to Lebanon, Egypt or the United Emirates. In this early phase, perhaps the most important media personality to take an oppositional stance vis-à-vis the regime was Jamal Suleiman, a prominent actor belonging to the same Alawite sect as the al-Asad family. After being repeatedly threatened and attacked by pro-regime militants, Suleiman – who later starred as the mafia boss in Hatem Ali's remake of 'The Godfather' – flew to Cairo (Kanaan 2011), where he spoke of his former enthusiasm for the president's reformist project, and his disillusion on realizing that it was not going to be implemented.[19]

Well-known media personalities have expressed their strong disagreement with this position, embracing rather a loyalist position. Najdat Anzour, one of the pioneers of Syrian realism in TV drama with his 1993 series *Nihayat rajul shuja'* ('The End of a Brave Man'), was at the forefront of an alliance of producers who declared a boycott against Syrian artists who had denounced the violent suppression of the protests in Daraa, the uprising's hub. Anzour, long considered a progressive, open-minded, *tanwir*-inspired filmmaker who had tackled crucial issues such as terrorism in his TV work,[20] had finally chosen to fully support the president's narrative which denied the existence of a grassroots, locally originated protest movement, and firmly believed the uprising to be the result of a foreign conspiracy aimed at undermining Syria's stability and national sovereignty.[21] In 2013, Anzour's filming of a *musalsal* inside the devastated Damascus suburb of Daraya – under heavy government attack for being a pro-opposition hub – generated heated polemics both inside and outside Syria (Mroué 2013). Debated even more fiercely was Anzour's dramatization of life under the self-proclaimed Islamic State of Iraq and Syria (ISIS or Daesh) in the 2016 long feature *Faniyya wa tatabadad* ('Decaying and Vanishing', Georgi 2016). Exclusively released in Syria and never distributed in movie theatres outside of the country, the film was produced in a joint venture with the government-owned film organization and telecommunication company Syriatel, backed by Bashar al-Asad's maternal cousin Rami Makhlouf. It fully embraces the Syrian president's rhetoric of reuniting the nation in the fight against Daesh, which according to the film's press release 'is the main reason behind Syria's destruction' (Syriatel 2016). 'Decaying and Vanishing' pushes a message of forgiveness and national reconciliation under the leadership of Bashar al-Asad who, according to Anzour and the scriptwriter, Diana Kamaleddin, has been the victim of a 'bad press' jointly promoted by Western and Gulf media (Georgi 2016). The filmmaker's staunch support for the Syrian president[22] finally received official recognition in June 2016, when Anzour was appointed Deputy Speaker of Syria's People's Assembly, a position he still holds (RT.com 2016).

A middle way between the oppositional and the loyalist position is that of the repentant artist – a sort of 'prodigal son' who, after expressing dissent vis-à-vis Syrian *sultat*, finally asks for forgiveness and is reintegrated into the regime, both as a citizen and as a cultural producer.

Here the story of Salloum Haddad is emblematic. In 2011, after receiving several threats, the actor was assaulted and beaten in a café in Damascus (Zamanalwsl.net 2011), which probably convinced him that it was time to leave the country as other artists had done (Kanaan 2011). Three years later, after deciding to return to Syria (Khitu 2014), Haddad was publicly celebrated with a long TV interview in which he appeared extremely emotional. Paying tribute to the president and the national army defending the country against terrorist groups and a 'zionist conspiracy',[23] Haddad stressed that 'the alternative to the regime is Daesh' and claimed that removing al-Asad would mean turning Syria into a 'backward Islamic country'.[24] When asked about other drama makers who had gone into exile, he called upon his colleagues to repent and return to their homeland, as 'Syria needs all its artists'.[25] In a blunt endorsement of the presidency, he then concluded that 'our leadership is merciful', as its sole demand is that one be 'a citizen and a nationalist'.[26]

In an effort to rebuild the national TV drama industry – once a major financial and PR asset for the country – the Syrian government and its supporters have publicly called upon 'defected' artists to return home. Filming in the stunning old city centre of Damascus, which has been so far preserved from destruction – and in its safe surroundings, such as the upper-class area of Yaafur – has been encouraged, and successful TV series like *Bab al-hara* have lately been produced inside the country. 'We will ensure the return of everyone who has not made any provocative statement against Syria by all possible means' (Enab Baladi 2017), Zuhair Ramadan, a popular actor and the president of the Syrian Artists' Syndicate, recently declared. He emphasized that those 'who abused the symbols of sovereignty in Syria … the Syrian flag, the army, the national anthem and the President of the Republic' (Enab Baladi 2017) will be permanently dismissed from the artists' union; Ramadan has also asked the parliament to prevent Syrian media from showing *musalsalat* featuring these artists, something that does not seem to have taken place, however.

The fragmentation of the drama industry and the divisions between its makers have impacted on the capability of Syrian *musalsalat* to provide a timely, critical reading of the events in the country (Alhamwi 2017; Enab Baladi 2016), even when these real-time events take centre stage in their storyline and characters. This is in the case of pro-regime media dealing with hot issues, such as religious extremism and terrorism, filmed inside Syria under the protection of the army or the *mukhabarat* – like Najdat Anzour's works. Yet also real-time drama crafted outside Syria by oppositional filmmakers, in an effort to construct a media platform for dialogue and reconciliation attracting both sides, appeals to a vague form of humanitarianism and patriotism which, in the end, fails to investigate or address the dramatic political and material causes behind the unfolding events, in Syria and in the wider Arab region.

This attitude is symbolically rendered in the final sequence of *Wilada min al-khasira*, season 3. Here two mothers – whose sons have both been killed fighting on opposite sides – have to come to an agreement, metaphorically suggesting an agreement over their country's future. One tells the other: 'Your son is a killer.' The other answers: 'Maybe your son is a killer, too. Who knows?' Because of its inability – or unwillingness – to clearly identify who is responsible for what, *Wilada* sends out '"ambivalent" messages based on phony patriotism and a romanticized notion that the people are the only way out of the crisis; where all of the political parties are equally corrupt, violent, and driven by personal and material interests, causing them to shift easily between the regime and the opposition' (Della Ratta 2014a: 13).

Similarly, a work like 'The Godfather' – which, according to the writer of its first season, Rafi Wahbi, aimed at unveiling and criticizing 'the inner reasons behind the social rebellion of 2011'[27] – turns out to be just another saga of a mafia family, with revenge killings, beautiful girls and luxury villas. Far from proposing 'a sociological analysis of the Syrian regime's material infrastructure', and of 'the period between 2000 and 2010 that changed the face of Syria, allowing a new class of corrupted businessmen to take control of the country',[28] 'The Godfather' is yet another *tanwir*-inspired TV drama that does not have enough steam – or lacks the willingness – to explore and criticize the power structure of the *sultat*.

Despite the declared intentions of its makers, and the timeliness of its topics, Syrian real-time drama fails to focus on the inner causes of the current conflict, and does not succeed – or, perhaps, is not interested – in questioning the representation of the latter offered by the dominant discourse. On the contrary, it reproduces this very discourse that reads the events on the ground as resulting from the combined action of an orchestrated conspiracy from abroad, aimed at undermining Syria's stability and sovereignty, and the inability of an allegedly under-developed Syrian society to claim civil rights and political freedoms, which pushed individuals to fight for their personal interests rather than for those of the country. This ill-concealed contempt and suspicion towards the masses is an inherent part of the *tanwir* ideology shared by political and cultural elites, and is constantly reproduced by post-uprising real-time drama. Failing in its original intention of providing a rational, deliberative platform for dialogue and reconciliation, it ends up moving away from questioning the politics of power and instead diverts attention towards society. Syria's political leadership is never critically examined by real-time drama, not even when its makers consider themselves to be oppositional artists.

This reluctance to question the seemingly reform-minded side of the Syrian *sultat* can be attributed to the long-standing elective affinities binding together cultural producers and the Palace, which find their common ideological ground in the philosophy of *tanwir,* and their ideal communication mechanism in the whisper strategy. Contrary to the generation of cultural producers raised under Hafiz al-Asad[29] – characterized by a confrontational attitude towards power,[30] and involved in a continuous struggle between the desire to criticize the regime and the obligation to compromise with it by negotiating forms of 'commissioned criticism' – the relationship between Bashar al-Asad and drama makers during his first decade was rather based upon dialogue. This new generation of cultural producers did not wish to hide its bond with the president; on the contrary, they used to boast about it in public, something the previous generation would have been unlikely to do.

Tanwir has inspired issues, slogans and awareness campaigns that the Palace has thrown into the public space to boost the president's reformist credentials, from 'the fight against corruption' in 2000 to the 2011 post-uprising media efforts to peddle the idea that 'every citizen is responsible', appealing to patriotism and individual responsibility in order to prevent people from demonstrating public dissent and criticism. Through whispers in public or quasi-public venues, these issues have been translated into edgy TV drama. Within this framework based upon affinities, mutual agreements and shared beliefs, even censorship has been emptied of its confrontational potential; rather than the sensitivity of the media product, what has been assessed is its *appropriateness* to the shared project of *tanwir*. The whisper strategy has made sure that everybody, from the drama writers and producers to the members of censorship committees,[31] is made aware of and agrees upon the issues deemed worth dealing with. Contrary to what one might think about an authoritarian country like Syria, overall during Bashar al-Asad's first decade *musalsalat* scripts were largely approved,[32] sometimes subject only to minor, cosmetic changes judged by the drama makers themselves to be a routine component of the 'artistic evaluation' (*taqiym fanni*)[33] of the product, rather than part of a process of 'censorship' (*raqaba*). The only exception to this trend was a few professionals from the former generation of producers who denounced the harshness of Syrian censorship contrary to its seeming openness to taboo-breaking topics.[34]

Because of these affinities between the reform-minded side of the *sultat* and the drama makers, the most sensitive topics – including the abuse of power perpetrated by other *sultat*, in particular the *mukhabarat* – have been open to discussion, as long as they served the shared standards holding society or individual members of the regime accountable for the malfunctioning of the system.[35] Even a TV product like *Laysa Saraban* ('It's Not a Mirage', 2008), focusing on the delicate relations between Muslims and religious minorities, particularly Christians, has not been censored or rejected by government-owned media. While the series' director publicly expressed his astonishment at not facing 'any problem … with such sensitive issues' (Forward Magazine 2008), it would have been unlikely for a work like *Laysa Saraban* to be redacted or banned, as it perfectly matches with the leadership's official rhetoric on religious minorities. The series suggests, in fact, that Syria's religious and ethnic groups can coexist in the much-advertised Syrian mosaic of cultures; yet they are not ready to merge in a proper multicultural society. The gloomy ending, where the two lovers – a Christian woman and a Muslim man – are obliged to split up and one of them dies, stands symbolically for a society that is not ready for in-depth inter-religious relationships, as it is still trapped in the backwardness of honour killing, sectarian revenge and arranged marriages. This message resonates with Bashar al-Asad's argument for having a religious minority – the Alawites – rule the country to protect other minorities and make sure that the state remains secular on the surface; while the population stays as controlled as possible in order to avoid – so the mainstream narrative goes – the chaos, social disorder and religious extremism that would arise in a society not yet ready to embrace multiculturalism.[36]

By dealing with the sensitive issue of honour killing (*jarimat al-sharaf*), *Laysa Saraban* shows once again how the whispers circulating between the *sultat* and the *tanwir*-inspired producers are rendered into seemingly progressive media, and then reformulated and re-injected in the public space. A public discussion around this sensitive issue did in fact exist in the country before the broadcast of the *musalsal*,[37] but only after *Laysa*

Saraban was aired, provoking a lively debate on honour killing (Mansour 2008), did Bashar al-Asad finally abolish Article 548 of the penal code,[38] which waived punishment for men guilty of having murdered a female family member involved in 'illegitimate sex acts' or in 'an extramarital affair.'[39] As the highest authority of (regime-backed) Islam, the Grand Mufti Sheikh Hassoun, had commented a few years before: 'it is difficult to change laws that people are used to ... and consider it as *Sharia* [Islamic law] ... What we need is to educate people and spread awareness among the society' (Sinjab 2007).

It is this foundational aspect of Syrian TV drama, it being 'revolutionary in form' yet 'reformist in content' (Dick 2007), that determines its failure to understand the profound changes within Syrian society leading to the outbreak of the uprising. Being 'reformist'[40] indicates the drama makers' attunement with Bashar al-Asad's political project, and their shared belief in *tanwir* as an elite-led process of engineering and managing society. While it has undoubtedly nurtured a ground-breaking 'visual language of critique', Syrian TV drama cannot be fully considered a 'prelude' (Salamandra 2012) to the unprecedented forms of creativity – web-based cartoons, short films, parodies, memes, mash-ups and mini soap operas (Della Ratta 2011, 2012c, 2012d; Halasa et al. 2014; Wind 2012) – that surfaced with the March 2011 street protests, mostly on the internet.[41]

Several cultural producers behind these new formats have in fact taken a distance from mainstream drama makers. Despite admitting to having partially adopted their languages – particularly dark humour and satire – they have underlined that *musalsalat* 'only skimmed the surface of Syrian issues ... because the authorities accepted them as a means of venting popular dissatisfaction' (Elali 2011). Among these young cultural producers there is a diffuse feeling of discontent concerning everything that used to symbolize the regime and the corrupted mechanism by which it operates. As Orwa al Mokdad, filmmaker and writer of the much-acclaimed web-series 'Top Goon. Diaries of a Little Dictator' (Batty 2013), has emphasized: 'Had the uprising not happened, we would have never been able to express ourselves as artists. Syrian drama was built around corruption, nepotism, money laundering and the secret services. It was created in the image and likeliness of the Syrian regime.'[42]

Besides the overt antagonism expressed by a web-inspired (and raised) generation towards the old guard of cultural production represented by TV drama, there is another component of the latter that contributes to

deepening the distance between the two. Lisa Wedeen calls it 'ambivalence', identifying this as the dominant trait of Bashar al-Asad's era as
opposed to that of his father, which was characterized by 'the ambiguities evident in overtly authoritarian logics of domination' (Wedeen
2013: 853). The current leadership sends out ambivalent messages using
all possible 'forms of market-oriented language' (Wedeen 2013: 858)
– including edgy TV drama – to forge what Wedeen calls, following
Lauren Berlant, 'an "ideology of the good life"' (Wedeen 2013: 842).
On the one hand, reforms that are implemented to grant wider market
and social freedoms to a select minority of the population secure the
accommodation of the latter group to the ruling *sultat* and its political
support for the president. On the other hand, this process of selective
openness generates exploitation, injustice and further social inequalities;
issues that, paradoxically, end up being the central themes of progressive
musalsalat aiming at enlightening a population deemed backward by
both cultural and political elites. This very ambivalence inherent in the
leadership's politics can be found in TV drama produced under Bashar
al-Asad, as even the most seemingly taboo-breaking works remain
suspended between holding the people's alleged backwardness responsible for the lack of political freedom while, at the same time, seeming
to suggest the inability – or unwillingness – of the regime 'to build state
institutions capable of ensuring the education of a citizenry' (Wedeen
2013: 870).[43]

In stark contrast with the new creative forms and formats emerging
in the post-uprising moment, all clearly aligned with their grassroots
producers' oppositional political stances, the ambivalence of Syrian
mainstream TV drama has remained unchanged. Rather than navigating
'through the perils of censorship, state repression, and co-optation in
order to create truly subversive work' (Joubin 2013: 11), Syrian drama
makers still seem to be bound – even when self-labelling as 'oppositional'
– to the country's political elites. The generation of cultural producers
raised during the 'era Bashar' (Perthes 2004: 110) are not 'complicit'
with[44] or submissive to the president, nor just 'passive participants'[45] in
the whisper strategy; rather, they seem to have enjoyed the benefits –
whether material or in terms of status, or both – of being close to the
leadership.

In a former authoritarian country turning into a 'neoliberal autocracy'
(Wedeen 2013: 843), where privatization has meant extreme wealth for
a few and rising social injustice for the many, these drama makers have

endorsed the president's reformist path, and vowed to help him move society forward through *tanwir*-inspired media. Yet, if during Hafiz al-Asad's era this ideology was materially supported by the ruling party's provision of mass education, development and greater social good, in the contemporary atmosphere of neoliberal reform *tanwir* has been emptied of its institutional infrastructure. The language of personal initiative, entrepreneurship and private competitiveness has overtaken the party's old paternalistic narrative of subsidies and social goods, while many public institutions have been dismantled in favour of the new class of businessmen acting as proxies of regime-business patronage networks. Here Syrian *musalsalat*, while gaining a reputation for being daring and taboo-breaking, have actually helped to disassociate the reformist project from institutional aspects and symbolically handed it over to 'enlightened' individuals, whether the president or the cultural elites themselves, as the only elements in society entitled to promote change.

Throughout the past decade, the neoliberal setting has consolidated this alliance to the extent that both political and cultural elites are now 'stakeholders and coinvestors in a political project where they concur in defining what is good and advisable for Syrian society' (Della Ratta 2015a: 64). This attitude, which is still perpetuated in post-2011 real-time drama, views society as a disoriented, headless mob that needs to be educated on how to think about religious tolerance, gender issues, citizenship and, eventually, freedom. No wonder that grassroots forms have emerged to revolt against this version of *tanwir* and to express defiance and criticism in completely novel, unexpected ways.

SNAPSHOT #4

The rise of 'the raised hands' meme, originated from user-generated remixes of a 2011 regime-backed campaign aimed at preventing people from protesting, hints at novel forms and formats of expressing creativity and dissent, far from seemingly progressive media inspired by *tanwir* and resulting from the whisper strategy. These networked cultural forms help Syrian citizens to visualize and recognize themselves as part of a collective entity debating contrasting ideas of nationhood and national belonging, yet they fail to construct a powerful enough discourse to challenge the regime or nurture a solid oppositional politics.

As the vicissitudes of the meme bring into bold relief, far from generating a Habermasian public sphere that would open up a democratic path, this collective formation thrives exclusively on the people's participation in making the remixes, and in the activity of sharing within the networks' economy of circulation. If the sharing and remixing of the meme during the early years of the uprising hinted at individuals trying to recognize themselves as a citizenry, its late disappearance from the networked environment marks a parallel fading away of Syrian civil society from public visibility, and the dramatic acceleration of the armed conflict on the ground.

4

The People's 'Raised Hands'

Once upon a time in a Damascus Spring...

My first encounter with the 'raised hands' dates back to spring 2011.[1] On a day like any other in that exciting and troubled time I was walking distractedly in the streets of Damascus, my head full of thoughts about the unrest that had been shaking the country since March 15, wondering what the future would hold for Syria and for all of us. The heavy Damascene accent of a passer-by shouting at me to pay attention when crossing the street brought me back to reality, to a familiar crossroads full of noise, cars, kids, street vendors, pollution. Something unusual caught my attention, though. It was a big white billboard featuring a blue hand which served as the first letter for the Arabic word *ana* ('I'), helping to compose the phrase *ana ma'al qanun* ('I am with the law'). The caption read: 'Whether young or old, I am with the law.'

The blue hand was just the first of its kind. Soon I realized that similar posters had mushroomed in the Syrian capital; the same visual pattern – a coloured raised hand – repeating slight variations on the slogan: 'whether girl or boy', 'whether progressive or conservative', 'whether emotional or rational', with the same conclusion: 'I am with the law.' The posters were part of a wider regime-backed campaign called *Kull muwatin masu'ul* ('Every citizen is responsible'),[2] aimed at stopping the demonstrations by reminding citizens that hitting the streets to protest, as many of them were doing that spring 2011, was an unlawful act. Before long, with all the coloured hands raised everywhere in public spaces, the city conveyed an Orwellian atmosphere, a Big Brother of sorts watching citizens from above and reminding them to comply with the law.

Yet, perhaps even more surprising than the raised hands looming on the billboards, were the other raised hands that suddenly started sprouting on the internet. Building on the same visual pattern, using the hand for the Arabic letter for 'I', these manipulated posters, mostly circulating on Facebook, carried a different message: 'I am free', said one;

Figure 4.1 'I am with the law' campaign, Damascus, Spring 2011 (photo: Donatella Della Ratta).

'I lost my shoes' echoed another – suggesting that the shoes had been thrown at the authorities, in a public sign of outrage and disrespect. 'I am with the law ... but where is it?', joked another, in a sort of imaginary conversation with the original message inviting citizens not to break the rules. The most meaningful for me was one that first surfaced on the Facebook page of a Homs-based group called *al-thawra al-siniyya* ('The Chinese Revolution'), whose name mocked the official regime narrative depicting Syria's street protests as having been fabricated using footage of unrest happening elsewhere. 'I am not Indian', stated the blue raised hand in the manipulated poster appearing on The Chinese Revolution Facebook page. By using this colloquial expression Syrians registered their firm intention not to be fooled by the regime as if they were foreigners in their own country. As a response to the 'I am with the law' poster, 'I am not Indian' – meaning 'I am not stupid, you cannot fool me'[3] – signalled the Syrian citizen's awareness that the regime had the exclusive control over the formal meaning of 'law' and 'lawlessness' in their country.

'I am not Indian' went viral on the internet, and became an avatar on several Facebook groups. An advertising poster created as part of a regime-backed campaign to remind Syrians not to protest had now

Figure 4.2   Remixes of the 'I am with the law' campaign (anonymous, Facebook).

taken the unexpected shape of a viral peer-produced work mocking the
regime-sanctioned message, and was widely shared on the internet. As
a result of the massive user-generated re-manipulations – particularly
those mocking the use of the word 'law' in a country that had lived under
authoritarian rule for more than 40 years – the campaign was redesigned
to reflect a more neutral, sober form.[4] New posters were released that
carried the colours of the Syrian national flag (red, white, black and
green). Repeating the same visual pattern as the earlier poster, the
redesigned raised hand stated *ana ma' Suriya* ('I am with Syria'), adding
the slogan 'my demand is your demand'. The new campaign attempted at
winning citizens' hearts and minds by appealing to a middle way, in the
generic form of nationalism, as if all the Syrian people's demands would
have to be exactly the same; as if it would be in the interest of the whole
nation not to protest. This idea was in line with the regime's official
narrative that the protests were not grassroots but had been fabricated
by foreign conspirators aiming at undermining the country's stability
and unity.

The 'I am with Syria' campaign was supposed to connect with ideas of
belonging and nationhood so as to imply that protesting was an unpatri-
otic act. By appealing to a supposedly safer, less controversial value than
that of 'the law', the regime-backed advertisement called upon Syrians to
regroup under a common platform of 'Syrianness'. Yet even this campaign
registered a wave of user-generated responses over the internet. This
time, though, the remixes went beyond the virtual spaces of the web,
as I witnessed myself. In a public square in central Damascus, the 'I am

Figure 4.3 'I am with Syria' campaign, Damascus, Spring 2011.

with Syria' poster was changed into 'I am with freedom.' Probably at night-time, armed with a marker, the unknown remixer had found the courage to descend from the virtual alleys of Facebook to the real streets of Syria, in a bold act of defiance of the tight security. On another poster, the mysterious protester had deleted the second part of the slogan – 'my demand is your demand' – and turned it into 'my demand is freedom'.

The defiant re-manipulations of the raised hands campaign are not an isolated example of the kind of user-generated creativity that erupted in the wake of Syria's uprising. Since March 2011, in fact, all sorts of grassroots-generated media, such as creative writing, video art, comics, songs, graffiti, political posters, jokes, as well as memes, have been flourishing on the internet, particularly on Facebook and YouTube (Della Ratta 2011). This overwhelming wave of creative insurgency has been largely welcomed as a sign of the 'resilience of revolutionary resistance and defiance', and the 'artist-activist' has been celebrated for contributing to 'the production of political change' (cooke 2017: 1–2). Creative insurgency is certainly not a new phenomenon in the Arab world (Kraidy 2016), yet the massive wave of user-generated creativity post-2011 presents the absolute novelty of being triggered by a technological platform, the web 2.0, that matches with a powerful human network, the so-called social or participatory web.[5] It is in light of the novel possibilities offered by this 'techno-human infrastructure' (Della Ratta 2017a) – in terms not only of self-expression and production, but also of re-manipulation and the circulation of messages – that networked communications technologies have been hailed as the quintessential site for empowering citizens and planning peer-to-peer resistance.

In a country where, for decades, the most prominent form of cultural production was the industry-backed and regime-sanctioned TV drama, the rise of web-powered user-generated content has introduced completely novel opportunities for expressing both creativity and dissent. Diffuse, ephemeral and often anonymous, these grassroots media do not depend on massive financial investments, government permits or friends in high places, thus making it unlikely that they will be engineered through a mechanism like the whisper strategy. These forms of content production – where the citizenry as a whole is turned into a potential army of savvy cultural producers – have put networked communications technologies centre stage in the discussion around self-expression and civic empowerment against authoritarian powers.

However, without wanting to downplay the incredible creativity of Syrian grassroots media post-2011 and its disruptive energy,[6] I am wary of these celebratory readings of the creative insurgency and of its potential as an enabler of political change.[7] I use the example of the raised hands campaign and its anonymous remixes to critically reflect on narratives of techno-utopias that have manifested in conjunction with the Arab uprisings, emphasizing the idea of citizen empowerment by way of technology and the belief that the latter should enable political change – to the extent of portraying the events in 2011 as 'Internet-enabled revolts' (Della Ratta 2017a). Particularly in the context of authoritarian countries, web-powered 'participatory culture'[8] has been celebrated as the quintessential site for nurturing oppositional politics, boosting grassroots mobilization, and finally triggering a quasi-democratic process.[9] This echoes the shared vision, jointly supported by the US State Department and Silicon Valley web entrepreneurs, that technology will eventually 'shake repressive governments', 'bring a meaningful change in the democratic process', and finally create what Google's top managers Eric Schmidt and Jared Cohen have defined 'a coalition of the connected' (Schmidt and Cohen 2010). Following this logic, even the simplest expression of user-generated creativity inherently implies the possibility of a sort of 'democratic subversion' (Shifman 2014: 123), as it would generate a virtual citizens' forum nurturing oppositional politics.

Far from supporting the belief that the making and remaking of cultural production implied by digital vernacular objects ought to lead to a deliberative, rational and decision-making oriented discussion – a public sphere à la Habermas (1989) – finally triggering a democratic process, the Syrian raised hands shed light instead on how even the smallest 'units of cultural ideas' – such as memes – 'that spread from an individual to another by copying or imitation',[10] are dynamic discursive sites (Huntington 2013) in which power can be imposed and exercised, but also contested and resisted. The regime-backed advertising campaign can be considered a discursive mechanism to regulate and discipline the production and circulation of concepts such as 'law' and 'lawfulness' in a time of unrest, in order to inhibit public manifestations of dissent and serve the political goal of maintaining power. Yet, at the same time, the grassroots user-generated responses and re-manipulations hint at how this very discourse can be addressed, reversed, and turned into a site of contestation. Sometimes, challenging a power discourse through massive user-generated responses may even result in hitting back the original message and forcing it to change, as happened when the 'I am with the law' posters were superseded by the 'I am with Syria' campaign.

This time, however, the emphasis on values such as 'Syrianness' pushed to the surface the complexity and contradictions in conceiving of Syria as a collective entity rather than an ensemble of individualities. Instead of hitting back at the regime's message and challenging its power discourse, the second wave of user-generated responses has rather generated controversies among citizens themselves over the meaning of nationhood and national belonging. In the end, they have signalled diverging opinions about how to think about 'Syria' and 'Syrianness' which have not resulted in shaping anything similar to a Habermasian public sphere, nor in building a collective, national platform for dialogue or a new online *agora* of concerned citizens. Without wanting to diminish their expressive potential, but taking a distance from readings that invest digital vernacular objects with the power of representing 'the idea of democracy itself' in authoritarian contexts (Shifman 2014: 144), I maintain that the Syrian raised hands register opinions. They are like sparkles,[11] spikes of intensity that do not have the strength to model any political formation. As forms of public address, they allow participants in the discourse they create 'to understand themselves as directly and actively belonging to a social entity that exists historically in secular time and has consciousness of itself, *though it has no existence apart from the activity of its own discursive circulation*' (Warner 2002: 105, my emphasis). In the end, they signal and express individualities that do not evolve into a political collectivity.

What do the raised hands say?

Before framing the analysis of the raised hands meme within the broader debate on the internet as a public sphere, and elaborating further on their condition as sparkles that fail to expand into a more mature political formation, I am interested in the relational dynamics that this meme is an expression of, both in the original regime-backed campaigns, and in the user-generated manipulations. What exactly gets to be manipulated and what to be repeated in the raised hands meme? What have the anonymous remixers opted to keep of the original message, and what have they changed and therefore challenged? And what does all this tell us about the current situation in Syria?

In her analysis of the production and circulation of memes, Shifman underscores three dimensions within which processes of imitation or, vice versa, re-manipulation, might take place: content, form and stance, the latter defined as 'the ways in which addressers position themselves in relation to the text, its linguistic codes, the addressees, and other potential speakers' (Shifman 2014: 40). During the first wave of grassroots manipulations of the raised hand meme, anonymous users mostly attacked the content of the 'I am with the law' campaign, and its stance. The remixing mainly originated from 'incongruity', an 'unexpected cognitive encounter between two incongruent elements' (Shifman 2014: 79). In the raised hands campaign, incongruity is generated by the use of the word 'law' in an authoritarian context, such as Syria, where complying with the rules would implicitly mean not joining in street demonstrations under any circumstances. The contrast between the representation of an ideal citizenry which sticks together on the basis of lawful compliance – as suggested in the advertising campaign – and the reality of laws that are entirely engineered and implemented by an absolute power, therefore excluding any possibility of citizens being included in the process, is what pushes the incongruity to the fore.

Irony and parody, as the prominent elements in the grassroots re-manipulations, serve to bring to the surface the incongruity of the original message. Moulthrop (2003) and Kuipers (2005) have underlined their importance as tools to subvert a given message and create 'anomalous juxtapositions' (Knobel and Lankshear 2007: 209), as in the 'I am with the law ... but where is it?' poster, which clearly hints at a cognitive dissonance between an ideal of law and lawfulness and the actual lack of it. The 'I am not stupid' remix adds a further sophisticated element to the grassroots wave of user-generated responses, i.e. the capability of memes to establish connections between different texts taken from a broader 'cultural repertoire' (Burgess 2008: 6). The original text of the remix in Syrian dialect literally translates as 'I am not Indian', drawing on a popular street saying to bluntly reaffirm the 'Syrianness' of the author(s)' grassroots response against a regime-backed message that treats them as if they don't know who makes the 'law' – as if they were strangers in their own country.

Yet perhaps the most interesting element in the raised hands meme is not what gets changed and manipulated, but what remains as a repetitive pattern throughout all the manipulations, i.e. the visuals of the original poster which, following Shifman's classification, I will refer to as the form. Visually speaking, the raised hand stands in for *alif*, the first letter of the Arabic word *ana*. This visual component, which also corresponds to a linguistic element, is constantly repeated throughout the manipulations, whether reacting to the 'I am with the law' campaign, or responding to the 'I am with Syria' posters. Here the raised hand, the 'I', stands for Syrian individualities; it visually evokes the very idea of citizens willing to express their opinions vis-à-vis an authoritarian rule whose linguistic and world-making power is bluntly reaffirmed through the monopoly exercised over concepts such as lawfulness, and through the disciplinary message suggesting what a 'good citizen' should do in order to comply with the law.

Responding to these disciplinary and non-negotiable concepts packaged by the regime in the first advertising campaign, the user-generated raised hands put forward their own versions of those very concepts. The 'I am with the law ... but where is it?' remix, for example, suggests the anonymous author's belief in law and lawfulness, at the same time ironically underlining her scepticism towards the latter in an authoritarian country. Other users' responses to the original poster counteract the regime's one-way disciplinary message by offering a multiplicity of alternative values, such as in the 'I am free' remix, where freedom replaces lawfulness and gets prioritized in an ideal scale of values defining citizenship.

By playing with the content and stance of the meme while keeping its original visual form, the first wave of manipulations of the 'I am with the law' advert managed to impact on the regime-sanctioned message to the extent that it led to a modification of the original campaign. The follow-up campaign was designed to replace a concept – lawfulness – which had proved to be highly controversial with a more neutral, possibly more inclusive idea, that of nationhood and national belonging.[12] Despite a second massive wave of manipulations showing that 'I am with Syria' could also generate contestation, this time the regime-backed advertisement was not adapted or changed. One explanation could be that, between the first and the second campaigns, the political climate inside Syria had dramatically shifted. 'I am with Syria' was released in May 2011, more than a month after the 'I am with the law' posters were published in reaction to the first street demonstrations in mid-March.[13] In a few months, particularly since his second official address on 16 April 2011 (Landis 2011a), Bashar al-Asad's public rhetoric on reforms had shifted, moving towards a more security-oriented solution to the crisis which did not leave room for progressive media (and politics). This is also suggested by the abrupt ending of other media projects that were inspired by the idea of opening a dialogue with citizens.

The user-generated responses to the 'I am with Syria' campaign failed to impact on the original message not only because of the changed political context, but also as a consequence of inherent features of the campaign message itself. In the former 'I am with the law' campaign, the user-generated responses were originated by anonymous citizens reacting to the unilateral and pretentious message of the regime, which had hijacked the concept of 'law' and 'lawfulness'. By replacing the latter with a much broader idea, that of 'Syria' and 'Syrianness', the new campaign succeeded in diverting attention from the regime's hegemonic discourse and refocusing it on a controversy between citizens over the meaning of national belonging in a society that is highly diversified in terms of ethnic and religious identity. This shift from lampooning the regime to igniting a debate among fellow citizens over contested meanings of nationhood resulted in grassroots manipulations of the 'I am with Syria' campaign that did not interfere with the regime-backed message as they did with 'I am with the law'. Rather, they focused on engaging in a debate with other anonymous users, remixing the latter's work. This led to a discussion that could sometimes become contentious, hinting at a society becoming more polarized and fragmented, which will eventually evolve, at a later stage, into a civil war.

The 'I am with Syria' manipulations shed light on the complexities and contradictions involved in understanding 'Syria' as a collective entity and negotiating a common ground for ideas and values such as 'Syria' and 'Syrianness'. What did it mean to be a Syrian back in spring 2011? Did it mean that one had to join the demonstrations, or not join them? To support the regime, or not support it? This indecisiveness is made apparent in the user-generated responses to the regime-backed statement 'I am with Syria'. For the anonymous author(s) of the 'I am with freedom' remix, standing by Syria means standing by freedom – a message that clearly builds a connection between being a patriot and endorsing the protesters' peaceful demands, as reiterated in the manipulated slogan 'my demand is freedom'. For another citizen, standing by Syria – and by freedom – entails the possibility of martyrdom. The 'I want to be martyred' remix suggests that supporting the people's demands might lead one to sacrifice one's life as a form of Islamic-inspired martyrdom, perhaps by joining the armed (and religiously denoted) resistance against the regime. In the end, 'I am with Syria' was such a broad concept that it even pushed pro-regime supporters to enter the debate. One raised hand poster featuring Bashar al-Asad's portrait stated: 'whether you like it or not, I love him'.

The user-generated manipulations of 'I am with Syria' radically changed over time. If the first phase immediately following the uprising was marked by the expression of singularities and individual ideas about what being with Syria could possibly mean, the remixes spotted in 2012 were dramatically different. As the peaceful uprising descended into a bloody civil war, the raised hand meme began to be employed to promote humanitarian campaigns and ask for people's support; as shown, for example, in the poster 'I want to help' and 'Volunteer!' The raised hands were also used to ask for reconciliation and forgiveness, and to strengthen national unity during a time of civil war, with one of the most powerful remixes stating: 'whether anti or pro-regime, you are still my brother ... and we care for the country'.

Recalling Shifman's classification, here the meme is not crafted following its content or stance; it is as if the original slogan 'I am with Syria' has been completely forgotten. These remixes have lost also

Figure 4.4   'I am detained', remix (anonymous, Facebook).

the visual coherence of the original meme, as the hand pattern has been modified for the first time. Despite reproducing the hand, these re-manipulations do not put it in a vertical position to form the letter 'I', as the two campaigns and the first wave of user-generated posters all did. The hands are no longer raised. They stand together in a chaotic space, moving away, even at a visual level, from the ideal of a peer-to-peer debate where each hand would depict and embody an individual opinion. The different spatial composition of these remixes, in which the hands move horizontally in a symbolic quest for mutual help, rather than vertically, as in a citizens' forum in which everyone expresses their own opinion, hints at a much more confused situation on the ground – which is, in fact, that of a fully-fledged civil war. It is as if the various phases of the Syrian conflict, from 2011 up to the present, could be summed up in the vicissitudes of the raised hand meme: 'from the politically active citizen forum of the first days of the street protests, to the following heated debates between opposed factions, to an attempt of reuniting a war-torn country in the name of national reconciliation' (Della Ratta 2016a).

The raised hand meme briefly resurfaced on the web in 2016. In the wake of yet another airstrike on the war-torn city of Aleppo, the hand returned, raised in a vertical position, in a grassroots viral campaign expressing solidarity and outrage. Against a blood-red background, a digitally designed white hand appeared on several Facebook walls and Twitter timelines composing sentences such as 'I am a Saudi from Aleppo'; 'I am a Moroccan from Aleppo'; 'I am an Iraqi from Aleppo'; 'I am an Algerian from Aleppo'.

It was the 'I am a Berliner' of Syria. Yet, this was not about a head of state like JFK addressing the masses, but rather the anarchist social media crowd virally disseminating red and white little memes everywhere on the internet, in the hope that somebody would pick up these digital cries and turn them into an action of sorts: stop the airstrikes, stop the killings. (Della Ratta 2016a)

The public outrage expressed in spring 2011 had returned and found a visual means of expression using the same meme. Yet the red and white hands very soon disappeared from the web, signalling despair and mistrust vis-à-vis the international community and its actual capability, or willingness, to help resolve the conflict.

In the end, the remixes following the 'I am with Syria' campaign exposed the lack of a shared national identity among Syrian citizens.[14] This later materialized on the ground in the dramatic shape of a civil war, which the regime has exploited to support and prove its narrative. Since the very beginning of the uprising, and despite the fact that the slogans chanted in the streets emphasized national unity,[15] regime-backed communications have repeatedly stressed the risk that the protests could lead to *fitna*:[16] a division of the country in the direction of sectarianism. This was likely a deliberate strategy by Syrian *sultat* to divide the population, exploiting its different religious and ethnic components in order to generate suspicion, violence and hatred among the citizenry in order to subjugate it.[17]

The raised hands remixes mirror this shift in the regime communication strategy, channelling contention, anger and mistrust towards Syrian citizens rather than the government. It is as if the individuals (and individualities) who emerged through the remixes of 'I am with the law', successfully challenging the regime's power discourse, had now been turned against each other, competing to define their own version of 'Syria' and 'Syriannness'. The raised hands, once manifesting a defiance of the regime, had shifted into a contentious 'multivoiced meme-based discussion'[18] over different understandings of national belonging, which sadly matched the civil war in the making on the ground.

The raised hands as public sphere(s)?

Rather than looking at the rise and fall of the raised hand meme as a failed opportunity to generate a public sphere à la Habermas, I will follow the trajectory of its proliferation and disappearance in order to reflect on it as a discursive formation that is temporary by nature and only exists by virtue of its circulation. The Syrian meme – similarly to other digital, user-generated vernacular objects – should not be regarded as a catalyst for change or as carrying the promise of igniting political mobilization merely because it operates within an authoritarian framework. Contrary to celebratory readings of the 'empowerment'[19] supposedly granted by networked communications technologies in such contexts, memes are, in fact, more about circulation than conversation.

A conversation presupposes the volitional agency of the subjects who engage in it, leading, in an ideal Habermasian public sphere, to a rational, deliberative process. Eventually, a link is established between this dialogue-oriented platform and the rise of democratic political action, both supposedly boosted by networked communications technologies (Rheingold 2000; Castells 1997; Burgess and Green 2009).[20] In this framework, mobs on the internet become 'smart' (Rheingold 2002), as they have the power to initiate committed actions and drive change. This voluntary, action-oriented potential pervades the subjectivities formed by virtue of networked communications technologies, from Rheingold's 'communities' (Rheingold 2000) to Jenkins' 'participatory cultures' (Jenkins 2006b). These social formations share 'a high degree of interaction, common objectives, and interests' (Schäfer 2011: 44), being the result of a voluntary process catalysed by motivated actions and shared goals.

Yet the formations catalysed around the manipulation and sharing of a meme such as the raised hands completely lack this volitional agency. There is no conscious act of coming together for a common cause, no willingness to gather and form a group of any sort – even if an actual gathering eventually happens around a shared text, which is the meme itself. Memes rather generate what Michael Warner defines as a 'public': an entity coming into being 'only in relation to texts and their circulation' (Warner 2002: 66). A public is a self-creating and self-organized space; no one is responsible for its existence, other than the text itself around which the public gathers. The discursive space generated around the text eventually inspires a sense of belonging among those who take part in it, even if they are strangers.[21] Yet this belonging is only temporarily defined, as it is contingent upon people's 'attention' and 'participation' in the making of the discourse, and the 'activity' which the latter generates (Warner 2002: 87–8, 74–5). Once that attention ceases, when activity and engagement with the discourse fade away, then the public dissolves,[22] as happened with the raised hands. The massive user-generated activity registered in 2011 was replaced by a second wave of remixes in 2012, which for the first time, as noted above, subverted the visual form of the original vertical meme. In 2013 I was able to spot only a few re-manipulated raised hands, which then seemed to fade away completely, only to briefly re-surface in 2016 in the context of renewed activist efforts to save Aleppo from indiscriminate destruction. The public that had been brought together by the intense activity of remixing and sharing the raised hands has dissolved into thin air, perhaps silenced by the violent conflict that has progressively gained ground in the country.

Temporality is key to determining the lifetime of a meme, and of the social formation that gathers around it. As Warner emphasizes, it is not texts themselves that create publics, 'but the concatenation of texts through time' (Warner 2002: 90). Linking texts with one another and building a network of 'cross-referencing' (Warner 2002: 92) between them is what helps the meme to survive and get replicated. The concatenation of user-generated texts created in response to the 'I am with Syria' campaign – e.g. 'I am with freedom', 'I want to be martyred', 'I like him', etc. – is an example of this process which is not about mere consecutiveness but is truly an interaction between discourses over time. Re-manipulated texts do not follow one another in a temporal chain; rather, they interact one with another, responding, attacking, lampooning and referencing each other in a much more dynamic space: 'a social space created by the reflexive circulation of discourse' (Warner 2002: 90).

Circulation is not only inherent to this process of connecting discourses that gives extra life to a meme and to its public; on a broader scale, it is also a key attribute and inner mechanism of the web 2.0, whose techno-human infrastructure is based on the idea of hyperlinking not only individuals among themselves, but also information and people, while granting non-stop circulation to the data created by their multilateral interactions. Yet, in this potentially endless and over-proliferating flow of content, everything – including opinions, messages and conversations – gets turned into a mere 'contribution' (Dean 2009: 26). Who produces the content and which kind of content is produced is, in fact, irrelevant within the infrastructure of networked communications technologies. It can be 'whatever being' giving life to 'whatever content' (Dean 2010: 88, 69), the only relevant factor being the possibility of circulating contributions in a non-stop flow of data that nurtures 'communicative capitalism' (Dean 2005, 2009, 2010), i.e. the form of late capitalism relying exclusively on communicative exchanges.

Communicative capitalism is the infrastructure beneath contemporary networked communications technologies, the 'strange convergence of democracy and capitalism' (Dean 2010: 4) that the latter nurtures. While ensuring a massive concentration of wealth in the hands of 'platform capitalism' (Srnicek 2017), as even the simplest or most personal communicative exchanges get commodified, at the same time these very exchanges are deemed to 'materialize the values heralded as central to democracy' (Dean 2010: 4). Participation, access, inclusion, discussion – attributes that come as a package attached to the very idea of democracy – are just fantasies serving as the ideological infrastructure for communicative capitalism (Dean 2009).

Coherently with Dean's analysis, understanding the internet as a quintessential public sphere – and believing it should inherently trigger a democratic process in authoritarian contexts such as Syria – amounts to an ideology that should be addressed through ideology critique (Dean 2003:98). The ideals of publicity, transparency, access, participation, etc. – which support an understanding of the internet as a public sphere, as well as other techno-utopias – do not ultimately foster democracy but, in fact, communicative capitalism. One might object that such a theoretical framework is only to be applied where it was developed, i.e. in neoliberal democracies. I maintain that it can be productively employed (Della Ratta 2014a: 6) to analyse the dynamics at play in countries such as Syria that have embraced an 'upgraded' authoritarianism (Heydemann 2007) featuring its own version of neoliberalism. Moreover, Syria's networked media environment – from its TV industry to its social networking sites – displays local dynamics that are dramatically intertwined with processes of globalization in terms of business models, capital concentration and platform ownership.

The emphasis on circulation offers a useful perspective from which to reflect on the raised hands, as well as on other digital vernacular objects generated in no matter what context, whether considered authoritarian or not. The viral circulation of the Syrian meme over time, and the cross-connecting between different discourses and cultural practices, has in fact merely generated a temporally limited social entity coming into being through the 'activity of its own discursive *circulation*' (Warner

2002: 105, my emphasis). Whenever this circulation stops or is stopped, then this temporary entity dissolves.

Even when still circulating, the raised hands do not produce anything other than a registering of individual opinions, signalling the existence of the latter to other participants in the discourse who are performing exactly the same action. They do not lead to the emergence of any virtual community, smart mob or citizens' forum, nor shape a critical, rational, deliberative dialogue of any sort. They cannot possibly do so, because of the very attributes of circulation and reflexivity that define such memes as discursive formations enhanced by the techno-human infrastructure of the web 2.0.

The raised hands simply rise and fall, signalling points of view, like sparkles and spikes blinking, then fading away, as yet another contribution to the endless data stream of the internet – *whatever* contribution. Contrary to the claims made for the quasi-magical power of enabling democracy attributed to networked communications technologies, it is precisely because of the latter's infrastructure that memes – and online cultural (re-)production in general – act as mere contributions, adding exchange value to the ever-circulating data stream of communicative capitalism, rather than fostering conversations leading to deliberative processes.

The performative value of the Syrian raised hands

Yet, reading the raised hands as if they were merely contributions to an undifferentiated data stream, serving exclusively the interests of communicative capitalism and a few internet platform owners, would be restrictive to say the least. Grassroots user-generated creativity should not be dismissed or belittled just because of its inability to shape public spheres and become a site for oppositional politics. A more fruitful approach to discursive formations such as memes and, in general, to the study of cultural production and reproduction on digital networks, would be to look at their performative dimension. Digital vernacular objects call into being identities and worlds whose 'poetic or textual qualities' have been disregarded 'in favor of sense' (Warner 2002: 115) within the dominant public sphere tradition employed to interpret networked communications technologies. As such, the Syrian raised hands should be looked at in terms of 'the work'[23] they are able to perform on behalf of the users who reproduce, manipulate and disseminate them.

The raised hands are a sort of declaration of status. 'I am not stupid', 'I want to be martyred', 'I want to help' are opinions, feelings, moods being aired publicly in the hope of being heard. Through the production and reproduction of the raised hand meme users visually enact the very thing evoked by the discourse; identities aren't 'antecedent facts about people that help determine their actions' (Wedeen 2008: 16) but are rather formed and brought into being precisely through public speech and acts. Here, as Lisa Wedeen has underlined in her seminal study of everyday practices in imagining the nation in Yemen, 'the utterance is the act itself' (Wedeen 2008: 15). In her understanding, performativity refers to a structural logic where the act 'brings into being the very thing invoked' (Wedeen 2008: 16), which is intimately connected to a process of identity formation. In a context where state institutions are weak, such as in Yemen, national attachments and a sense of national belonging are produced not only through rational, deliberative dialogue, but also through everyday performative practices that constitute the self through its very performance.

This key link between performative practices and identity formation – and the relevance of the latter in terms of shaping a political and national self – takes also centre stage in Olga Goriunova's reflections on the processes and dynamics that bring to life digital objects in a networked environment. Goriunova talks about memes as mainly aesthetic performances that are nonetheless able to 'exhibit the capability to propel a political voice, an idea, problem, discontent' (Goriunova 2013) by virtue of the fact that they enable a process of individuation described as 'the becoming of being'.[24] Borrowing from Simondon and Bakhtin, her work goes beyond the domain of the psychic to embrace a social and collective dimension, which frames the process of individuation – whether individual or collective, whether concerning human subjectivity or political acts – as an act of creativity that is *performed*, enacted: a creative expression in its relational element.[25] From this perspective, a meme is 'an aesthetic expression which is performed *with the promise of social response*' (Goriunova 2013, my emphasis). It does not exist outside of a collectivity, or a network that reproduces and redistributes it.

With the raised hands meme this collectivity or network corresponds precisely to the networked techno-social infrastructure of the web 2.0, in which dynamics of individuation, once occurring mostly in private (yet always 'technologically' mediated through meetings, informal chats, etc.), are now manifest publicly and openly – whether the context is that of teenagers using social networking sites to form their identities and build relationships with their peers, or that of citizens shaping their political identities around shared grievances. The visual form of the raised hand standing for *ana*, 'I', beautifully hints at this process of individuation in the making. Yet, the fact that it surfaces and becomes visible in a moment when that process is still ongoing makes the raised hands appear in a 'semi-clad, raw and bare state' (Goriunova 2013). Here these digital objects and behaviours enjoy the double nature of being at the same time the devices through which individuation takes place, and the technological and aesthetic platform displaying this very process in the making.

The Syrian raised hands both shape a process of individuation of the citizen-self vis-à-vis a collectivity, and display it as it unfolds, even if it has not yet reached completion. The latter, in Goriunova's understanding, might entail giving life to an art movement, or the coming into being of a political event. Yet processes of individuation happening openly and publicly on platforms such as the web 2.0 might also stay confined in a sort of 'grey zone between the pre-individual and individual and the collective, between culture, art and politics' (Goriunova 2013). In the end, these digital objects and practices can evolve in both ways: either reaching the stage of 'brilliance' of aesthetics and political completion, or, failing individuation, remaining trapped in the grey zone of indecisiveness, with the perennial status of 'try-outs, objects soon forgotten' (Goriunova 2013).

The raised hands are in this in-between state, a transitory phase of individuation visibly rendered by the visual form of the hand itself and by its content, or what it stands for: the *ana*, the 'I' of the individualities trying to melt into, and recognize themselves in, a collective formation, that of the Syrian citizenry. The multiple *ana*, the raised hands that have been re-manipulated and shared on social networking sites since 2011, register the ongoing pursuit of an individuation not strong enough to reach completion, yet continuously calling upon a collective to be. They signal a constant effort to reach a state of brilliance, yet they seem to remain trapped in the form of flashing sparkles. While they were once relegated to private or quasi-private settings before reaching completion, processes of individuation are now publicly exposed on the web 2.0 as they unfold, taking on raw, incomplete forms between the individual, the semi-individual and the collective. Even in this unfinished state, the Syrian raised hands might have managed to survive on social networking sites for some years thanks to their ability to convey a 'poetic world-making' (Warner 2002: 114), finally slowly disappearing in parallel with the extension of the armed conflict.

Despite not bringing public spheres into being, or injecting disruptive revolutionary politics into an authoritarian context, the raised hands, like other vernacular digital objects originated in Syria, should not be diminished or disregarded given their performative capacity for poetic world-making. Visually, they stand as a memento of a Syrian civil society airing its contrasting opinions, eager to express its individualities. By being continuously repeated and replicated virally, they suggest a process of individuation in the making, of citizens trying to become and recognize themselves as a citizenry, at the same time functioning as the devices through which this very process is displayed publicly and openly on the internet. Unfortunately, the raised hands have remained digital flashing sparkles, trapped in a limbo between creativity and politics, individual expressions and shared ideas, subjects and society. The fading of the meme from social networking sites sadly marks the slow descent into invisibility of Syrian civil society, the vivid subject that the meme itself once brought to life.

SNAPSHOT #5

The tragic end of my dear friend and work partner Bassel Safadi, an open-source engineer who has become an icon of the 'Arab Spring', together with my first-hand experiences in the field of Arab digital activism, invite a reflection on the challenges of the latter at a time when a variety of Syrian grassroots-generated media does not seem to have crafted a powerful narrative to counter that of the regime.

A critical look at the political economy of digital activism suggests that assumptions about the liberating, democratizing power of networked communications, and a fascination for the technological fetish, have shaped the myth of the 'Arab Spring' as tech-powered revolutions, removing the agency of local activists, and paradoxically pushing the latter to co-author and self-produce a new form of digital Neo-Orientalism.

Caught between the desire to have its voice heard after decades of repression and the need to adapt to formats and rules set by foreign governments, non-profit organizations and commercial internet platforms, Syrian (and Arab) activism reveals its inner fragility. Its precarious political economy brings into stark relief the volatility and uncertainty of local storytelling, suspended between the imperative to gain attention in the overcrowded domain of digital media and the need to counteract Bashar al-Asad's propaganda. Its fragility includes the questions of distribution, and of the storing and access to content, since the bulk of the diffused archive of the Syrian uprising lies in the hands of internet platform capitalists.

5

Fear and Loathing on the Internet: The Paradoxes of Arab Networked Activism

Where it all began

Bassel Safadi is a geek.[1] I meet him for the first time on a cold winter's day in 2008 at the Zero One cafe, a place where Damascus expats and internet-addicted Syrians gather and chat, either face to face or through computer screens. At the time, I am overseeing the formation of the Arabic-speaking community of the Silicon Valley-based non-profit organization Creative Commons. We foster a culture of legal sharing in the domain of information goods, proposing a flexible copyright licence that makes immaterial items sharcable under conditions set according to the author's wishes.

Bassel is a talented software developer, and an active member of international web communities devoted to open source software, such as Ubuntu and OpenClipArt. He earns his living by working as chief technology officer for al-Aous, a publishing house and research institution dedicated to the cultural preservation of Syria's heritage. He looks excited at the prospect of introducing Creative Commons in Syria, a country in which there is no such thing as knowledge or respect of the author's rights and intellectual property. He believes that original content creation and widespread distribution of locally originated knowledge are key to getting Syria and the Arab region as a whole to progress and secure effective independence from cultural and political domination – a data-driven, post-colonial strategy in the era of web 2.0.

Soon, Bassel becomes Creative Commons Syria's project lead, playing a prominent role in shaping its regional community, translating licences into Arabic, participating in gatherings and meetings, both in the Arab world and internationally. In July 2010 we launch Syria's first hacker-space, Aikilab, which Bassel describes as a 'collaborative technology and art space' where 'we hold FLOSS events, Open Content workshops, teach classes, have geeky parties, and do pretty much anything related to sharing, creation, collaboration, research, development, mentoring, and of course, learning'.[2] In October 2010 Aikilab hosts Mitchell Baker, co-founder and chairperson of the Mozilla project.[3] The Syrian Computer Society (SCS), founded in 1989 by Hafiz al-Asad's deceased son Basil, and later headed by Bashar al-Asad, refuses to let her speak at a public event aimed at reaching out to computer science students. We are not given a formal explanation, but we can feel the government's determination to control all things computer-related, and its silent pushing of the practice of pirating copyrighted content and software,[4] rather than spreading awareness of open-source initiatives which would risk encouraging community-building, solidarity and peer-learning that are more likely to lead to political activism.

But at the time nobody seems to pay too much attention to geeky initiatives, so Aikilab is able to host talks, tech workshops, hackathons and a Creative Commons *iftar* dedicated to the culture of sharing.[5] Before March 2011, the *mukhabarat* are not really interested in the computer skills that many Syrian youths have developed due to the lack of other alternatives, while government-sanctioned media seems to be focused on encouraging the consumption of tech-related goods in order to foster a material culture of the 'good life'.[6] The crowd attending Aikilab initiatives, or just visiting the hackerspace for the free use of desks and an internet connection, is made up of people in their twenties and thirties, mostly university students from a variety of ethnic and religious backgrounds, including some veiled girls. They all come to learn new skills, or to use the available technologies for freelance work, dreaming of finding a well-paid job or setting up their own business.

The word 'politics' is barely heard. In 2009 a 19-year-old female blogger, Tal al-Molouhi, was arrested for her online activity allegedly related to political activism (ElGohary 2010; Alabaster 2016). Prominent social networking sites, such as Facebook and YouTube, were blocked in 2007 (Oweis 2007). Online activism was close to non-existent, and even at a regional level, prior to 2011, very few Syrians had ever attended community gatherings revolving around the use of technology for social and political change. In 2009, Bassel was one of the few Syrians to join the Second Arab Bloggers' Meeting in Beirut (Ben Gharbia 2009), a gathering of hundreds of activists coming from 18 Arab countries. I will never forget what he told me on the way back to Damascus: 'political blogging or any other form of online activism cannot develop in Syria. There is no breathing space, no margins to grow anything barely related to politics, even in the wider online domain. We'd better focus on more neutral stuff, such as coding, making open source projects and applications.'[7]

In less than two years things changed dramatically. 'Syria went from being an information black hole to one of the biggest YouTube video producers in the world', Reuters remarked in a tweet in November 2013.[8] One year later, in a study entitled 'Syrian Emerging Media' commissioned by the Danish NGO International Media Support, we counted a total of 93 grassroots media outlets including news agencies, publications, radio and TV stations, most of them operating online.[9] Syria had quickly become the set of 'the most socially mediated civil conflict in history' (Lynch et al. 2014). In less than five years, the country's youth had shifted from using the internet for activities safely deemed 'non-political' (including coding) to understanding it as the quintessential 'technology for freedom' (de Sola Pool 1983).

I experienced this change first-hand, both in my professional career as Creative Commons' Arab world community manager, and in my daily life, as a personal friend of Bassel and many other youths from the Aikilab crowd. In 2011, I witnessed the Creative Commons community in the region becoming politicized and actively engaging in the changes affecting the Arab world since December 2010, when Mohammed Bouazizi set himself on fire in Tunisia, inaugurating a season that was too quickly dubbed 'the Arab Spring'.[10] In February 2011 I attended a sit-in in front of the Libyan embassy in Damascus.[11] Formally, we were protesting against Qaddafi's regime and calling upon the Libyan ambassador to defect. In reality, the protest was a sort of general rehearsal for the Syrian uprising; the regime sensed this, and the sit-in ended with several people being beaten or temporarily arrested. Many of those who would later become well-known activists, bloggers or YouTubers were present at the embassy sit-in.[12] Bassel was there too, although still very sceptical about the possibility of political change – and political activism – in the country. Less than one month after the sit-in, however, a protest held in Damascus city centre marked the official beginning of the Syrian uprising. In the immediate aftermath of the 15 March 2011 demonstration, I saw the Aikilab crowd suddenly changing. Some 'techies' stopped coming, others started to come more often. People without a tech background would come to learn new skills, especially how to film with their phone cameras and upload and share the footage safely. Information became the primary and most sought-after good: days and nights and, sadly, human lives were sacrificed on its altar.

It is beyond the scope of this book to reflect upon the complex set of events that have shattered the Arab world since 2011, or to investigate the multiple causes – social, economic and political – that have led its people to mobilize and revolt at great risk to themselves, in Syria as elsewhere in the region. My aim, rather, is to shed some light on the media ecosystem that was formed as a result of those mobilizations, specifically in Syria, and on what this ecosystem has generated, or failed to generate, in respect of the movement for political change at the basis of its very creation. It immediately struck me, not only as a scholar but as an activist, that the overwhelming amount of information generated by anonymous, brave citizens – university students, shop keepers, graphic designers, artists, traders, geeks like Bassel and his Aikilab crowd – did not have the strength to form a narrative powerful enough to counter that of the regime. The 'wealth of networks' (Benkler 2006) generated by Syrian online activism not only failed to create a new public sphere à la Habermas; the superabundance of information it produced created a 'state of disarray' in what was initially framed as a 'networked revolution' (De Angelis 2011).

Several years have passed since the beginning of the uprising, yet still, at a communication level, the Syrian regime's narrative of a foreign conspiracy and violent revolt shaped by sectarianism seems to be holding – perhaps now more than ever, since the fight against Daesh has succeeded in building a coalition of international interests, from Russia to the United States.[13] How did it happen that the once over-celebrated peaceful 'protester' – the iconic *Time Magazine* person of the year for 2011, a clear tribute to the Arab uprisings (Della Ratta 2017b: 142–3) – had been completely forgotten in such a short period of time? It was not only the international community who abandoned the once attractive idea of a peaceful, digital, revolutionary vanguard. In 2014, only a few years after *Time*'s 'The Protester' issue, Syrian photographer Laura Haddad released yet another iconic image that was later widely shared on social networking sites. Under the telling title 'The Retired Activist', the picture featured a young woman sleeping on the floor – possibly Haddad herself – mirroring the state of despair and powerlessness that had invaded the hearts and minds of many Syrian youths.

How did Syrian networked activism end up in depression and despair? Why did the grassroots-originated content, despite having revealed a vibrant culture of creative resistance (Della Ratta 2011), seem to have generated neither new publics nor robust counter-narratives to the

Figure 5.1 'The Retired Activist', 2014 (photo courtesy of Lara Haddad).

regime's rhetoric? My aim here is to critically reflect on these questions, and highlight the multifaceted dynamics behind the rise and fall of Syria's networked activism. I pursue this as a researcher who has invested the major part of her professional career investigating media and networked communications technologies in the Arab world; as an activist who has co-founded a web portal, SyriaUntold, with the objective of preserving the creative experiences of civil disobedience and grassroots activism that have blossomed in the country since March 2011; and as a human being who has a personal investment in Syria in terms of friendship ties, starting with Bassel Safadi.

This account is therefore not only the result of several years of eth-nographic research and scholarly reflection on networked activism in the Arab region (Della Ratta and Valeriani 2012, 2017). It is also, first and foremost, an exercise in auto-ethnography (Ellis 2004) that draws on my first-hand experiences as Creative Commons' Arab world manager[14] and on my personal involvement in Syria's activist scene: I have actively contributed to Syria's grassroots media ecosystem through the activities of SyriaUntold, and have activist friends who have been tortured, imprisoned, persecuted and, sometimes, killed. Bassel was jailed in March 2012. In October 2015, while imprisoned in Adra civil prison on the outskirts of Damascus, he was executed with no formal charges made, or justifications given. His death has left an unsurmountable void for his family and friends.[15]

Bassel's thoughts and personal life experience have deeply inspired my scholarly reflection on Syria's networked activism. Since our first trip

Figure 5.2 'Bassel' (photo: Joi Ito, via Flickr, https://tinyurl.com/yb7yvtme licenced under Creative Commons).

together to attend the Second Arab Bloggers' Meeting in Beirut, Bassel and I had many insightful conversations on the issue of digital activism, in person or on Skype. On the one hand, we were part of an international network of activists, techies, journalists and NGOs that deemed networked communications technologies to be an essential platform for achieving social – and eventually political – change. On the other hand, our experience of the original protest movement in Syria taught us that the uttermost violence was not inflicted on cyber dissidents, but on those bodies who physically hit the streets, on those who marched, those who sang, those who carried protest signs, and those who filmed the demonstrations.

While international media focused on finding testimonials to promote the idea of a 'revolution 2.0' in Syria,[16] anonymous people were being imprisoned, tortured or killed, not for having liked a Facebook page or tweeted anti-regime slogans, but for having joined actual demonstrations on the ground. In early 2012, less than one year into the uprising and only a few weeks before his arrest, Bassel tweeted: 'activism is another word for crap, at least in #Syria, real people who die each day or lose their families don't talk about what they do', and 'media don't know the real people and they will never do'.[17] He concluded: 'In the new regime of #Syria non (*sic*) of the famous *Internet icons* of the Syrian revolution will have a place.'[18]

Bassel's words were prophetic: up to today, none of the Syrian 'internet icons' has any visibility in international media, let alone in a hypothetical 'new regime' that, at the time of writing, has not succeeded in replacing Bashar al-Asad's rule. Why did this happen? Why were the once trendy 'Arab DIY revolutions' (Della Ratta 2017b: 144–6) so quickly dismissed, and the defiant, peaceful protesters put into early retirement? I am approaching this question from two angles. On the one hand, I look at the political economy shaping contemporary digital activism, and reflect on how Syrian grassroots media, spontaneously born from the urge to foster free expression and resistance to power, were quickly forced to adapt to financial and cultural models set by foreign non-profit organizations and by commercially driven internet platforms, in order to survive a hyper-crowded global media environment. I understand 'digital' (and networked) 'activism' (Joyce 2010) as the ensemble of activities and practices that make use of, and are performed and executed on, a networked infrastructure, where the latter hints not only at the technological layer defining the web 2.0, but also at 'the human fabric' underneath this very technology, i.e. the 'social environment, linking people to one another, and combining people and information together in what defines the very core of Internet cultures, that is, its participatory and sharing practices' (Della Ratta 2017a: 4). Digital networked activism is conceived as powered jointly by networked communications technologies, and at the same time by the human social networks that exist by virtue of the web 2.0.

On the other hand, I reflect upon the issue of why none of Syria's emerging activist media has succeeded in 're-establishing any regime of truth' (Gonzalez-Quijano, in De Angelis 2011) in the country. In the aftermath of the 2011 uprising, Syria has fully entered the 'post-truth'[19] era, where 'the production and reproduction of an epistemic insecurity'[20] seem to have favoured the regime's project at the expense of thousands of activists' lives, sacrificed on the altar of information and free speech.

The production of Arab Networked Activism and the rise of Digital Neo-Orientalism

Five years after that first visit to the Arab Bloggers' meeting in Bassel's company, I flew to Amman, Jordan to attend the fourth regional activists' gathering.[21] Bassel could not be with us, as he was locked in a Syrian jail. Another prominent activist, Alaa Abdel Fattah, who was among the founders of the bloggers' network and a pioneer in the Arab Techies movement,[22] was also imprisoned in Egypt. Although a gloomy atmosphere surrounded the meeting due to the absence of Bassel and Alaa – and the fact that the vaunted 'Arab Spring' was descending into a complicated phase of violence, unrest and civil war – the gathering's programme was filled with feel-good expressions describing the workshops and training activities on offer, such as 'marketplace', 'pitching of ideas', 'self-sustainable initiative', 'digital storytelling', 'empowerment'. This jargon, quite unusual for a political meeting, made me think of an image that had been buried in my memory for a while: the poster of the previous gathering, the Third Arab Bloggers' Meeting in Tunis 2011, pictured a crowd marching together in what looked like a street protest carrying, instead of slogans and signs, mobile phones and icons of the most famous Silicon Valley-based internet brands, from YouTube to Facebook. In the bloggers' meeting poster, the political message of the imaginary protest had been sealed in an envelope … and given to the Twitter bird to be delivered to the outside world!

This language and iconography hint at two major themes that have shaped the issues, practices and concerns of Arab networked activism and, ultimately, its political economy: civil society and the empowerment granted by virtue of networked communications technology. Both, as I discuss below, are of political and strategic interest for the Western part of the world. By arguing that such ideas, and the set of practices deriving from them, have dramatically influenced the making of Arab networked activism, under no circumstances do I want to endorse theories claiming that foreign institutions and governments plotted to effect political change in the region, albeit in a peaceful, non-violent way.[23] Neither do I want to suggest that Arab activists lacked agency, being mere tools in the hands of Western manipulators who were able to set an agenda modelled on their own interests rather than on local needs.

Rather, my argument is, on the one hand, that the emphasis put on the idea of civil society and its progressive battles, such as promoting freedom of expression and access to knowledge and communication, is the result of a historic process which began globally after the fall of the former Soviet Union with the aim of dismantling the welfare state and creating proxy institutions like NGOs, taking over some of its tasks while lacking its symbolic and political potential as a collective aggregator (Carapico 2013: 150–98). On the other hand, this neoliberal project has found the perfect ally in networked communications technologies which have provided the techno-human infrastructure materializing fantasies of equal access, participation and wholeness that come attached to the very idea of democracy (Dean 2009). Particularly since the beginning of the 2000s, these phenomena – the rise of civil society as a counter-hegemonic power to the authoritarian state, and the rise of the networks as the quintessential platform for implementing the idea of a democracy – have marched in parallel in the Arab region.

Reviewing the history of civil society in the Arab world, Amani Kandil (2010) has highlighted that, although the practice of volunteer-run non-profit initiatives outside the family and the state has been rooted in the region since the nineteenth century, the employment of the concept of 'civil society' as a political subject, and the implementation of institutions shaped around this very idea, have been boosted during the past two decades. In the years following the fall of the Berlin Wall, in fact, a trend emerged in the region that emphasized the role of the market as a counter-balance to the corrupt authoritarian state, and promoted the idea of a non-state subject, civil society,[24] which would defend human rights and open a path towards progressive reforms. This civic-centred culture was further strengthened after the events of 9/11,[25] in consequence of which a number of funding tools and programmes were implemented in the region by Western governments and NGOs with the aim of fostering the growth of this counter-hegemonic subject.

The rise of Arab civil society as a political subject was matched by 'a package of concepts and development approaches' (Kandil 2010: 9) that became part of the daily jargon of the region's growing civic culture. Expressions such as 'participatory development', 'partnership', 'good governance', 'empowerment', 'capacity building', 'advocacy', 'strategic planning', 'social capital' and – of course – 'citizenship', were largely employed in meetings, conferences and training sessions, and became the primary vocabulary used in the writing process to secure international support and funds (Kandil 2010: 10). These concepts were far from being rooted on the ground, and sounded 'emptied from a realistic content' (Kandil 2010: 10). Even so, this language was further boosted in the early 2000s with the rise of technology-centred activities, workshops and training sessions supported by Western donors, whether governmental (such as USAID) or non-governmental (such as Global Voices, Creative Commons, the Heinrich Böll Foundation, etc).[26] The virtuous circle between civil society and technology as factors encouraging the development of a more open and 'democratic' culture was celebrated by Barack Obama in a speech delivered in 2009 in Cairo. The speech heralded a 'new beginning'[27] in the relationship between the United States and the Arab world, announcing a funding programme to support tech development, innovation and entrepreneurship, and 'help transfer ideas to the marketplace so they can create jobs' (*New York Times* 2009).

These funding policies – and, indirectly, the supporting bodies and donors behind them – have dramatically impacted the development of Arab activism and over-emphasised the latter's civic and technological component, as reflected in the structure of the training programmes, the type of activities supported by grants and donations, and the workshops and meetings held in the region throughout the 2000s, such as those of the Arab Techies and the Arab bloggers. As an example of this trend, during the fourth Arab bloggers' meeting in Amman, surveillance and online censorship – issues that were debated on international media after Edward Snowden's revelations about the NSA, and that were the core interest of donor organizations such as Tactical Technological Collective and Global Voices[28] – became the main themes of its visual communication.[29] The poster for the event featured a sort of Orwellian Big Brother's eye with a spy-cam at its centre and a caption stating: 'surveillance is bad for your Internet'. It is quite hard to imagine how cyber surveillance could be the Arab activists' main preoccupation in a year, such as 2014 was, when countries like Syria and Yemen were descending into bloody armed conflicts, and Egypt was experiencing the harsh restoration of authoritarian rule. In the words of the Yemeni scholar Walid al-Saqaf, who was also present at the Amman meeting: 'according to the findings of my PhD research, circumvention is not a big issue here; yet we heavily invest in training on such tools in every single event, conference, and gathering held in this Region' (Della Ratta and De Angelis 2014).

As emerged during a period of critical reflection at the gathering, very often the training sessions, workshops and funding programmes for the Arab world were designed following the donors' requirements rather than taking into account local needs. This was underlined by Lina Atallah from the Egyptian collective Mada Masr: 'I ask myself: why are we doing a training about digital storytelling if we are not even able to write a political communiqué when our main goal is to get more people to Tahrir square?' (Della Ratta and De Angelis 2014). Echoing Atallah's words, Wafa' Ben Hassine from the Tunisian multi-award-winning web portal Nawaat also pointed out the fallacy of employing human and financial resources exclusively in the domain of the digital: 'after investing in the training we realized that, although more local stories were produced, they did not get any attention or visibility. We take for granted that we should train more people to produce more content, because it is good to empower citizens and have more stories out, but is this really needed?' (Della Ratta and De Angelis 2014).

In short, the main themes and concerns of Arab networked activism – and the way in which they are rendered visually – have been heavily influenced by Western NGOs' advocacy programmes implemented in the region throughout the 2000s with the aim of creating a domestic counter-balance to local authoritarianism, and at the same time nurturing a form of 'deterritorialized activism' (Carapico 2013: 164) that could operate 'beyond and above the level of (national) sovereignty' (Carapico 2013: 167). Networked communications technologies have provided the platform and the ideological grounds for nurturing this type of 'commodity activism' (Banet-Wiser and Mukherjee 2012), in which communication and the production of data and knowledge-based goods – a core aspect of neoliberal communicative capitalism – have taken centre stage in articulating political struggles and even resistance.

This joint emphasis on technology and civil society – the non-state subject that, empowered by technology, would have finally confronted authoritarianism and helped bring about political change in the Arab world – has dramatic implications. It heavily contributed to shaping the myth of the 'Arab Spring' as Facebook and Twitter revolutions, a myth largely promoted by international media and Silicon Valley platform capital. The latter had in fact long nurtured the dream of a global, tech-savvy youth that would bring about political (and bloodless) change in the region: the 'coalition of the connected', as it was dubbed by Google CEO, Eric Schmidt, and Jared Cohen, director of Google Ideas and a former aide to both Condoleezza Rice and Hillary Clinton at the US State Department, in their telling piece 'The Digital Disruption: Connectivity and the Diffusion of Power' (Schmidt and Cohen 2010), published almost at the same time as the outbreak of the Tunisian uprising in December 2010. 'The advent and power of connection technologies', Schmidt and Cohen argued, 'will make the twenty-first century all about surprises. Governments will be caught off-guard when large numbers of their citizens, armed with virtually nothing but cell phones, take part in mini-rebellions that challenge their authority.' Cohen described this new kind of regime change as the quintessential form of '21st century statecraft' (Silver 2010), warning that without their keyboards these youths (referring to non-Westerners, particularly Muslims) would assume 'a *real-life* political, religious, ethnic, or nationalist identity' (Cohen 2009, my emphasis), i.e. would become a potential threat to the West. The fostering of a tech-centred culture would result in creating cool, cosmopolitan, interconnected '"like us" activists' (Della Ratta 2017b: 146–50), which is precisely the narrative at work in the making of the 'icons' of the Arab uprisings, such as Wael Ghonim and his 'revolution 2.0' (Ghonim 2012); or the elite of English-speaking 'bridge bloggers' described by a famous Harvard University study on the Arab blogosphere (Etling et al. 2010).[30] Yet this overemphasis on the technological aspect of the uprisings takes agency away from Arab activists, implicitly suggesting that they are 'compelled to action as a response to superior Western technology' (Burris 2011).

In this construction of the 'like us' activist a form of digital Neo-Orientalism has emerged, which is also a form of digital neo-colonialism,[31] where the techno-fetish is the new colonizer; it is subtler and less visible than the traditional manifestations of Orientalism described in Said's seminal work (1978). Digital Neo-Orientalism (Della Ratta 2017b; Della Ratta and De Angelis 2014) is co-authored and self-produced by Arab activists, probably unwillingly and unconsciously. In their use of networked communications technologies they perpetuate the idea that by virtue of the latter they are (re)empowered to tell their stories in a seemingly free and non-hierarchical way. Nonetheless, 'while apparently allowing the production of Arab identities, narratives, and iconographies in a free and horizontal way, the networks force all sort of content into a pre-set framework which Korinna Patellis has called "blockbuster software"' (Della Ratta 2017b: 149), i.e. software designed and owned by Silicon Valley proprietary and commercial platforms. Moreover, in order to have their voices heard and gain international support to their causes, Arab activists need to get hits on global news outlets and to be widely liked, shared, retweeted, tagged. In this way, they involuntarily contribute to 'building the fantasy of the Arab blogger, the activist who was once prevented from having her voice heard by repressive authoritarian regimes but who is now, thanks to networked communication technologies, finally able to re-seize her right to self-expression and to share her thoughts' (Della Ratta and De Angelis 2014).

Networked communications technologies look innocent. They seemingly embody horizontality and equal access, materialize fantasies of wholeness and participation, and suggest that all voices and stories produced within their environments are native, genuinely grassroots and 'authentic'. In the way they are engineered and designed to function, the networks pre-set the formats through which stories and identities should be narrated, and outside of which the latter simply do not exist. Hence, the emphasis on the communication and tech aspects of activism should not be regarded as innocent, but as revelatory of the networks' political economy in a way that calls for further reflection and investigation.

Fear and loathing of Syrian networked activism

To a certain extent, Bassel Safadi was a 'like us' activist. He had a clean face, spoke good English, owned all sorts of tech gadgets, and was a secular Muslim who drank alcohol. He used to hang out with an international crowd at tech gatherings, barcamps, geek fests, pecha-kuchas, TED talks, conferences and un-conferences; he mastered their jargon, and was loved by journalists, international human rights organizations and Silicon Valley entrepreneurs. After he mysteriously disappeared from Adra civil jail in October 2015, we launched several international campaigns to push the Syrian government to release at least some information on his whereabouts. In one of these many outreach efforts the public was invited to print out Bassel's face and wear it as a mask, in public places, with the hashtag #WhereIsBassel. I remember the comforting beauty of seeing so many people across the planet becoming 'Bassel' in solidarity.[32] Yet the fact of his being 'like us' did not prevent him from dying in the most horrible, most 'traditional', most 'non-2.0' way: Bassel was brutally executed, with no right even to make the last phone call to his loved ones.[33]

Like Bassel – who is probably among the 'lucky' ones, as his name and work will always be remembered through a fellowship that Creative Commons and other Silicon Valley organisations launched after his death (Merkley et al. 2017) – so many other 'like us' Syrian activists have lost their lives in silence, completely forgotten by the international media, public opinion, and the politicians who celebrated them at the beginning of the promising 'Arab Spring'. Once upon a time, there was a general feeling of excitement about the virtue of digital activism and citizen journalism, which was translated into articles, conferences, funding (Brownlee 2017), and even awards. In 2012 Google teamed up with Reporters Without Borders in establishing the 'Netizen Prize', which was, not by chance, awarded on the World Day Against Cyber

Censorship. 'The Netizen Prize proves that our voices were heard and that we succeeded in delivering the stories of millions of Syrians who are struggling on the ground to achieve what they have always dreamed – to live in freedom and dignity' (Reporters Without Borders 2012), a 27-year-old Syrian activist exiled in Canada declared at the ceremony in Paris, accepting the award on behalf of people like Bassel, who were still active inside the country at the time.

Years later, nothing seems to be left of this excitement. No more conferences, articles, awards, and, apparently, much less funding (Issa 2016: 24–5) for the media development sector in Syria which, throughout the 2000s and in the aftermath of the uprising, was deemed a key 'vehicle to achieve far-reaching goals such as to increase citizens' participation in politics, strengthen the respect of human rights and democratise institutions' (Brownlee 2017). The technological fetish, i.e. the idea that technology has the quasi-magical power of 'empowering' human beings (Della Ratta 2017b: 142–6), still inhabits the global imagination and visual culture. Yet instead of materializing in the form of cool, cosmopolitan, 'like us' activists à la Bassel, it is shaped around another trope: that of the tech-savvy, barbarian Daesh militant. Since the seizure of Mosul in June 2014 – widely echoed on social media thanks to the Twitter hashtag campaign #AllEyesOnISIS (Katz 2014a) that cleverly infiltrated the circulation of news on the World Cup taking place in Brazil – Daesh has been widely deemed a 'tech-savvy' (Coker et al. 2015) terrorist group capable of mastering, 'together with Kalashnikovs and knives, the modern language of the participatory Web 2.0' (Della Ratta 2014b). This 'hype', mostly on Western media, about the organization's alleged influence on social networking sites (Della Ratta 2014b) betrays our obsession with technology as an empowering tool: whether in the hands of peaceful activists struggling for freedom and dignity, or in the hands of brutal jihadis aiming at generating violence and death, both are just two sides of the same coin. The technological fetish lies at the core of the issue.

A few months before the outbreak of the Tunisian uprising, the activist and blogger Sami Ben Gharbia authored a prophetic piece entitled 'The Internet Freedom Fallacy and the Arab Digital Activism' (Ben Gharbia 2010) in which he reflected upon the risks of fetishizing technology and attributing to it the capacity of driving political change, particularly in authoritarian contexts such as the Arab world. Underlining the danger behind the hyper-politicization of Arab networked activism – and its possible misuse as a diplomacy and foreign policy tool to achieve the dreams of an alliance that net-critic Evgeny Morozov (2010) has dubbed the 'invisible revolving door between Silicon Valley and Washington' – Ben Gharbia's essay pointed out the strengths and weaknesses of this grassroots movement. Arab digital activism was born out of the local 'necessity' of finding a public space in which to discuss and practice politics, and not from technological hype. It experienced a first phase of total 'independence' from both Western donors and domestic opposition parties intent on infiltrating or exploiting it for their own benefit. It enjoyed the 'complexity' of being a multi-faceted movement, with substantially different strategies and tactics in resisting local powers from one Arab country to another (Ben Gharbia 2010). For these reasons, during its incubation stage in the early 2000s, none of the digital activities undertaken in the region (campaigns, online protests, dissident websites)[34] were supported or funded by Western NGOs or governments.

Things changed dramatically with the so-called 'Arab Spring' and the fantasies of bloodless political change it had triggered through the technological fetish. Arab networked activism is now caught in a dramatic contradiction. On the one hand, after the outbreak of the 2011 uprisings and the increasing need to process a formidable amount of information almost in real-time, and, sometimes, from places – particularly Syria – where no other sources were available, volunteer-based digital activism sought to adopt a more professional approach. This was a consequence both of the need for material survival in countries where the unrest had caused inflation, financial instability and unemployment, and of the demand of international news outlets for more accurate and verified data. On the other hand, in order to move towards more professionalisation, Arab activists needed financial and professional support and advice that they were unlikely to find locally. As foreseen by Ben Gharbia (2010) long before the 'Arab Spring', digital activists faced a dramatic restructuring of their ecosystem, and had to readapt to the emerging political economy of the media development 'industry', caught as they were 'between authoritarian regimes aggressively engaged in repression, Internet filtering and monitoring on the one side, and growing attention from Western public agencies and associated NGOs on the other' (Stanley 2007: 118–34).

Syria underwent a very similar process to that described by Ben Gharbia, from almost entirely lacking a local digital activism 'scene' throughout the 2000s,[35] to counting around 196 active media outlets (the majority of which operate online) launched in the aftermath of the uprising and which have managed to survive at the time of writing (Issa 2016: 6). A director at *Enab Baladi*, a prominent independent Syrian media outlet, explained the reason for this blossoming of counter-information by emphasizing that, 'after 40 years of repression, media was an avenue to express ... newly discovered freedom' (Issa 2016: 3). Since its foundation in 2011 in Daraya[36] – a suburb of Damascus widely considered as the cradle of the peaceful side of the uprising – *Enab Baladi* has managed to improve professionally, growing from a volunteer-based, amateur-run news service into an independent organization that packages multiple information products[37] and whose profile is featured on the BBC Syria Media page (BBC News 2018). As if to ratify this successful shift from amateurism to professionalism, in 2015 Majd Sharbaji and Kholoud Helmi, two of its co-founders, won respectively the US State Department Women of Courage Award and the Anna Politkovskaja Journalism Award.[38]

Other web-based grassroots initiatives originated post-2011 have taken an analogous development path. My first-hand experience with SyriaUntold – which I co-founded together with the scholar and activist Enrico De Angelis, the journalist Mohamed Dibo, and several other friends and colleagues from Syria – tells a similar story. In early 2012, sensing that the creative, peaceful side of the uprising was starting to be neglected by international media, and reflecting upon how to archive the digital past of the non-violent movement, we set up the English-Arabic web portal in the hope of drawing attention to the 'many aspects of the Syrian struggle that remain uncovered, many stories that we would not like to see forgotten'.[39] As the peaceful uprising descended into civil war and SyriaUntold staff inside the country were exposed to increasing personal risk and financial insecurity, we had to provide more funding to ensure sustainability.[40] There was no other way for us to do this than to seek support from international donors with an investment in developing oppositional media to counter the regime's one-sided narrative. Luckily, we have found in the Danish NGO International Media Support (IMS) a very honest and reliable partner, who has since helped make SyriaUntold a sustainable media operation, shifting from a grassroots outlet to a full-fledged organization, legally registered in Brussels and subject to European laws.[41]

To say that this financial support was translated into strict guidelines in terms of content production, or led to external pressure and interference, would be inaccurate and unfair. Yet forming a Syrian staff capable of adapting to rules and standards set elsewhere has definitely involved a huge effort in terms of cultural mediation. As an example, Syrian media that traditionally lacked a culture of accountability had to adapt quickly, for their own survival, to produce the paperwork required by international donors in order to document financial expenses, receipts for services, and reports about activities carried out during the year. This was extremely unusual for citizens of a country where media had been an integral part of a non-transparent, non-accountable and corrupt system nurtured by an authoritarian regime for more than 40 years. Training and workshop sessions also had to be shaped around the needs of international donors and NGOs, often including a focus on how to 'pitch' ideas on the marketplace, how to promote content on social media – 'if it doesn't spread, it's dead' (Jenkins 2009) – and how to become self-sustainable.

As in the case of the Arab bloggers' meetings, there seems to be no escape from this neoliberal, market-oriented language in defining the concepts and practices of contemporary digital activism. Finally, Syrian networked activism – having suddenly sprouted from a spontaneous desire for information on the events of the March uprising, and from the need for citizens to freely express their opinions after decades of repression and fear – became a faction among factions engaged in the Syrian conflict.[42] A non-violent, non-armed faction that spoke the language of a cosmopolitan, global civil society, of international solidarity, of activists 'like us', and yet it had sincerely and genuinely emerged at a local grassroots level.[43] Paradoxically, in order to survive in an environment heading towards a violent conflict involving regional and global powers, it was soon obliged to embrace rules, formats and standards set by foreign governments, non-profit organizations and commercial internet platforms, thereby fuelling the regime's accusations of conspiracy and foreign interference in domestic affairs.

The sacrifice Syrian grassroots media had to make on the altar of the political economy of contemporary networked activism was a loss of its initial enthusiasm and innocence. Without nostalgia for this lost 'purity', or judgment in respect of the neo-colonial role once again played by Western governments and organizations in the Arab world, even in the domain of the digital, I underline the fragility of contemporary Syrian alternative media in light of its political economy. A fragility that affects not only the production of digital content, but also its distribution over the web 2.0, as revealed by the fact that the diffused archive of the Syrian uprising mostly lies in the hands of Silicon Valley-based platform capitalists.

Dreams of freedom, sectarian fears, and the uncertainty of the digital

A few days into the March uprising the streets of Syria started to be filled with posters from a regime-backed advertising campaign saying 'no to sectarianism, no to chaos'. Meanwhile, Buthaina Shaaban, Bashar al-Asad's media advisor and spokeswoman, emphasized in her first public speech after the outbreak of the protest movement that its target was 'the beautiful coexistence in this country' (Al-Marashi 2011), its ultimate goal being to make the Arab world 'a sectarian, parochial, and ethnic-based region'. And when Bashar al-Asad himself finally decided to release an official statement about the unfolding events, he solemnly declared: 'Syria faces a great conspiracy, the webs of which spread from close and far away nations, and some of whose strings reach inside the country' (Al-Marashi 2011).

Sectarianism was a recurrent word in these official communications. The video documentation of these first days, weeks and months of the uprising – and my own ethnographic experience, having personally joined several protests at the time – hinted at a radically different situation than the one evoked by the regime's rhetoric. In the country's streets and squares people were chanting 'the Syrian people are one' or 'One hand, one hand'; slogans that underlined the protesters' wish to inject into the public space an idea of a population united in demanding a civic state and the rule of law, despite ethnic and religious differences. Yet the regime responded to this legitimate grassroots protest movement by recycling the old 'Baathist interpretative framework' (Al-Marashi 2011) based on conspiracy theories about foreign plots most likely designed in Israel with the support of Western governments.

This framework has been present across the spectrum of regime-sanctioned media, from advertising campaigns to *musalsalat* like the popular *Buq'at al-daw* which, in Ramadan 2012, featured the episode *Id Wahda* ('One hand'), mocking the Syrian people's capacity to act together and overcome their differences and individual interests. Even seemingly oppositional TV drama like real-time drama *Wilada min al-khasira* hinted at sectarianism as an evil deeply rooted in the country's history.

In a telling sequence from season 3 (2013),[44] the *musalsal* features a teacher (played by the director of the series, Seif Sbei, a staunch regime supporter) trying to convince his former students not to seek sectarian revenge for a friend who was allegedly killed by the protesters (Della Ratta 2014a). He insists that emphasizing sectarianism would surely lead to a civil war, the price of which would be too high for anyone in the country. The group, clearly identifiable as *shabbiha*, responds: 'We are with the regime and those who want to kill us will be killed by us', while the dialogue escalates into open violence.

The regime's official rhetoric, and the country's mainstream cultural production, seem to have been working coherently in the direction of strengthening the sectarian narrative since the very beginning of the uprising. After several years, this interpretative framework based on the same old Ba'athist tune and aiming at instigating fears connected to sectarian division and chaos, still holds, at least communication-wise. It is a leading theme in Bashar al-Asad's official communications to the Syrian public and in his interviews with international media. As an example, in the talk given at the University of Damascus in June 2011, the president reiterated the idea that Syria has traditionally been subject to foreign plots and interventions: 'the seasons of flowering and fruition have been replaced by seasons of conspiracy and killing ... I do not think there is a stage in Syria's history where it was not the target of some sort of conspiracy, both before and after independence. These conspiracies took place for many reasons, some relating directly to the important geo-political position that Syria occupies' (al-Asad 2011b). The entire speech was built around a rhetoric of national unity as a response to a foreign conspiracy that, in 2011, would have been orchestrated employing media channels and tech tools. 'What do we say about all of this media pressure? What do we say about these sophisticated phones that are found in Syria in the hands of vandals? What do we say about all the fraud that we witnessed recently? We certainly cannot say that this was an act of charity. It is definitely a conspiracy' (al-Asad 2011b).

In these official communications sectarianism is always paired with foreign conspiracy,[45] and both are used to undermine the legitimacy of the demonstrators' demands.[46] In the July 2014 inaugural speech after the presidential elections, Bashar al-Asad goes even further, calling the citizens who have managed to stay in the country 'free Syrian revolutionaries' opposed to the 'storm of sedition' and 'the winds of division' that those who 'chanted: "The Syrian people are united"' tried to spark (al-Asad 2014). Here the denigration of the 2011 protest movement is carried out through the appropriation of its 'purest' slogans, those appealing to the unity of the population in asking for a civic, multicultural state, in opposition to the regime's accusations of the uprising's sectarian nature.

Since the outbreak of the protest movement, Bashar al-Asad's presidency has cleverly adopted a twofold strategy. On the one hand, as underlined above, he has perpetuated by all means possible the narrative of a foreign conspiracy aiming at generating a sectarian divide in order to drag the country into a bloody civil war. On the other hand, he has worked extensively to undermine the demands of the protest movement and its claims to being peaceful and non-sectarian. In order to do so, he has exploited the domain of digital activism in particular. While revolutionary youths and oppositional formations have been mesmerized by the technological fetish, tasking it with carrying out their political struggle for dignity, pluralism and freedom of expression, Bashar al-Asad's communication strategy seems to have acknowledged the fragility and uncertainty of the digital, exploiting it to the advantage of the counter-revolutionary project.

Two points can be made in support of the argument that Syrian activists' good faith in the liberating power of technology was exploited by the regime to undermine their political project. Firstly, there is a widespread fantasy among digital activists that networked and participatory media are the quintessential domain of the progressive, 'as if radical left politics is somehow built into the technology' (Dean 2009: 147). This is a global fantasy that traces back to the libertarian 'Californian ideology' (Barbrook and Cameron 1995) of the first Silicon Valley-based tech companies. Deeply rooted in computer-inspired visual culture, the idea of a progressive, liberating technology is perfectly rendered by Apple's famous 1984 Macintosh commercial, which features a dystopian society of the future controlled by a Big Brother-like dictator who is finally murdered by a bold female runner. The caption reads: 'On January 24th, Apple Computers will introduce Macintosh. And you'll see why 1984 won't be like "1984"'[47] – the reference to George Orwell's famous novel implicitly suggesting that a computer-driven society of the future will be liberal and progressive *by default*. This tech-related visual culture has travelled globally, and also impacted on the Arab world. In 2005 a remix of the Macintosh commercial was released by Tunisian activist Riad Guerfali under the pen name of Astrubaal.[48] It featured the bold runner destroying a picture of the authoritarian leader Ben Ali and, once again establishing the connection between tech-powered activism and progressive politics.

Syria has proven this view of digital activism to be a fantasy as it can equally be the domain of progressive, liberal politics, or serve as the battleground where counter-revolutionary tactics and strategies are implemented by pro-establishment militants. Only a month after the uprising had started, when Syrian digital activists were at the peak of their excitement about what networked communications technologies could help them achieve, the pro-regime online hacker group Syrian Electronic Army (SEA) was formed. SEA never disguised its direct connection to Bashar al-Asad's presidency, and appears to be 'unbothered by the fact that its domain name is registered inside the country with the Syrian Computer Society (an institute previously headed by Bashar al-Asad)' (Aouragh 2014). The group has carried out several Distributed Denial of Service (DDOS) attacks against pro-uprising activists and prominent media outlets such as al-Jazeera (Baiazy 2012), also succeeding in disabling Anonymous' platform AnonPlus (Aouragh 2014). SEA's counter-revolutionary hacking strategy has been further strengthened and supported by two phenomena happening simultaneously in the digital domain: 'corporate complicity' and pro-active, 'online propaganda' (Aouragh 2014). On the one hand, international corporations and tech companies have provided the Syrian regime – sometimes in violation of the sanctions imposed on the country – with surveillance software, cyber espionage tools, online censorship and monitoring systems, thus increasing its capacity for policing and repressing pro-uprising activism (Aouragh 2014; Baiazy 2012). On the other hand, several grassroots initiatives have been established by pro-regime groups and ordinary citizens that contribute to building a positive image of al-Asad's presidency, at the same time as undermining the narratives promoted by the pro-uprising groups. In a recent study of post-2011 Syrian media, Antoun Issa has counted 72 pro-regime initiatives, mostly online, representing the 37 per cent of the total offer against the 36 per cent of openly pro-opposition initiatives – a further 20 per cent is listed as 'independent' for not siding with the official political opposition (being openly anti-al-Asad, though).[49] The strength of these pro-regime media is that they are truly grassroots and volunteer-run, confirming once again that digital, participatory activism can indifferently be revolutionary or counter-revolutionary, progressive or conservative, liberal or authoritarian.

The second point to problematize is the illusion that the domain of the digital can somehow produce credible *evidence*. In the firm belief that more documentation would generate more information and awareness, and that the latter would eventually lead to active mobilization, Syrian activists produced masses of data and audio-video material as evidence of what was happening on the ground (Della Ratta 2017c). Yet very early on in the uprising the domain of the digital revealed its fallacy. In June 2011, Amina Arraf, a Syrian-American blogger internationally known as the 'gay girl in Damascus' was allegedly arrested by the security forces. A global campaign was initiated to free her:[50] petitions were signed and articles were published in the international press, presenting Amina as a champion of freedom of speech and gender diversity embodying the quintessential peaceful activist repressed by a brutal regime. Yet the over-celebrated 'gay girl in Damascus' finally turned out to be Tom MacMaster, an American graduate student who had engaged in an internet-era literary exercise (Bell and Flock 2011). The revelation was followed by shock, frustration and a sudden feeling of 'loss of certainty about the digital itself – a sense that the stability and knowability of this sphere, from which the Arab Spring was supposedly born, was now shattered' (Kuntsman and Stein 2011: 3).

The fragility of all things digital was not new, or peculiar to the Syrian uprising, as underlined by Kuntsman and Stein (2015) in the context of the 2012 Israeli military campaign in Gaza. At the time, an Israeli amateur had revealed how a picture of a weeping father carrying the body of his dead child that went viral on the internet was actually a photoshopped image from Syria re-purposed by Hamas for political advantage. The discovery of the manipulation led many to believe that the bulk of the user-generated visuals from Gaza were fakes or had been doctored. This suspicion of the digital triggered the active partic-ipation of regular Israeli citizens in a work of digital forensics aimed at revealing more hoaxes and manipulations; a work that was celebrated by the Israeli government as patriotic. In the end, no matter how many evidence-images (Didi-Huberman 2008; Della Ratta 2017c) Pales-tinian (or Syrian) activists produce to shed light on the human rights violations in Gaza (or in Syria), patriotic Israeli (and Syrian pro-regime) data-activists will still believe them to be fake, or photoshopped, or adapted from another context.

No matter how much effort (and actual blood) Syrian activists have put into the production of data as evidence, this permanent state of 'digital suspicion' – 'directed against the digital image and archive as such, articulated most prominently on social media, mostly in the language of amateur digital forensics' (Kunstman and Stein 2015: 58) – has represented the leitmotif of the 2011 uprising from the beginning, leaving international public opinion, observers and media in the position of being unable, or maybe unwilling, to decide what is *really* happening in Syria – a situation that the regime has cleverly played to its own advantage. A 2016 interview with Bashar al-Asad on the Swiss TV Channel SRF 1 epitomizes this attitude (Sana 2016). When asked to comment on a photo of Omran Daqneesh – a young boy covered with blood, scared and traumatized, who had become the viral symbol of the regime's violence against civilians, the 'new face of the Syrian civil war' (Calamur 2016) – the Syrian president calmly answered:

> There's something I would like to say to you first of all, because I want you to go back after my interview, and go to the internet to see the same picture of the same child, with his sister, both were rescued by what they call in the West 'White Helmets'[51] which is a facelift for al-Nusra[52] in Aleppo. They were rescued twice, each one in a different incident, and just as part of the publicity of those White Helmets. None of these incidents were true. You can have it manipulated, and it is manipulated. I'm going to send you those two pictures, and they are on the internet, just to see that this is a forged picture, not a real one. We have real pictures of children being harmed, but this one in specific [*sic*] is a forged one.

To which the journalist was only able to answer back: 'but it's true that innocent civilians are dying in Aleppo' (Sana 2016).[53]

One year later, little Omran resurfaced. He was shown by Syrian and Lebanese pro-al-Asad media quietly sitting on his father's knee (McKernan 2017; Sanchez 2017). His father said that he supported the Syrian president and had rejected all international offers to leave the country, as this would undermine the reputation of the Syrian armed forces. Kinana Allouche, the prominent Addounia TV journalist whose celebratory selfie with corpses in the background had gone viral the previous year, tweeted pictures of herself interviewing 'the ambulance boy' with the caption: 'The child Omran, those who tried to shed Syrian blood misled the news that he was hit by the Syrian Arab Army. Here he now lives in the Syrian state with its army, its leader and its people' (Sanchez 2017; Gordon 2017). In such a short time frame, on international media and social networking sites, little Omran went from being a symbol of the violence against civilians in Syria, to becoming a 'fake' (Katz 2016; Frisk 2016), to being classified as an undecidable case, since very few publications problematized the latest public appearance of the child and his father on pro-regime media.

A similar issue has been raised in relation to the White Helmets, the volunteer rescue organization twice nominated for the Nobel Peace Prize who, in the same interview with the Swiss TV channel, were accused by al-Asad of being a 'facelift' for a jihadi group (Sana 2016). Among the most effective 'evidence' to support this claim was a video provided by Vanessa Beeley, a staunch pro-al-Asad British blogger (Solon 2017). The video was a contribution that, probably in the hope of getting people to talk about the situation in Syria, the White Helmets had provocatively sent to 'the mannequin challenge', a viral internet video competition featuring people staging actions and imitating mannequins (Molloy 2016). Beeley took the contribution out of its original context and spread it virally with the caption 'Here is [sic] the White Helmets caught faking a rescue after a fake attack' (Solon 2017). Later she admitted that the video was produced in the context of the mannequin challenge, yet still exploited the event to trigger a polemic under the provocative title 'A Publicity Stunt that Backfired?', where she argued that the clip had generated 'widespread doubt, even among diehard supporters, as to the veracity of their much edited slick video reports' (Beeley 2016).

Even if on several occasions the accusations against the White Helmets have been deconstructed and counter-balanced by accurate analyses undertaken by professional researchers and journalists (Worrall 2016; Solon 2017), what is left from this example – as much as from Omran's case and countless other stories emerging from Syria – is the continuous (re)production of digital uncertainty which has been exploited by Bashar al-Asad to the advantage of his regime. Unlike what most Syrian activists have genuinely thought – and with them, many of us who have long advocated for the digital as progressive – networked communications technologies neither help in the production of evidence, leading to the enforcement of international human rights and justice, nor foster the establishment of pluralistic views, opening up a democratic path. We have set about producing ever more data and 'evidence', taking it for granted that this would be assessed on the basis of 'a consensus regarding the rules and conditions for establishing truth and falsity, not to mention a shared notion of reality' (Dean 2009: 147). This is yet another fantasy triggered by networked communications technologies whose participative, viral (and vital) mechanism of non-stop circulation of 'whatever' (Dean 2010) contribution prospers on the contrary on 'dissensus, incredulity, and competing conceptions of reality' (Dean 2009: 147), i.e. on the same conditions under which communicative capitalism thrives.

While Syrian activists have been busy producing alternative sources of knowledge and information, this proliferation of data has not only proved vital to the preservation of corporate media's investments and global platform-capitalism's interests; it has also created 'conditions amenable to the flourishing of psychotic discourses' (Dean 2009: 173) that would generate a state of 'constituent anxiety' (Dean 2009: 171) in the Syrian and international publics. None of the newly formed conceptions of reality has been powerful enough to oppose the long-established Ba'athist narrative framework, in a situation in which the over-proliferation of digital voices, often materialized in pixelated, blurred frames,[54] has rather produced uncertainty, mistrust and disbelief. As if one were to fire a bullet into the sky and suddenly kill a flying Dumbo, everything is unreal, everything is surreal, in Syria. And perhaps the first casualties of this bloody war – as Banksy's mysterious viral video from 2013 seems to suggest[55] – are truth and innocence, or the capacity to trust and believe.

SNAPSHOT #6

A wave of user-generated videos filmed with camera phones emerged with the outbreak of the 2011 uprising, a pervasive smartphone culture which paralleled the peaceful protest movement unfolding on the ground. Contrary to what regime-sanctioned and elite-managed communications had envisaged, mobile networked technologies, particularly social networking sites, were not employed to seize the opportunity of enjoying individual freedoms and commodified experiences of consumption, but rather to claim civic and political rights, and express dissent.

Filming turned into a continuous life activity flourishing in the realm of politics, yet it was soon appropriated by all the factions involved in the conflict, including torturers, regime officers and armed gangs. Filming and killing became two inherently intertwined dynamics in Syria's everydayness, generating multiple aesthetic languages and formats: from the blurry, pixelated shots that are the signature of the protesters' videos, to the static, 'caught on camera' sequences marking the performance of violence.

Yet in the networked environment, and in the visual economy of warfare, no matter what image becomes a commodity to be copied, appropriated, manipulated and reproduced as a result of a supply and demand process involving multiple subjects, from foreign governments and NGOs, to private media, commercial and art ventures. Syrian image-makers are no longer the keepers of their own images, which have been appropriated by Silicon Valley's platform capitalists, and by those activists who abandoned the idea of the revolutionary 'commons' and claimed back ownership, once they realized that Syrian visual production was in high demand. This split between image-makers and image-keepers, which takes on a global dimension in moving between local activists and the Californian internet giants, opens up an emerging political economy of the image post-2011, one whose material, legal and ethical implications are yet to be fully explored.

6

Screen Fighters: Filming and Killing in Contemporary Syria

It's Friday – let's go out and protest

The young man looks straight into the camera. He can see us, yet we can't see him, his face being entirely covered with the Syrian national flag. He wears a white baseball cap with the word *hurriyya* written in red. In his hands is a shiny silver iPod. 'First of all, I will film using this iPod', he begins with a sort of sacrality in his voice, explaining that the device ensures better quality and frame rate than any other, hence it is ideal to serve as a hidden camera. Then he demonstrates how to sew a secret pocket into his shirt that will function as a hidden case inside which the iPod will be firmly secured, in order to continue filming even in an emergency situation.

This video resembles thousands of DIY and how-to clips that populate the internet nowadays. Yet its unique appeal comes from it being shot in Syria by an unknown activist filming another unknown activist showing how to film without being seen, as being caught holding a camera means a death sentence in the country.[1] The video has recently resurfaced, yet it dates back to August 2011, a few months after the outbreak of the uprising: a moment in which its peaceful side was enjoying its momentum, both internationally and on the ground, the Free Syrian Army being still in its early days.[2] The Syrian citizen journalist on the frontline, armed only with a mobile camera, had become a trope in the narration of the events, especially on the international stage. In 2012, this iconic figure was publicly praised by the Google-sponsored Reporters Without Borders Netizen Prize, a prestigious award celebrating freedom of expression which was symbolically offered to all 'Syrian citizen journalists and activists' (Reporters Without Borders 2012). 'The Internet allows courageous individuals in Syria and elsewhere to tell their story to the world', Google France president Jean-Marc Tassetto declared at the time. While Reporters Without Borders's Dominique

Gerbaud emphasized the 'instrumental' role of Syrian citizens 'in the news gathering process', which had turned them into targets and victims of 'increasingly sophisticated methods of censorship, surveillance and repression' (Reporter Without Borders 2012).

The use of the mobile camera phone as a tool for political participation and citizen engagement in a country where access has been severely restricted to international reporters is truly unprecedented, to the extent that, as noted earlier, Syria has been dubbed 'the most socially mediated civil conflict in history' (Lynch et al. 2014: vii). More than that, the massive employment of smart devices in the production of 'civic media' (Roque 2011) also represents a completely unforeseen circumstance from the perspective of the ruling power. Ironically enough, less than one year earlier and only a month prior to the outbreak of the uprising, the Syrian government had taken the surprising decision of lifting a three-year ban on social networking sites. At the time, many human rights organizations, as well as the US Secretary of State, warned that the government might have finally allowed the use of sites such as YouTube or Facebook in order to monitor people more closely in case the unrest that was taking other Arab countries by storm spread to Syria (Preston 2011). Yet for others, such as the Syrian tech entrepreneur Abdulsalam Haykal, this was a step in the direction of 'a commitment to build confidence with the country's young people. "The power of social media is an important tool for increasing participation, especially by engaging young people"' (Preston 2011), he declared at the time. This belief reflected Bashar al-Asad's official rhetoric about Syria being on the verge of significant reforms in the media and investment sectors, including information and communication technology. 'We are the fastest growing Internet user in the Middle East', the Syrian president had proudly announced in an interview with *The Wall Street Journal* at the end of January 2011, a few days before lifting the ban on social networking sites in early February.

Less than a month later, in early March, billboard ads started to appear introducing a brand new 3G-enabled smartphone that had just been released by an internationally renowned brand. The campaign posters featured a Twitter timeline displaying conversations among *tweeps* (avatars of people) discussing food and lifestyle issues. Using the Twitter style 140-only characters, 'Fashion France' talked about its 'autumn collection launch' being a 'success!'; while a Twitter handle under the name of 'JuliaW72' had typed: 'It's Friday – any recommendations on a good film?' Whereas the displayed Twitter conversation was in English, the poster caption read, in Arabic: 'quintessentially social' (*ijtima'i bi-l-imtiyaz*). The new smartphone featured in the campaign seemed to convey expectations of new friendships and novel opportunities for leisure, fun and business that the always connected, networked environment would eventually open up. Once the ban was lifted, the world of social networking sites – symbolized by a trendy new platform, Twitter, still little known in the country – seemed to be promising in Syria. In this context, being 'quintessentially social' meant rendering commodified urban experiences, such as dining out or buying fashionable clothes, into opinions and conversations to be shared and commodified in their turn, to the advantage of social networking platforms.

The fantasies suggested by these new, exciting urban freedoms, reflected the atmosphere of the neoliberal Syria that Bashar al-Asad had tried to shape, particularly since the second half of the 2000s. Within this framework, social and consumption-oriented freedoms were deemed more important than political freedom. Stability and development before reforms had been a recurring, long-time mantra in the regime's official discourse (*The Wall Street Journal* 2011) – a clever strategy that not only delayed political reforms but also widened the regime's support base by appealing to the new urban elites emerging as a result of the selective liberalization policy implemented throughout the 1990s.

The 'quintessentially social' campaign targeted precisely these new elites who were familiar with the English language and intrigued by the latest gadgets and trendy devices – a class of people who wanted to

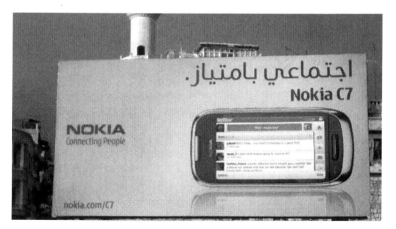

Figure 6.1   'Quintessentially social' advertisement campaign, Damascus, March 2011 (photo: Donatella Della Ratta).

be up-to-date and cosmopolitan, and who populated the stylish cafés in the city centres of Damascus, Aleppo and Lattakia, drinking exotic *lattes* or *mochaccinos* while surfing the web non-stop thanks to the wi-fi connection offered with their beverages. A crowd that, most likely, was fascinated by Bashar al-Asad's vision of moving the country forward (*Forward* was also the title of the progressive, English-language magazine managed by Abdulsalam Haykal) at a market freedom and entrepreneurship level, rather than guiding it through a process of political opening. Yet, contrary to what the ruling power and its marketing advisors had wished for, the popularization of networked communications technologies on a large scale happened thanks to a radically different target group who used their smartphone devices in ways other than those envisioned by the 'quintessentially social' campaign.

In early 2011, small protests had started to occur simultaneously throughout the country, demanding very different freedoms from those promoted by the market's seductive languages: freedom of speech, the right to work and live in dignity, the rule of law and a civic state (Sinjab 2013). In Daraa, a city in southwestern Syria with a strong tribal component, the spark of the protest movement manifested after young children who had allegedly painted anti-regime slogans on the school walls were arrested, and eventually disappeared (Marsh 2011). In Damascus, a small group bravely walked the heart of the Old City chanting 'the Syrian people are one' and 'peaceful, peaceful' – in the very area that was being transformed into 'a politically neutered museum, a playground for new middle class money spenders', by the president's plans for the new Syria (Salamandra 2004: 135). A month before, on 17 February 2011, a much bigger crowd of workers and shopkeepers of the Old City's market had gathered in front of the local police station after one of them had been beaten by an officer (Williams 2011). 'The Syrian people will not be humiliated', they had chanted, together with 'thieves, thieves, thieves'.[3] Although spontaneous and not politically organized, this was undoubtedly the first mass protest witnessed in Bashar al-Asad's Syria.[4]

Other attempts at gathering in a public space – although rather elite-led and promoted by prominent public figures such as Suhair Atassi (al-Jazeera 2011b) – were also initiated in February 2011. These resulted in sit-ins and assemblies in front of the Egyptian and Libyan embassies (Williams 2011), in solidarity with those two countries' popular uprisings, and urging the official representatives of the Mubarak and Qaddafi regimes to leave their posts. However, in a country like Syria, with an emergency law that had been in place for more than four decades (Allain 2017: 216–26), these peaceful sit-ins and candle vigils represented ways of publicly rehearsing discontent, showing defiance, and gaining visibility in front of a political power that had carefully erased any manifestation of dissent from public spaces (Hamadeh 2016). These defiant 'rehearsals' did not go unnoticed by the *sultat*. In an atmosphere of extreme tension between the small crowd of peaceful protesters and the much more significant number of armed policemen sent to contain them, they finally ended in harsh repression, severe beatings and arbitrary arrests.[5] It was a clear warning sent by the ruling power to the Syrian people who, through the internet and satellite channels, were witnessing live the Tunisians, the Egyptians and the Libyans revolting and toppling their authoritarian rulers. The repression was thus a sort of preventative advice not to try to emulate their Arab brothers.

This strategy of restraint did not work, however. After the first protests in Daraa were crushed with bloodshed (Marsh 2011), more cities started to join the popular movement: Banyas, the Damascus suburbs Duma, Harasta and Jobar, and later Homs and Hama. The demonstrations throughout the country gathered together a very different crowd: from the disadvantaged working class of the suburbs cut off from the selective liberalization process – whose daily lives and troubles *tanwir*-inspired TV drama had often portrayed in its aspiration to tackle sensitive, cutting-edge topics – to the urban youth who had studied hard under the illusion that education would enable them to escape a highly corrupted job market based on *wastat* ('recommendations') and personal connections within the upper echelons of the regime and the *mukhabarat*. Cultural producers were also involved in the protest movement at its outbreak: beside the already mentioned Suhair Atassi, the actress May Skaf, the scriptwriter Rima Fleihan, the writer Khaled Khalifa and the actor Fares al-Helou not only took public positions supporting the popular uprising but also physically joined the demonstrations (one of which was famously dubbed 'the demonstration of the artists'[6]), sometimes with severe consequences for their personal safety.[7] And although the majority of TV drama makers preferred to stay silent during this first phase, or publicly supported the regime's position, it should not be forgotten that the actress Fadwa Suleiman[8] and the actor Jalal al-Taweel took a leading role in mobilizing the crowds during mass gatherings in, respectively, the city of Homs and in Midan, a popular neighbourhood in central Damascus – to the extent that they soon had to be smuggled out of the country in fear of their lives.

Unlike the Damascus Spring of 2000–1, which was a markedly elite-led movement, the March 2011 uprising had succeeded in attracting very diverse crowds in terms of class, social status, ethnicity and religious beliefs. They were united by a common aspiration towards a more dignified life, meaning the end of the system of arbitrary abuse perpetuated by the *mukhabarat*, and the establishment of the rule of law (Al-Shami and Yassin-Kassab 2016). Although embracing a whole spectrum of personal beliefs, lifestyles and religious faiths, from conservative Muslims to Christians to staunch secularists and nonbelievers, this varied group managed to gather in mosques across the country every Friday and, immediately after prayer, start demonstrating together. For several months the Friday protest was a well-consolidated, recurring pattern in the Syrian uprising,[9] leaving many international observers doubtful about the latter's non-sectarian character.

In a country under strict surveillance and subject to emergency law, Friday prayers at mosques were virtually the only public assemblies allowed, although strictly for religious reasons. Thus for many Syrians the Friday prayer represented a unique occasion to start a protest in significant numbers, as it provided an acceptable excuse to gather in a public space. Instead of being an opportunity to experience new urban lifestyles, buy fashionable clothes or consume exotic foods, as the 'quintessentially social' campaign advertised, Friday became instead a symbolic celebration of public defiance. Far from a commodified or communication-driven experience, being 'social' finally meant *being political*.

Ironically enough, Twitter, the trendy internet platform chosen to symbolize (and sell) the new smartphone, was soon turned by the protesters into a political tool for mobilisation and communication with the outside world (Lynch et al. 2014). As a co-organiser of the 2011 Damascus 'Twestival' – the Syrian edition of a simultaneous global gathering involving several international cities to celebrate sharing and communicating across borders – I soon experienced this political turn of Twitter first-hand. Having secured the authorisation[10] to host the Twestival on 26 March, partly at Aikilab and partly at the Danish Institute in Damascus, on 18 March my co-host Bassel Safadi received an informal visit from the *mukhabarat* 'advising' him to cancel the event immediately. The Syrian secret police who before 15 March had not been too worried about the political use of social networking sites (as signalled by the fact that we had secured their initial approval), suddenly realized that the 'quintessentially social' world unlocked by networked communications technologies was in the process of being turned into the quintessential site for politics. Our initially harmless Twestival was now deemed dangerous and abruptly cancelled, since in the aftermath of 15 March a Twitter conversation would most likely have started with: *'it's Friday – let's go out and protest...'.*

An emerging smartphone protest culture

'Politics in the Middle East is now *seen*' (Khatib 2012: 1). Lina Khatib's remark about the markedly political visual culture that has (re)surfaced in the Arab region since 2011 is nowhere better illustrated than in Syria, where a tiny mobile camera phone defiantly held against a gun has become iconic of the peaceful phase of the 15 March revolt. The use of the camera phone as a counterpart to weapons – which symbolically makes it into a weapon in its own right[11] – is so intrinsically intertwined with the imagination of the Syrian conflict that a little girl can surrender to a camera thinking it is a gun.[12] This widely circulated image suggests the extent to which protest culture in the country has embraced the visual form.

The mobile camera phone *is* indeed a gun, the only tool an unarmed protester has to shoot back at his killers, 'trying to provoke them into producing an image of *his* death, so that at least there will be some evidence of their murderousness' (Snowdon 2016: 92). In this way the protester and his murderer are jointly condemned to the immortality of images, Snowdon remarks. Yet, as Hamadeh's fascinating analysis suggests, 'the threat that the protesters pose by parading cameras against the Syrian armed forces' might be read less as a defiant gesture of documenting the violence against civilians and more as 'an act of rebellion' against the 'practice of disappearance' from public spaces and collective memory that has been systematically carried out by the regime (Hamadeh 2016: 17, 35, 36). The most (in)famous symbol of this joint erasure of dissent – from both the physical and the immaterial space of Syria's collective imagination – is undoubtedly the 1982 massacre perpetrated by the Syrian armed forces against a Muslim Brotherhood-led rebellion in the city of Hama, during which between 10,000 and 40,000 people were killed, in the complete absence of any recorded evidence or visual documentation (Hamadeh 2016: 25). Such was the climate of fear that parents would hardly talk to their children about what they dared to refer to only as 'the Events' (Omareen 2014), without giving any more specific name to the bloodshed: an *obliteration* of the visual and of language that resembles what Georges Didi-Huberman defined as a 'machinery of *disimagination*' (Didi-Huberman 2008: 20) when describing the Nazis' systematic project of destroying all evidence of the violence committed in order to deny its historical existence. In this 'world that the Nazis wanted to obfuscate, to leave wordless and imageless', four photographs were 'snatched from hell' by brave members of the Sonderkommando[13] (Didi-Huberman 2008: 20, 3): four blurred, undefined, almost unrecognisable frames from Auschwitz that Didi-Huberman calls 'images in spite of all', because, 'in spite of their low technical quality, their lack of framing, and their blurriness, they stand as powerful evidence' (Della Ratta 2017c: 116) of what the Nazis attempted to eradicate from collective memory and imagination.

Syria's pixelated, mobile-generated, blurry frames are indeed images *in spite of all*; images that have been shot and uploaded in spite of the danger and against all the odds, like 'signals to be emitted' (Didi-Huberman 2008: 5) to the outside world in order to resist oblivion. Before serving as evidence-images (Didi-Huberman 2008: 90; Della Ratta 2017b) and seeking to become historical testimony – even in such a fragmented, unfinished way – the Syrian frames produced since the beginning of the uprising are counter-actions to the regime's project of removing any trace of dissent from public spaces and from the space of history: a resurgence, as Hamadeh calls it, in the 'virtual space inaugurated by the act of filming,'[14] 'of what was determinately erased in full presence somewhere else' (Hamadeh 2016: 17). The videos themselves become substitutes for a space that was violently subtracted and appropriated by the ruling power; they turn into the quintessential place to perform and manifest dissent, making the latter visible not only to other Syrians and to the entire world, but also to the person simultaneously filming and live-witnessing the events filmed (Hamadeh 2016; Rich 2011).

The question of visibility is crucial in reading Syria's uprising video archive as a collective 'statement against this forced disappearance' that the regime has condemned its people to since 'the Events' in Hama (Hamadeh 2016: 36). In the eyes of the ruling power, Syrians who oppose the regime simply do not exist, they have no visibility in public space; and if they do manage to gain this visibility, as during the 2011 uprising, then they should be treated as 'conspirators' (al-Asad 2011a) or individuals whose 'Syrianness' is to be questioned and denied.[15] From this perspective 'the lives of those who dared to desacralize the national ideal had no critical mass, no political visibility, no representability, and thus their extermination held no ethical claims or consequences'. Unlike the Nazis' disimagination strategy, erasure from the public space in Syria does not serve 'to cover the traces of a despicable crime, but as [a] negation' of the very fact that those lives have ever existed (Hamadeh 2016: 14). Hence, before being a 'rational act of a "citizen journalist"' (Snowdon 2016: 91) determined to capture evidence-images, the compulsive, non-stop filming inaugurated in 2011 stands as a powerful reaction to the decades-old denial strategies of the ruling power: the denial of public visibility, and the denial of 'Syrianness' in those whose values of nationhood and identity diverge from the mainstream narrative.[16]

The first citizen-generated videos casually filmed during the spontaneous protest of 17 February 2011 in a central Damascus market already demystify these two strategies. Firstly, the footage shot by unknown citizen-protesters in itself represents a reclaiming of stolen visibility, as it testifies to the *being there* of the people in that very moment. Yet visibility is not only regained through the frames documenting protests as the main object of the filmed material, but also by virtue of the fact that the footage itself is the living testimony of more people filming, as active subjects in the unfolding of the events. Here visibility is multiplied, expanded, as it concerns the visibility of the crowd: not that of an isolated person filming as 'a spectacular, narcissistic thing', but that of the individual '*being there* together with others' (Snowdon 2016: 68, my emphasis). Secondly, the collective, spontaneous chant – 'the Syrian people will not be humiliated' – as the immediate reaction to the police brutally beating a fellow citizen, reaffirms an idea of 'Syrianness' in which a shared identity *in defiance* is shaped in contrast to the blind acceptance of the abuses perpetrated by the ruling power, defined by the crowd as 'humiliation'.

After this first wave of spontaneous, grassroots videos, the footage filmed by unknown protesters throughout 2011 has often emphasized these two recurring elements:[17] the (re)establishment of the visibility of the crowd, in combination with a different, defiant idea of 'Syrianness'. A protest pattern can be clearly identified in the Syrian uprising: the simultaneous surfacing of a network of sporadic and loosely connected demonstrations,[18] at first exclusively on Fridays, and later spread throughout the entire week. Unlike the Egyptian uprising, in which Tahrir square served as a centralized and monumental protest and filming hub, in Syria's heavily surveilled public space protesters had to reinvent the time and space of the political protest, at the same time as finding new ways of documenting it. The new formats of the *muzahara tay'ara* – a flash demonstration starting unexpectedly and lasting only a few minutes – and of the *'itisam manzili* – a home sit-in organized mostly by women fearing the danger of being in the streets – are innovative responses to the violent repression perpetrated by the Syrian armed forces and secret services since March 2011. The act of filming takes centre stage in forging these emerging practices on the aesthetic level, as it shapes a visual culture of dissent which is peculiar to Syria, establishing its own sort of grammar, creating its own tropes, formats and genres for documenting political activism. More importantly, it operates at a political, symbolic level by creating a 'virtually augmented space of contention' (Hamadeh 2016: 18) that extends much further the tiny alley where the flash mob happens, or the secret home in which the sit-in is held; once uploaded and injected into the realms of web 2.0, in fact, the filmed material finds a new online life – an *onlife* – as it circulates and is re-circulated by thousands of unknown users.

The videos thus perform an operation of (re)connection at a double level. On the one hand, they reunite visually what the regime has historically worked to isolate spatially, in order to avoid the formation of a cross-cultural and inter-religious solidarity across very diverse cities that would threaten the mainstream narrative on minorities in the country (also perpetuated through TV drama). Finally, in 2011, Syrians managed to talk to each other through protest videos. The chant 'by our blood, by our souls we will defend you, oh Daraa'[19] resonates in the footage filmed in Damascus, Banyas and other protest sites since the first demonstrators were killed in the southwestern city on 18 March; and it reaches out to its population once the material is uploaded and circulated on the web.

Thanks to the uploaded video footage, in a spontaneous domino effect, after one city had somebody killed during a protest – its own martyr[20] – the material filmed in other parts of Syria would feature a crowd chanting: 'by our blood, by our souls we will defend you' followed by the name of the martyr's city, in a sort of endless and fascinating 'intertextual visuality' (Hamadeh 2016: 21) between cities that were once divided, geographically and culturally. On the other hand, once uploaded to the internet, the footage connects the Syrian space of contention with the broader networked space of the web 2.0, linking it to other spaces, people, and data, and circulating it within a much wider, transnational spatial dimension. This way, the symbolic and political function of reclaiming visibility performed by these videos vis-à-vis the Syrian ruling power meets with their communicative and informative function directed towards a more general, international public.

Together with (re)establishing the visibility of the Syrian people, both at a local and at an international level, the 2011 protest videos work to affirm a different idea of 'Syrianness' in stark contrast to that of the regime. The video shot in Damascus on 15 March – which has become iconic as it marked the official 'start' of the uprising[21] – features a small crowd of about 50 people descending the tiny alleys of *suq al-Hamidiyya* (a famous market in the Old City) and chanting 'the Syrian people are one', a recurrent slogan both in later demonstrations and in the footage documenting them. 'One hand' is another chant often resonating in 2011 videos, sung by crowds that progressively increase in size, by hundreds, then by thousands, sometimes managing to take control of a public square and stage a sit-in, as it happened in the city of Homs.[22]

These slogans, and the way in which they are bodily performed in the protest videos, testify to the participants' desire to inject into the public space – both the physical space of the protest and the virtual space of its video documentation – an alternative idea of Syrian identity. Whereas the regime's rhetoric asserts the impossibility of Syrian religious and ethnic minorities living together in peace and stability,[23] other than under the leadership of al-Asad's family,[24] these chants suggest that demanding a civic state and the rule of law is, in fact, a common and shared request across the Syrian cultural mosaic. At a time when the ruling power widely disseminates the words *fitna* (a Koranic expression evoking sectarian divisions) and *ta'fiyya* ('sectarianism') in the public space – from Buthaina Shaaban's first speech after the uprising (Al-Marashi 2011) to street billboards[25] – as a strategy to suggest that protest will lead the country into chaos and conflict, the protest videos uploaded across the country testify of a very different situation on the ground. The protesters hold the regime accountable for having generated fears and anxieties over sectarianism in order to justify the tight surveillance and the continuous abuses perpetrated by the secret police, and they respond by demanding instead the establishment of a 'civic state' (*dawla madaniyya* [civic state] is in fact another recurrent expression in the footage documenting the protests).

Figure 6.2   Advertising campaign 'No to sectarian division', Damascus, Spring 2011.

The idea of 'Syrianness' emerging from the protest videos is that of a mature population wanting to live together despite the cultural and religious differences, and to do so not under an authoritarian rule, but governed by the rule of law – a vision in stark contrast with the *tanwir* ideology supported by the political and cultural elites. It is not by chance that *tanwir*-inspired TV drama has tried, after the outbreak of the uprising, to lampoon the idea of unity in diversity emerging from the protests. In the 2012 episode of the multi-season *musalsal Buq'at al-daw* with the telling title *Id Wahda* ('One hand') the protagonist seeks to convince his fellow citizens to act together and stay united, only to discover, on 'the day of his death, that he has been totally left alone by society' (Della Ratta 2012a). Several other episodes of the same TV series – widely deemed progressive and cutting-edge – also try to debunk the idea that the Syrian people are ready to live in a multicultural, multi-religious society regulated by the rule of law, as the protesters demand (Della Ratta 2012a). This does not necessarily indicate the drama makers' full support for the regime, but it does signal the patronizing attitude vis-à-vis Syria's population that is widespread among the country's elites.

This scepticism towards the protest movement and, more generally, towards the capacity of Syrian society to embrace a political path leading to the establishment of a civic state, is not, however, shared by the entire drama-maker community. The videos Fadwa Suleiman recorded from her hiding place during the peak of demonstrations in the city of Homs, defiantly talking to the camera about the civil rights brutally stolen from Syrian citizens,[26] stand as a striking counter-narrative to that of the political and cultural elites; even more so as the actress belongs to the Alawite community, the same religious minority as the al-Asad family. In stark opposition to the idea of a society deemed backward and not ready for political reform, such protest videos finally conquer a physical and immaterial space of dissent. For the first time in Syria's history, they manage to inject into the public space a portrayal of society that is radically different from regime-sanctioned elite communications. Through these videos' pixelated frames, Syrian society finally (re)gains visibility, as much as a public, markedly political, space.

Filming and killing, dying and filming in contemporary Syria

Since those very first grassroots videos, spontaneously surfacing from the February 2011 protest in a Damascus' market, a smartphone protest culture has taken over in Syria. Protesting and filming, filming and protesting, have become dramatically intertwined activities, mutually influencing each other. A 'new protest culture has developed ... through images and sounds' (Boëx 2013),[27] as image-making in Syria has finally found an opportunity to flourish in the realm of politics in the guise of a collective life activity accessible on a mass scale.

Once the project to keep technology in the 'safe hands' of the upper-middle class had fallen apart, and the 'quintessentially social world' of commodified urban experiences imagined by regime-backed spin doctors had collapsed, the activity of filming – completed by networked processes of uploading and sharing – lost its elitist nature as an art separated from life, and eventually turned into an ordinary matter of the everyday. In his seminal manifesto 'For an Imperfect Cinema',[28] Cuban filmmaker Julio Garcia Espinosa defines this process of life re-appropriating art as the latter's disappearing 'into everything' (Espinosa 1979). 'Cultivated art', as Espinosa calls it, traditionally referred to an individually centred, unique occupation, directed towards self-fulfilment and carried out as labour; unlike 'popular art', which was just an activity among other life activities, where the line between 'creators' and 'spectators' remained blurred. In a perspective on art understood as a continuous life activity, cinema also has to transform itself, and become 'imperfect' by virtue of the fact that it becomes 'committed':[29] no longer preoccupied by the aesthetic qualities of images, its raison d'être now lies in using the latter to serve revolutionary goals.

As much as in Cuba in the 1970s, in Syria in the 2010s filming seems to have become an ordinary, ongoing life activity:

> Peaceful activists, street protesters, regime officials, torturers, armed groups, unknown citizens; everyone films and everyone is a filmmaker in contemporary Syria. All relationships – whether political, material or human; whether within Syria or between Syria and the outside world – have been shaped and processed by images and through images. Filming literally disappeared into everything, as Espinosa envisioned. (Della Ratta 2017c: 114)

This *everydayness* of filming is powerfully rendered by Osama Mohammed's[30] *Ma'a al-fidda* ('Silvered Water: Syria's Self-Portrait', 2014),[31] co-directed with Wiam Simav Bedirxan in collaboration with '1001 Syrians', as the credits acknowledge, paying tribute to the thousands of unknown filmmakers whose anonymous YouTube uploads appear in the film. 'It is Syria filming herself' (Badt 2014), Mohammed declared, underlining the Syrians' compulsive practice of video recording every 'routine' action in a time of war, from the brutal torture inflicted inside the prisons, to protesters running away and filming, filming and running away, during street demonstrations that quickly resulted in bloodshed.

Yet, far from removing the aesthetic from the everydayness of filming, or ascribing the latter's potential to the realm of the political and the revolutionary – as Espinosa does – throughout *Ma'a al-fidda* Mohammed's voiceover is haunted by the cinematic language powerfully yet unconsciously emerging from those anonymous shots abruptly taken from the flow of life. Only after watching – and making us watch, as powerless spectators – thousands of anonymous frames rescued from YouTube, does the director finally realize that the *murderer* and *murdered* make two very different cinemas.

> Only those who commit a crime, in fact, have the time to look for the most spectacular angle, fix the camera, and finally render their violence into an aesthetic performance that can be reproduced and re-enacted for the sake of the camera-eye. The protester, the tortured,

the victim, must run away in an attempt to escape death; their cameras are shaky, their images blurry. It's the 'cinema of the murdered' versus the 'cinema of the murderer' – ultimately, the luxury of a static shot belongs to those who perform violence, not to those who risk their lives to document it. (Della Ratta 2017c: 115)

In post-2011 Syria, the image has dramatically taken centre stage in the execution of violence as well as in its denunciation. On the one hand, the gaze of the perpetrators – like those who mercilessly torture a young kid in the opening sequences of *Ma'a al-fidda* – is complacent: their 'on-screen boasting' reflects 'their cinematic fantasies to dramatize their roles in the killings' (ten Brink and Oppenheimer 2012: 9–10).[32] As a Syrian filmmaker who was jailed in the first phase of the uprising has remarked: 'They dress up to torture, as for a day of feast; they are brutal and have no mercy on you, but some of them, after their shift is over, come to see you, as if nothing had happened. They look completely different.'[33] This performance-like aspect of torturing aesthetically translates into sophisticatedly filmed static shots in which the camera surgically records the execution of the violence step-by-step. The static shot, or 'caught on tape' form, as film studies scholar Catherine Zimmer notes, is a common aesthetic trait both of the early cinema and of contemporary surveillance cameras (Zimmer 2015: 8). It lies at the 'intersection of spectacle and surveillance' (Zimmer 2015: 15), in between the amazement caused by the first public projections of the Lumières' *Arrival of the train at La Ciotat* (1895),[34] and the anxiety of being constantly followed and watched that surveillance cameras, so dramatically familiar to contemporary global cities, generate. The mix of spectacle and surveillance aesthetically conveyed by the 'caught on tape' shot embodies the quintessential visual mode of 'a decade politically and culturally saturated by the "war on terror"' (Zimmer 2015: 53). Terror is the politics behind the static shot;[35] vice versa, the latter aesthetically transposes the logic, rhetorics and tactics that, since 2001, have occupied a key place 'in the world's political reality, not to mention its imaginary' (Zimmer 2015: 32). An imaginary that, thanks to mass media and networked communications technologies, has circulated globally, thus normalizing and standardizing the imagination and the performance of violence worldwide.[36]

On the other hand, the protester also films. He does so in an unprecedented way, performing several roles at the same time: the role of the victim and that of the hero, as he is able to move the camera away from the crowds demonstrating on the streets and turn it towards himself, filming his own death. *He shoots while being shot at,*[37] producing blurred, shaky, pixelated images that are the stylistic trait of the condition of emergency in which they were generated.[38] As Jon Rich has poetically put it, 'the protester in Syria is simultaneously a victim of bare repression and a historian … who writes history with his own blood' (Rich 2011). This (re)gained agency, even at the time of his own death, is probably the most significant achievement of the Syrian protester; finally, nobody is entitled to speak for him, 'neither the Syrian regime nor the western reporter/spectator', because he has succeeded in 'appropriating the double enunciation as victim and historian' (Hamadeh 2016: 26). The 'three-dimensional presence' of embodying at once the victim, the narrator and the spectator constitutes, as Hamadeh observes, a 'complex layering of viewing perspectives' that stands in stark contrast and blunt opposition to the oversimplified 'monocular voyeuristic view' (Hamadeh 2016: 27). Perhaps this constitutes the tragedy of the Syrian image: because it (re)acquires its own agency and takes control of self-narration even when death is at stake, it 'confronts the spectator with the impossibility of being Syrian' (Rich 2011), whether victim or killer, let alone the videographer who is simultaneously the viewer of the narrated events. This simultaneity of performances, this 'inter-changeability of positions' (Hamadeh 2016: 27), and the multilayered perspective it offers, powerfully opposes a 'politics of producing and consuming death imagery, what Hannah Arendt calls a *"politics of pity"'* (Hamadeh 2016: 26, my emphasis), preventing viewers from identifying with Syrians.[39]

In short, from the perspective of both the perpetrator and the victim, the camera is a weapon. For the former, it serves the spectacular goal of documenting his own performance of violence; for the latter, it captures that very performance on a film whose blurry frames will stay as a living testimony to the condition of emergency and fear in which they were produced, sometimes at the cost of the narrator's own life. One films his own death, the other films the death of others. One films with the aesthetic perfection of the static shot – 'the static shot is beautiful', Osama Mohammed tells his protester friend, before realizing that it embodies the gaze of the murderer (Della Ratta 2017c: 114–15). The other creates *images in spite of all*, like the undefined, barely recognizable frames produced by the Sonderkommando in Auschwitz.

Yet, although they seem so diametrically opposed, the first-person-camera aesthetics of self-representation and that of the objectified, static, 'caught on camera' shot characterizing surveillance actually converge in what Zimmer calls a culture of 'compulsive documentation' (Zimmer 2015: 78). The global diffusion of consumer recording technologies – the pervasiveness of the smartphone protest culture – implies, among other things, that everything can be documented by everyone; this peer-to-peer surveillance is ubiquitous, reproducible and accessible on a mass scale. As such, power – the state, the media, *the killer* – is no longer the only subject entitled to surveil and punish, to manage violence and render its performance in the objectified gaze of the static shot; other agencies – individuals, citizens, *the victim* – have their own ways of striking back, thanks to the pervasiveness of the amateur video gaze. Aesthetically, this convergence between self-representation and surveillance cultures signals a 'mingling of explicitly subjective perspectives' – such as the blurry frames captured on the move by a camera phone – 'with more traditionally "objective", evidentiary representational forms' (Zimmer 2015: 78) – as in the 'caught on camera' genre.

This mixing of languages and perspectives is naturally encouraged by the techno-human infrastructure of the web 2.0, as the sharing and participatory cultures shaped by the latter promote the non-stop production of self-representations in order to boost an economy increasingly driven by the commodification of self-disclosed data and ubiquitous peer-to-peer surveillance (Zimmer 2015: 113). The prosperity of a social networking environment is intimately connected to the rise of compulsive documentation cultures enabled by forms of live recording and sharing, such as the smartphone, that have turned into 'stand-ins for existence itself' (Zimmer 2015: 93). Real-time updating has become the other side of non-stop surveillance which is, again, intimately related to the post-9/11 logic of terror, from the very first user-generated mobile camera shots that randomly captured the collapse of the Twin Towers (Berg 2011), to Osama Bin Laden quietly talking with an AK-47 on his back, in the most sinister static shot cinema has ever produced.

The logic of commodification and terror, of self-documentation and surveillance, smoothly captures 'whatever' (Dean 2010: 61–90) content produced in the ever-circulating stream of data supporting the economic infrastructure of networked communications technologies, thereby assimilating 'what could be resistance back into an increasingly totalizing system' (Zimmer 2015: 114). In the end, even the heroic gesture of the Syrian videographer filming and narrating his own death is caught in this logic of compulsive documentation that finally nurtures profit and communicative capitalism. In the context of the latter, the exchange value of a message, 'its contribution to a larger pool, flow, or circulation of content' (Dean 2009: 27), acquires more prominence than the *meaning* of the content itself. From the perspective of the circulation and reflexivity that defines the infrastructure of web 2.0 (Dean 2010), the use value of a message injected into the data stream – even that of a video documenting the cruel spectacle of the filmer's own death – does not really count; since 'a contribution need not … be understood', but only 'repeated, reproduced, forwarded' (Dean 2009: 27).

The increasingly commodified aspect of the networked environment in which Syrian acts of rebellion and defiance are injected and circulated together with 'whatever' other messages, requires us not only to focus on the fascinating aesthetic questions raised by the Syrian images, but also to reflect on the material and political implications of the act of filming, understood as a continuous life activity. As Tarnowski rightly points out, the dichotomy, upon which several readings of Syrian image-making are based, between 'the elusive, revolutionary, low-res image and the commoditized, compromised, high-res image' (Tarnowski 2017) does not account for the complexity of the situation in which those images were produced. Not only can several subjects – the market, the state, international NGOs, foreign journalists, etc. – appropriate, make and re-make the blurry, pixelated revolutionary aesthetics, using it to serve their goals and agendas;[40] the pixelated images can also be the result of a supply and demand process even when generated by anonymous citizens and videographers, uploaded and shared free of charge on social networking platforms.

The Syrian documentary *Jellyfish* (2015)[41] sheds light on the heavy commodification of citizen-generated content that was once deemed innocent, by showing the extent to which amateur protester-videographers got caught up in a commissioning process where several subjects, from international NGOs to the armed forces, from media outlets to medical associations, all requested tailor-made videos to serve their purposes and agendas. Tarnowski (2017) refers to a similar process when remarking that a UK- founded organisation helped create a centralized media office for the Free Syrian Army, whose job was to commission and package user-generated videos for their YouTube page.

Just as much as the seemingly objective 'caught on camera' shot, the pixelated, low-fi image can no longer be deemed innocent. Its charming aesthetics, its poetic value, the sense of emotional proximity it renders, so close to the *being there* of its filmer, might distract from the exceptional material conditions in which it was generated, diverting attention from the power struggles it conceals, and of which it is a result. These seemingly innocent blurry clips are 'commodity images, active in the economy of war, and contributing directly to it' (Tarnowski 2017). Finally, the everydayness of filming in Syria seems to have resulted in its inevitable hyper-commodification. Part of the catastrophe of Syria's imperfect cinema is that it no longer serves the revolutionary goal, as Espinosa and the original amateur videographers had wished, but rather other, more opaque and still to be unveiled projects.

Here and Elsewhere: *Image-makers and image-keepers in contemporary Syria*

International and Pan Arab media outlets often refer to Syrians who use a camera to document street protests, political activities and human rights violations on the ground as 'video activists' or 'citizen journalists' (Harding 2012; Listening Post 2012; Platt 2014; Baraniuk 2016; Omari 2017). However, the latter in particular, as al-Ghazzi rightly underlines, carries the indirect danger of projecting the Western-centred, 'liberal democratic values implied in both journalism and citizenship' (al-Ghazzi 2014: 2) into a dramatically different context such as Syria. Moreover, applying the citizen journalism frame to Syria's grassroots-originated videos implicitly charges the latter with a unilateral (and simplistic) goal – to witness and produce evidence in order to mobilize for the political cause – and over-emphasizes the empowerment allegedly granted by (Western-made) networked technologies that would gift Syrian activists with the ability to produce alternative narratives to that of the ruling power.[42] This definition does not take into account the fact that the grassroots videos were originated by a variety of politicized activists – including 'state agents, soldiers, and torturers' (al-Ghazzi 2014: 6) – who, rather than just witnessing or generating evidence, crafted digital items for multiple purposes including staging events, producing media propaganda, instigating terror and performing violence.

Other scholars and media practitioners have employed expressions that instead emphasize the aesthetic and formal qualities of the grassroots-generated videos. The Lebanese artist Rabih Mroué, in his touching non-academic lecture performance 'The Pixelated Revolution' (2012), refers to these unknown individuals as 'cameramen' (Mroué 2012), charging them with a sort of implicit professionalism, and praising the blurred frames they produce, often at the cost of their own lives. By calling them 'videographers', Ziter (2015) and Marks (2015) also emphasize the aesthetic and formal qualities of this user-generated footage, produced in exceptional conditions where protesters are simultaneously involved in the act of demonstrating and filming. Wessels goes even further, comparing them to modern 'kinoks', an expression coined by the avant-garde Russian filmmaker Dziga Vertov to describe his own film collective whose goal was to merge political engagement in the 1917 revolutionary cause with the aesthetic aim of documenting reality 'as it is' (Wessels 2017: 161).

Wessels' comparison carries the risk of assuming that all Syrian activists who took up filming in 2011 did so with the deliberate objective of serving the uprising's goals, and employed a realistic aesthetic in the belief that it would strengthen the political cause. As observed above in relation to 'video activists' and 'citizen journalists', this assumption does not take into account subjects who engaged in visual media production with multiple agendas and political projects often radically different from the revolutionary one – including those of the regime or other armed groups. Moreover, even among activists who embraced the revolutionary cause there were different perceptions about how to serve the latter, and what sort of aesthetics and formal approach to visual media should be employed – whether a realistic one or other, more elaborated forms of sense-making that would include storytelling, fictionalisation and the staging of events.[43] In a piece with the telling title 'Cinema of Death', Orwa al-Mokdad, a former activist and now an internationally recognized filmmaker,[44] quotes Gilles Deleuze's remark on how the widespread belief among Vertov's generation of politically engaged filmmakers that cinema should change the world by presenting the shock of reality would raise 'a smile today' (al-Mokdad 2017b). By contrast, al-Mokdad confesses, his 'dream is to make a fiction film', wishing to be set free from the imperative of real-time documentation dictated by what he calls the 'cinema of death' (al-Mokdad 2017b).

Taking a distance from definitions that implicitly attach an inherent democratic potential to Syrian video works, or a liberating power to the technology behind their making and distribution, yet also trying to avoid the trap of aestheticizing them as a new avant-garde, I want to look at the Syrian images not as mere narrations of war, but as 'actions and weapons' implicated in that very war (Keenan 2012: 24). This means shifting the focus towards the historically determined, material conditions in which they were produced and distributed, and the power struggles shaping these processes, i.e. their political economy. This approach was pioneered by Ernst Jünger in the aftermath of the First World War, when, reflecting on the 'trove of images' generated by the pervasive technology of photography in wartime, he deemed it necessary to look at them not so much as reproductions, but as a production of '*labor*' (Jünger and Nassar 1993: 24–5, my emphasis). Emphasizing the material dimension of the chain of production behind the process of image-making, rather than its language and aesthetics, Jünger prophetically anticipated that future historians would have to face 'the excess' rather than 'the lack of sources' (Jünger and Nassar 1993: 24). The sheer amount of visual media generated in the extraordinary context of warfare had mesmerized Jünger, who was convinced that violence and technological reproduction were mutually (and almost magically) interconnected phenomena, to the point that 'there can be no war without photography' (Cadava 1997: 51). In Jünger's view, the pervasiveness of technologies of reproduction, combined with the enactment of war, generated 'a specifically modern form of perception organized around the experience of danger and shock'; with the latter invading the once reassuring territory of everyday life to the extent that 'a space of absolute danger' – rather than one 'of absolute comfort' – would likely constitute 'the final aim concealed in technology' (Jünger and Nassar 1993: 30).

The writer and filmmaker Pier Paolo Pasolini also shed light on the inner connection between technology and violence in the last interview before his tragic death, under the telling title 'We Are All in Danger'. Discussing his fascination for 'the violent life' (Pasolini 1975), the filmmaker reflected on how the latter, once uniquely experienced by risk-lovers like himself within the private sphere, would soon take on a collective dimension. Capital, with its logic founded on accumulation/possession and destruction, would make the violent life publicly available and consumable on a large scale through technologies of mass reproduction.[45] Having summed up his argument about violence, capital and technology with the prophetic words 'Hell is rising towards the rest of you' (Pasolini 1975), Pasolini was brutally assassinated in unclear circumstances only a few hours after releasing the interview.

Technologies of mass (re)production reveal this potential violent nature in their adherence to the rationale of capital that reduces everything to the 'logic and labor of the assembly line: a "chain of images", "arranging memories", "chaining them in a certain order"' (Drabinski 2008: 44). Jean-Luc Godard's seminal film-essay *Ici et ailleurs* ('Here and Elsewhere', 1976) unveils this violence-based relation between technology and capital, suggesting that 'the events of history are given exchange values' only 'when they become *images*, because it is as images that these events are able to circulate within the system of capital' (Morrey 2005: 112). Technologies of mass (re)production work according to capital's imperative of accumulation and circulation; images are given a value only if exchanged and circulated. The violence of technology is exercised as a violation of the 'here' – the place where the images are generated – in favour of the 'elsewhere' – the place where they are later consumed.

In *Ici et ailleurs*, images are produced in the Palestine of the early 1970s, while a revolution is unfolding, with the goal of celebrating its 'victory'.[46] After the uprising is violently crushed, Godard realizes that its protagonists, the people he had passionately filmed in the excitement of the revolutionary moment, are either dead or disappeared; therefore, he decides to edit the original images using a sophisticated technique of alternating montage with newer footage shot in France. By violating the 'here' of the images, their place of origin, their revolutionary goal, technology finally transposes them into an 'elsewhere', where their fate is to be distributed and commodified just like any other good, and digested, together with a hot meal, in front of a TV screen. Godard seems to imply that the violence of technology unfolds through the violence of capital and chain labour. As the film critic Serge Daney remarked when commenting on *Ici et ailleurs*, 'the real pornography lies' precisely 'in this change of scene' (Daney 1976: 120), i.e. in turning the 'here' into an 'elsewhere'.

This displacement of images, the fact that they are injected into the ever-circulating flow of information and data of global capital, causes their devaluation, their fading away into meaningless objects – as Godard shows by juxtaposing images of Nazi Germany, atrocities in the Middle East, and families having dinner in front of television, all together in a row. The proliferating image-based economy introduces a disjunction between those who make images and those who keep them. 'Poor revolutionary fools, millionaires in images' (*Ici et ailleurs*) – as

Godard calls the Palestinian activists who produced a massive amount of visual material to document the revolutionary moment – later ending up losing control of its circulation. The revolutionaries have not only lost the political struggle, and perhaps their own lives, but also the ownership of the visual media produced as evidence to document and celebrate the revolutionary goal. Paradoxically, the proliferation of images and a fast-growing visual economy are matched with the 'loss of influence over the reality of events' (Morrey 2005: 11). Image-makers are no longer image-keepers.

As in Godard's 1970 Palestine, so in contemporary Syria image-makers have lost control and ownership over their own creations. Here, too, we witness the failure of a once promising uprising, in favour of chaos, violence and destruction. Here, too, we silently ratify the disjunction between processes of production and processes of distribution, as the Syrian image is appropriated by subjects other than its makers. Image-keepers are those who exercise (direct or indirect) control over the storing, archiving and distributing of the Syrian image, maintaining a de facto ownership over it. Like Silicon Valley's platform capitalists who, although not formally or legally owning the images, yet have the power to determine their online fate – their *onlife* – as the episodes of content removal that have occurred in recent years proved (El Deeb 2017). The keepers of the Syrian image are also those activists who, having filmed for the collective 'we' (Snowdon 2016: 18) in the excitement of the revolutionary moment, started claiming ownership back once they realized that Syrian images were in high demand, from international NGOs, journalists and TV networks, the global art market and festival venues. Several ownership controversies have occurred between Syrian image-makers and those claiming to have the legal right to keep the images under their control, often resulting in the disputed content being kept from distribution, therefore from being seen in public.

Rather than its aesthetic and formal qualities, it is precisely this materiality of Syria's contemporary visual production that has to take centre stage if we want to understand the relation between violence and visibility in a time of warfare. And even more so in the networked environment, where exchange value is generated through restless circulation and shareability, while the production of sense gets lost in what Kracauer called a 'strike against understanding', an 'evacuation of meaning from the objects' that may be turned into a detonator of violence (Kracauer 2005: 58, 53).

SNAPSHOT #7

Selected visual productions from Daesh and non-violent Syrian activists highlight the 'camera as a weapon' as a common trope used by both groups to formulate their demands and frame their ideologies. Despite radically different objectives and strategies, they both articulate their worldviews around a framework in which values of solidarity, camaraderie and brotherhood contribute to forging their identity, together with ideas of revolt, risk-taking and the capacity to imagine and aspire to a revolutionary future. Non-stop filming is a strategy that gives visual form to the groups' imaginative demands – be they the invitation for international public opinion to (re)act against the Syrian conflict, or the call to carry on media jihad.

Having injected them into global but largely Western-owned communication platforms, both groups have lost control of their own media. Yet, while non-violent activists struggle to preserve their digital commons as a shared and publicly available good, Daesh seems to have understood the dynamics of circulation and reflexivity upon which the networks thrive. Despite the joint efforts of proprietary web 2.0 platforms and governments to police and eliminate Daesh-made media, the latter have found a way to come back to *onlife* in the domain of the open web, turning the internet pioneers' libertarian dream of openness and accessibility into a nightmare of anonymous recirculation and the sharing of terror.

7

Syria's Image-Makers: Daesh Militants and Non-Violent Activists

The camera as a weapon

The opening scene of the video features a man with an Arabic book in his hands, and a handgun on the table in front of him. The man prepares his camera and picks up his military equipment. The black flag of Daesh emerges behind him. He opens his car and puts the AK-47 on the passenger seat. We see a Sony HD camera right next to the weapon, while the title of the video appears on the screen in Arabic: 'Media Man You Are a Fighter, Too' (Jihadology 2015). A series of military actions are featured: shootings, bombings, all calmly followed by a cameraman. Then a black-dressed man wearing a gun and a pair of sunglasses starts talking in classical Arabic. He explains how the media battle has been employed since the time of Prophet Mohammed as a key element in fighting enemies. He reminds the viewer how the West has been conducting a media war to heavily damage the Muslims' image, yet even the 'enemy' has acknowledged the so-called Islamic state's skills in creating powerful media products to counteract its propaganda (Jihadology 2015). Despite these achievements however, the black-dressed man underlines, Daesh needs skilled media people to join up and put their talents at the service of the organization: 'you are the martyrs of the media', he solemnly concludes (Jihadology 2015).

Another opening scene from another video: we hear heavy shooting but can only see the floor and the hand of the person carrying the camera. More gunshots are heard in the background as voices seem to come closer, screaming in Arabic 'God is great, God is great', several times, in a clear state of fear and anxiety. Here the frame starts to shake, and the camera falls to the floor, leaving the viewer with a totally black screen that implies the sudden death of the image-maker.

These videos originate from two radically different sources. The first, 'Media Man You Are a Fighter, Too', was released by Daesh in May 2015, at a time when the terrorist organization was at the peak of its media success, having become infamously known for its Twitter campaign #AllEyesOnIsis during the seize of Mosul. The second is a raw 40-second clip shot by the Syrian image-maker and peaceful activist Basil al-Sayed at a checkpoint in Homs: while filming security forces opening fire at protesters, he was suddenly hit by a bullet with the camera still rolling (al Omran 2011). Despite the radical differences in terms of goals and tactics between an armed terrorist organization and a group of peaceful activists, both videos suggest a way of using the camera as a weapon. On the one hand, Daesh's video calls upon media men to use their camera to support and document the violence inflicted by its militants on other people. On the other hand, Basil al-Sayed symbolically employs his camera to counteract the security forces' brutality, eventually becoming a victim of the latter himself. The former films in order to document the death of others; the latter shoots to the point of documenting his own death.

Yet both groups employ the metaphor of the camera as a weapon as a central and recurring theme in their visual production. For Daesh, the media man is a *mujahid* ('fighter') having the same importance as a soldier fighting on the ground, because, as a 2005 letter addressed to the group's ideologue al-Zarqawi emphasized, 'half of this battle is taking place in the battlefield of the media' (al-Zawahiri 2005: 10). Spectacular videos of extreme graphic violence, such as the burning alive of the Jordanian pilot Muath al-Kasasbeh, or the destruction of statues and historical artefacts in Mosul, are military tactics used by Daesh to instigate terror and fear, and at the same time to gain support and attract new militants.

Figure 7.1   Syrian activist Basil al-Sayed's camera (photo: Rami Jarrah).

Figure 7.2 'Media Man You Are a Fighter, Too' (Jihadology 2015).

Cameramen are gunmen, and filming is a fully-fledged propaganda strategy in which the images produced should not be understood as accounts and reports of war, but as 'actions and weapons' in that very war (Keenan 2012: 24). They are 'killer images' (ten Brink and Oppenheimer 2012).

The idea of the camera as a weapon also plays a key role in shaping the imagination of Syrian non-violent activists. Having refused to arm themselves, they replaced real weapons with the camera as a metaphorical weapon, the only one capable of producing lasting accounts that defy the regime's narrative of the uprising being rooted in a foreign-fabricated conspiracy and sectarian conflict. Videos such as the one shot by Basil al-Sayed constitute a trope in Syrian peaceful activism's visual culture: they literally embody the idea that filming is like shooting, an act of defiance responding to the violence of the bullet with the eternal visibility granted by digital pixels.

The analysis of the two groups' visual productions serves to underline the main features of their ideology, and the concepts around which their vision of the future is built. For despite their profoundly divergent attitudes vis-à-vis the use of violence in achieving their objectives, both Daesh and the peaceful activists share a radical approach to politics – if by 'radical' we mean to advocate fundamental or revolutionary changes in current practices, conditions or institutions. To borrow from Arjun Appadurai, they both present a 'capacity to aspire' (Appadurai 2013: 179), a potential for imagining a political future: whether a Syria conceived as a civic nation state applying the rule of law and equal rights to all citizens, or a Sunni-exclusive caliphate submitted to the Islamic *shari'a*.

This capacity to dream and imagine, to project into a future which will surely bring change – whether through non-violence and civil disobedience, or by establishing a permanent state of chaos and terror[1]

– originates from a shared generational feature, as both groups enjoy a strong youth component. According to the UN agency IFAD (International Fund for Agricultural Development), 58 per cent of Syria's population prior to the 2011 uprising was composed by people below the age of 24 (IFAD 2011). However anecdotal it might appear to be, several elements seem to suggest that this generational factor is a key component of the Syrian non-violent protest movement.[2] For example: the crowds featured in the uprising video productions; the civil disobedience actions documented by Pan Arab and international media coverage (Della Ratta 2012b; Atassi 2011; Khoury 2013); and the profiles of activist groups on social networking sites.[3] As for Daesh militants, several scholars focusing on extremism (Roy 2017; Bertho 2016; Atran 2015) have emphasized the fact that 'contemporary jihadism … is a *youth* movement', deeply 'rooted in wider youth culture' (Roy 2017). Atran has reported a poll conducted in August 2014 whose findings revealed that 'a quarter of France's young adults of all creeds, aged 18 to 24, had at least a "somewhat favourable" attitude towards ISIS' (Atran 2015). This markedly youth component shaping Daesh's activism seems to find confirmation in the group's visual production, both in terms of employing the compelling languages of a digital-native culture, such as a 'selfie' aesthetics, and content-wise, since many videos and magazine articles feature young militants from different nationalities and a variety of ethnic backgrounds.

Connected to this generational factor, both groups articulate their worldviews around a narrative framework in which values like solidarity, camaraderie and brotherhood jointly contribute to forging their identity together with ideas of revolt, risk taking and a radical break with the status quo. As noted by cooke (2017) in her account of the creativity of the Syrian uprising, the latter's emergence in the forms of graffiti, poetry, street chants and dancing attests to a collective dimension of solidarity and defiance finally gaining public visibility in a country that has traditionally repressed both. Peter Snowdon, in his fascinating analysis of post-2011 'vernacular videos', speaks of these anonymous creations as '*tokens of trust* formed out of socially cementing speech and embodied gesture that signify shared destiny to those that recognise them, and that are used to build those relations of practical solidarity upon which the revolution depends' (Snowdon 2016: 148, my emphasis). This collective 'we' that surfaced with the protest movement – not only in political acts of mobilisation and defiance, but also in a social and cultural dimension – has also been recalled by Syrian activists. In the words of the collective

'Syrian Revolutionary Youth': 'We did not only protest, we used to turn our demonstrations into nights out. Most Damascene activists would join our protests, and we would stay out and enjoy our freedom' (SyriaUntold 2013). Many clips produced during the first, predominantly non-violent phase of the uprising highlight this state of mind, featuring young activists involved in animated discussions on the meaning of a peaceful revolution, while drinking together, occasionally playing music, hosting social gatherings and parties, or driving at night to deliver revolutionary leaflets.[4]

What is certainly less acknowledged than the values of solidarity and camaraderie expressed by Syrian non-violent activists is the role that culture plays in jihadism. Only recently, in fact, have scholars started researching and exploring 'the cultural dimension' (Hegghammer 2017) of armed groups such as Daesh. Great emphasis has been put on studying the terror tactics employed by Daesh through its media production and its unorthodox 'military' strategies, described by one of its alleged ideologists as 'the management of savagery' (Naji 2006). However, as provocatively suggested by Hegghammer, jihadism should be regarded as a 'subculture' in respect to what it produces in terms of 'rituals, customs, … jokes and food': jihadis, apparently, 'love poetry', 'talk regularly about dreams', and even 'weep-a lot' (Hegghammer 2017: 1). Which echoes Scott Atran's controversial conclusion in his thoughtful study entitled 'ISIS is a Revolution' (2015): while the majority of politicians, journalists and scholars 'dismiss radical Islam as simply nihilist', very few recognize 'its genuine appeal' or acknowledge 'the joy' that joining a collective fight with other young peers might provoke (Atran 2015). Atran's analysis underlines that more than 80 per cent of the militants who join Daesh do so through peer-to-peer relationships that become prominent when, having left their own countries, 'they seek new families of friends and fellow travellers to find purpose and significance', experiencing what social psychologists call 'identity fusion' (Atran 2015), i.e. melting their individualities into the collective 'we'. These conclusions resonate with many Daesh-originated media which I discuss in the next pages, showing how ideas of brotherhood, camaraderie and peer solidarity are deeply embedded in the group's visual culture, as much as ruthlessness, brutality and extreme violence – often manifesting in the same video.[5]

To conclude, no matter how radically different they are in terms of their political goals and the strategies and tactics adopted to implement them, Syrian non-violent activists and Daesh militants share similarities in terms of generational features; a *Weltanschauung* built around values of brotherhood, camaraderie and peer solidarity; and a markedly future-oriented imagination. All these elements are condensed in the metaphor of the camera as a weapon, as for both groups the latter becomes a key tool to disrupt the status quo and defy the powers that be. Filming is an open act of subversion, whether performed with the intention of securing visual evidence of the Syrian regime's brutality, or with the aim of generating spectacles of terror targeting local and international audiences and governments.

Shoot Me, Shoot at Me!: *Syria's non-violent protest culture*

'The ony weapon I shall carry in this life is my camera.' Thus Syrian filmmaker Ziad Kalthoum ends his beautiful debut documentary film *al-Raqib al-Khalid* ('The Immortal Sergeant', 2014), an account of his daily life in Damascus between 2012 and 2013. Obliged to serve in the Syrian army, Kalthoum succeeds in smuggling out from the barracks a bunch of pixelated frames of his military life which he will edit, once out of Syria, together with footage from the backstage of director Mohammad Malas' feature film *Sullam ila Dimashq* ('Ladder to Damascus' 2013), shot in a schizophrenic Damascus experiencing daily violence and bombings, yet pretending not to see the civil war in the making. Like Syria, Kalthoum himself, as Lisa Wedeen writes, is 'internally divided, evidenced by repeated images of division – the split screen like a children's butterfly painting made by folding the paper in half, as well as juxtapositions of scenes shot professionally with a proper camera to ones shot surreptitiously on a handheld cell phone' (Wedeen 2019). In the final sequence, however, Kalthoum finally opts for his filmmaker self, forever giving up to his military doppelgänger, choosing exile and defection over the daily performance of violence.

The theme of the splitting of the country into separate and irreconcilable pieces mirroring an individual self torn between the daily exercise of violence – of which silence and collusion with the authoritarian power is a part – and its absolute refusal – affirmed through its non-stop documentation – recurs in another Syrian debut documentary film, *300 Miles* (2016) by Orwa al-Mokdad. The inner conflict of the filmmaker is reflected in two characters who have chosen very different paths in relation to their belief in the revolutionary cause: Adnan, a young non-violent activist from Aleppo, and Abu Yaarub, the leader of a loose battalion with the Free Syrian Army (FSA). Neither of them, however, is a hero. Abu Yaarub's romantic justification for taking up weapons in order to defend the city (and the revolution) is confronted by the chaos and confusion generated by the daily violence, in which this Don Quixote type is no longer able to identify who the real enemy is. And when al-Mokdad asks him 'Where is the revolution?', he reacts firmly, to cover his embarrassment for lacking a real answer: 'I won't answer you'. As for Adnan, his faith in civil disobedience and peaceful resistance has to confront not only the brutality of the Syrian regime and that of the jihadi groups taking over Aleppo, but also the plethora of initiatives on dialogue and reconciliation sponsored by international NGOs in a purely cosmetic attempt to support non-violent forms of anti-regime opposition through feel-good gatherings. In a final sequence featuring him and his friends gathered in a safe house before leaving for exile in Turkey, an enraged Adnan tears a poster for a dialogue initiative to pieces and throws it on the floor.

These dramatic figures reflect al-Mokdad's personal life experience: a former student at Damascus University, in March 2011 he became, like many Syrian youths, a self-taught image-maker, mostly filming the events unfolding in his home city of Daraa, which resulted in his imprisonment and torture in a Syrian *mukhabarat* branch.[6] Once released, al-Mokdad thought of abandoning peaceful resistance and taking up arms.[7] He finally ended up in war-torn Aleppo, working with an FSA battalion to document the rebels' fight with his camera, rather than embracing a gun. The camera became his one and only weapon, yet this choice did not completely reconcile him to his original dilemma. Instead of protecting Syrians from death, the camera had rather become a way to live-document the latter without being able to escape it. 'Filming and the desire to make films have become wooden weapons in the hands of quixotic characters fighting the invisible windmills of the world that we are not quite able to confront', al-Mokdad concludes in his bitter reflection on the 'cinema of death' (al-Mokdad 2017b) produced by Syrians during the past years.

Why should the camera have protected Syrians in the first place? Why would conceiving of the camera as a metaphorical gun provide a shield from a real gun? Once more, it's the character of Adnan who gives voice to questions that are so common among Syrian image-makers. 'If someone in Japan cared...' he laments, cursing the general indifference to Syrian activists' efforts to engage international public opinion in finding a solution to the conflict. Yet at the same time he admits that he has himself never cared about crises and conflicts in far-away countries.

In the privileged position of a former anonymous image-maker filming in revolutionary times now turned into an internationally recognized filmmaker, al-Mokdad offers a bitter reflection on this widespread attitude among Syrian activists:

> We thought that images would help us ... Yet our images are ambiguous: they fluctuate between appealing to an international audience that we want to seduce and mobilise to our cause; and the Syrian public whom we aim at convincing of the justness of our revolution. We are caught in this indecisiveness of not knowing, or perhaps not wanting to determine, to whom exactly we are talking. Unlike the regime who aims its media propaganda towards the domestic public and the army, our images have become self-complacent of their aesthetic beauty and of their inner heroism in confronting violence; to the point that they have lost their communicative value. We are not aware of whom we are talking to when we film our beautiful images.[8]

In stark opposition to al-Mokdad's assessment of the Syrian images being lost in narcissism and lacking a communicative value, Wessels argues that 'video activism from Syria is actually a form of conflict communication' (Wessels forthcoming) and, as such, has deeply contributed to its escalation. Initially, Syrians picked up cameras as 'alternative non-violent weapons' to denounce the repression of the peaceful protests, which was then followed by the documentation of torture and abuses perpetrated even on children,[9] and the live-recording of street funerals targeted by the regime's gunfire: all 'extra-ordinary events' that have, according to Wessels, generated the 'mutual social energy' necessary to break through the wall of fear of a decades-long authoritarian rule, and motivated more people to join the protests and demand the fall of the regime (Wessels forthcoming). The extra social energy indirectly produced by the sheer number of videos has pushed larger crowds to gather in public and express defiance and outrage, which in turn generated more repression from the regime side, which once more pushed activists to live-document the latter, in a non-stop circle of violence and visibility, physical repression and viral online circulation.

Paradoxically, the choice of using cameras as non-violent weapons has resulted in creating a format of conflict communication in which visibility and violence are dramatically intertwined. The non-stop, real-time documentation of the violence has become a key mechanism in triggering the conflict on the ground through the production of awareness, empathy, moral and emotional outrage.[10] This escalation mechanism involves not only Syrian image-makers and the regime, but also international players such as NGOs and media outlets. The more the conflict becomes violent and recorded on camera with the aim of denouncing this very violence, the more these outside subjects become invested in it, demanding further documentation and often commissioning it according to their political goals and agendas. Finally, all these players are active in the political economy of visibility and violence in which the non-violent camera eye has become a military device in spite of the initial premises, *in spite of itself.*

Yet if the non-stop documentation of violence contributes to the escalation of the conflict on the ground, watching that conflict from a distance has not, in its turn, generated the reaction of global solidarity and pro-active engagement that Syrian image-makers had envisioned while shooting and putting their lives at risk. 'We used to be killed in the dark, now we are killed in the light' (Wessels forthcoming) – this is the bitter remark of a Syrian activist on the hyper-visibility granted by processes of live-recording and uploading that, rather than protecting the people, has instead condemned them to die on camera while their deaths are endlessly reproduced for the sake of viral circulation and sharing.

The Syrian film collective Abounaddara has pointed out that 'never before in history has a crime against humanity been filmed day by day, turned into a spectacle with the cooperation of *both victims and executioners*, broadcast by the big television networks and streamed on social media, intercut with ad breaks, consumed by the general public, and commodified by the art market' (Lensculture n.d., my emphasis). In response to the sheer amount of war-porn, the group has called for re-establishing the Syrians' right to a 'dignified image' (Elias 2017): an image that is not crafted according to the imperative of commodifying violence in order to shock viewers and push them to act, and over which local civil society would exercise total control.[11] Yet, in stark contrast to Abounaddara's reading, the fact of filming their own deaths live on camera might be interpreted as the Syrians' ultimate defiant act of regaining agency over the regime or other international subjects, rather than as a submission to the latter's narratives and formats of storytelling and production of history (Rich 2011; Hamadeh 2016).

Beyond the controversy of whether these *shooting while being shot at* videos should be framed in terms of a loss of dignity and compliance with the rules of the spectacle or, conversely, as a fierce subversion of these very rules, offering an unsanitized vision of self-immolation, it is rather on the assumptions behind the act of showing at all costs that the discussion should focus. Ethnographic work (Della Ratta 2017c; Wessels 2017, forthcoming; Elias and Omareen 2014) has emphasized the commitment of Syria's post-2011 activism to the 'evidence-image' (Didi-Huberman 2008: 90): an image that, in spite of being low-definition, blurry and shaky, would carry a value inherently connected to the emergency and fear in the context of which it was crafted. Following Jacques Rancière's reflection on how aesthetic formats shape and determine the form of politics, we could relate the Syrian evidence-image to what the French philosopher defines an 'ethical regime' in which images are assessed in terms of 'their origin (and consequently their truth content)' and 'their end or purpose' (Rancière 2013: 20).

Within an ethical regime, the aesthetic qualities of images do not matter so much as their potential to reflect the truthfulness of the moment in which they were generated, and their capability to affect behaviours and reactions. It is irrelevant how pixelated the Syrian revolution is, or how blurred, unstable and fuzzy its frames are, as long as they are able to connect to the instant of fear and extreme danger in which they surfaced, and push their international viewers – whether politicians, journalists or public opinion in general – to act and put an end to the violence on the ground, through diplomatic pressure or military intervention (Elias and Omareen 2014; Wessels 2016; Snowdon 2016). This is 'the unbearable lightness' (Della Ratta 2017c) of the Syrian image, whose pixelated frames apparently carry no aesthetic value, no consistency, no weight; yet they are burdened with an ethical demand which the aesthetics of the handheld camera helps to construct. On the one hand, 'hypermobility, opacity, non-narrativity, and raw audio' (Andén-Papadopoulos 2013: 345) are employed to establish the authority of the image-maker around the latter's *being there* during the unfolding of the event, as if this makes the conveyed information inherently trustworthy. On the other hand, the 'liveliness, immediacy, and co-presence' (Frosh 2009: 52) granted by images thus produced shape a specific aesthetic format to the affective demands of empathy and compassion addressed towards viewers.

I once asked Syrian image-makers who gravitated around the Aikilab hackerspace, 'Why do you risk your lives to film?' 'The world does not know what is happening in Syria', they replied. 'Once the world knows, the world will act. As soon as information flows, mobilization will start' (Della Ratta 2017c: 117). Which resonates with the words of a Raqqa-based activist: 'I have filmed everything. My people were being killed and I needed the world to know this' (Wessels forthcoming). Like them, many Syrian youths have filmed to death in the deep belief that 'ethical' images would mobilize by virtue of their origin – 'their truth content' (Rancière 2013: 20) – and their final end. Yet they have not considered the fact that, while their blurred frames convey spontaneity, immediacy and a sense of proximity to the event that contribute to constructing 'the "claim to reality" and morality' (Andén-Papadopoulos 2013: 348), at the same time these images transmit an ambivalence with regards to the context, and indecisiveness about their legibility, verification and interpretation. 'The highly emotional load generated by this footage makes the latter *affective* but not always *effective*; at least from the perspective of an audience who is used to reading detachment and distance, i.e., objectivity, as the founding values of the authority of professional journalism' (Della Ratta 2017c: 119). Rancière himself had warned that 'there is no straightforward road from the fact of looking at a spectacle to the fact of understanding the state of the world; no direct road from intellectual awareness to political action' (Rancière 2009: 75).

Syrian image-makers have tasted the bitterness of these words first-hand. Having turned their cameras into metaphorical weapons and produced an unbearable amount of visual media at the risk of death, their faith in the evidence-image seems now to be over. Some of them have abandoned their once pixelated revolution to embrace tripods, fix their cameras, and start filming static shots: a dramatic shift that 'reflects the loss of the ethical aspiration of the image and the process of it becoming a mere aesthetic performance produced, re-adjusted and repackaged for the sake of commodification and material consumption' in international circuits (Della Ratta 2017c: 123). And while a 'clip' produced and distributed in the context of the networks is, as Treske underlines, a mere recording of life in progress that should not be treated as representation, the shot bears the inherent quality of 'an intentional cinematic approach' which '"extracts" significant detail and through this builds an explicit meaning' (Treske 2015: 85).

The Syrian evidence-image has succumbed to the loss of its innocence, of its capacity to represent and testify to principles of truthfulness and morality. A new form is emerging from the rubble – a form that Daesh had comprehended and embraced very early in its visual production, and that Syrian non-violent activists on the contrary could not have foreseen at a time when they were mesmerised by the evidence-image. With the fading away of the latter, 'the networked image' (Della Ratta 2015c, 2017a, 2017c) rises: an aesthetic form based on a new 'fictionality' (Rancière 2013: 33) which does not refer to the creation of a fictitious universe but, rather, to an aspiration to construct new realities and propose alternative framings of the empirical world, boosted by the decentralized authorship and diffused ownership that are inherently part of the techno-human infrastructure of networked communications technologies. Unlike evidence-image which aims to establish a connection between its maker and the viewer that ultimately translates into an ethical address, networked images do inhabit an 'aesthetic regime' (Rancière 2013) and forge a wider interaction between the temporal, ever-changing database of people, places, objects and algorithmic relations defining the networked environment of web 2.0.

The networked image opens up a new visual political economy in which multiple makers and keepers emerge and clash. While the Syrian activists' faith in evidence-image seems to have faded away, there is something that still struggles to survive as its everlasting memento. Peter Snowdon calls it 'the vernacular anarchive' (Snowdon 2016: 25), where both terms are employed to hint at a non-authoritative and anti-authorial repository of the Syrian image. The 'anarchive' is anarchic because it prospers on a form of order independent of those accommodating the distribution and consumption logic of capital, or the policing and surveilling authority of the state. Instead, it is constructed around the power of the 'vernacular': not the amateur, user-generated images typical of the web 2.0 remix and participatory cultures (Lessig 2008; Jenkins 2006a, 2006b), but the politically savvy collectivity behind the production of those images that implies, rather than indifference to authority, 'the authority of *anyone* to speak to and for' it, signalling a 'distributed leadership' (Snowdon 2016: 121) distinct from the over-romanticized horizontality and leaderless-ness preached by digital utopians.

According to Snowdon, the images inhabiting this vernacular anarchive should be interpreted as '*amara*', i.e. as 'tokens of trust formed out of socially cementing speech and embodied gesture that signify shared destiny to those that recognise them, and that are used to build those relations of practical solidarity on which the revolution depends' (Snowdon 2016: 148–52). *Amara* refers to a 'common moral horizon based on shared everyday practices of speech and gesture' (Snowdon 2016: 151), a horizon that has been made visible and recognizable through visual culture. It expresses the general feeling that 'the Syrian people know their way', as a grassroots art and civil disobedience collective had suggested in the immediate aftermath of the 2011 uprising.[12]

'Media man you are a fighter too': Daesh's visual warfare

'In societies reduced to blur and glut, terror is the only meaningful act. There's too much everything, more things and messages and meanings than we can use in ten thousand lifetimes' (DeLillo 1991: 157). These words were written by Don DeLillo back in 1991, yet they could not sound more appropriate than now, with the spectacular rise of Daesh amidst the over-saturated information environment defined by networked communications technologies. Yet the image of Daesh as tech-savvy barbarians that has haunted and attracted us for the past several years has also misled us, and still does. The tech-savvy jihadi is a quasi-mythological figure, the offspring of the technological fetish that took over the global imagination and visual culture at the beginning of the 'Arab Spring'. It is the reverse shot of the 'like-us' activist: whereas technology empowered the latter to seize his future and demand freedom and democracy, it now provides tech-savvy jihadis with the networked tools to spread chaos and fear. But overemphasizing the fascination and terror that Daesh generates via its visual production; spotlighting the glossy, professional quality of its videos and magazines; and complaining in horror that a bunch of barbarians have appropriated our networked communications technologies, does not help us to understand why 'ISIS is [still] a revolution' (Atran 2015), even when it has been declared (temporarily) defeated on the ground.[13]

Taking a distance from analyses of Daesh-generated content within a classical propaganda perspective, I focus rather on the context in which the terrorist organization acts, and to which it reacts: a complex eco-system defined by the techno-human infrastructure of networked communications technologies where human agency combines with algorithmic design, and where machine automation and users' creativity meet. Here content does not really matter so much as the operations that set up the conditions for the perpetual regeneration cycle of its *onlife*. The social features of platforms – such as likes and shares, tweets and retweets, encrypted apps or circumvention tools, anonymous imageboards, online content hosting services, mirror sites and pastebins – all make up the apparatus of contemporary networked communications technologies on which Daesh relies and from which it continues to prosper at a time when it has been declared militarily dead (Semati and Szpunar 2018).

'Rebutting a message is futile when the medium itself is the message' (Kraidy 2017: 13); here the message has dissolved into a mere contribution in the circuits of 'drive' (Dean 2010, 2015) upon which networked communications technologies thrive, turning a psychoanalytical mechanism that captures individuals in a repetitive process of pursuing enjoyment (yet never reaching it) into actual labour, an 'affective labour' (Dean 2015: 98). This affective dimension, as Jodi Dean remarks, does not foster active engagements or rich emotional practices; rather, a negativity of drive characterizes contemporary networks and their economy. Precisely when we (seemingly) move in the circuits of drive, we are in fact stuck in the pursuit of something we feel is lacking – information, for example – and that we should possess; and so we write, we post, we share, we read over and over again, in order to reach full enjoyment. Negativity of drive is about stuckness in movement, or stuckness achieved through (the illusion of) movement: we feel compelled, obliged, driven to act, tweet, like, post, share, upload, comment; yet the more we do so, the more we are irremediably glued to the starting point, caught in the repetitive gesture of circulation for circulation's sake.

It is precisely within this stuckness in (the illusion of) movement that Daesh's visual production should be understood. Marwan Kraidy suggests reading the group's visual media as 'self-conscious martial forms made for global circulation and designed to inflict hard on a wide scale: geopolitical visual projectiles' (Kraidy 2017: 13). Daesh's visuals are indeed like projectiles for the actions they attempt to inspire, the trajectory they draw, the movement they trigger regardless of their content. Whether they are circulated by wannabe supporters, who upload, copy-paste, re-upload and mirror them in online venues other than the mainstream social networking platforms; commented on and hashtagged by horrified users who micro-blog, post and comment; referenced to or redacted by mainstream media who are nevertheless compelled by the news cycle to talk about the group's infamous actions; Daesh visual media do circulate *regardless of their content*. The motivations triggering the circulation process do not really matter as, in the end, either a propaganda action or an action to inform or denounce are exactly the same from the perspective of drive.

Not only is content indifferent to the circulation of affect that we see disguised as contemporary communications (deprived of any real communicative power); the latter are also paired with a disturbing feeling of perpetual anxiety. Excess enjoyment, a surplus in discovering 'the unexpected, the marvelous and occasionally even the miraculous' in the circuits of drive immediately becomes a descent into hell, 'into the void of a sheer bottomless amount of videos, with their proliferation of images, their banality or obscenity in sounds and commentary' (Elsaesser quoted in Dean 2015: 98–9). That same 'too much everything' evoked by DeLillo, noting that, in such 'blur and glut, terror is the only *meaningful* act' (DeLillo 1991: 157, my emphasis). Meaningful because, paradoxically, it has grasped the indifference to meaning that characterizes networked communications technologies, therefore operates accordingly.

Between the two world wars, the German cultural theorist Siegfried Kracauer, in his essay dedicated to photography,[14] spoke about a loss of meaning in relation to the rise of visual technologies on a mass scale. By giving visibility to an object, a moment, an action in a space-time continuum, these technologies would reduce knowledge to something made visible, accessible and reproducible only in that very spatiotemporal configuration, excluding all other forms and possibilities of knowing. Because of that, the visibility granted by mass technologies would not ultimately generate understanding but, conversely, a 'strike' against the latter, an 'evacuation of meaning from the objects' (Kracauer 2005: 58, 53). Kracauer's prophecy seems to have been fulfilled in the era of the networks, in which meaning has not disintegrated by virtue of an exclusive visibility granted to a one and only space-time continuum but, quite the opposite, thanks to a plurality of spaces and times, layers, hyperlinks, digital copies and re-copies of people and data collapsing simultaneously in the circuits of drive. *Too much everything.*

In this networked context where meaning has come apart, Daesh-generated visual media are operative. In Harun Farocki's understanding,[15] 'operative images' are those 'that do not represent an object, but rather are part of an operation': they are 'made neither to entertain nor to inform' (Farocki 2004: 17). This idea was elaborated by the German artist in reference to his video work 'Eye/Machine' (2001): an accounting of US-led techniques of automated warfare in the 1991 Gulf War, where violence dramatically manifested itself in its mutual interconnection with visibility. Farocki seems to grasp the fragile and ambiguous status of the digital image, fluctuating between its visual and data components, which puts it in a loose relationship with the thing represented, and subtracts it from the domain of the representational, handing it over to that of the operational.

From the six months of the 1991 Gulf war, to the 2011 Syrian uprising turned civil conflict entering its seventh year at the time of writing, the shift of the visual's main function from showing towards acting, from representing towards doing, has been fully accomplished with the help of image-based software applications and the algorithmic regime of networked communications technologies. Syrian non-violent image-makers have experienced this move first-hand, after realizing that their faith in the evidential and ethical attributes of the image had fooled them. Conversely, since its spectacular appearance on the global online scene, Daesh seems to have fully grasped the new function of the visual in the networked environment, and its absolute indifference to meaning.

With networked communications technologies granting the utmost visibility, and the performance of violence turning into a mundane life activity among others, the image has acquired a new agency which combines human and algorithmic features and connects with web databases as much as with networked global publics. Farocki's operative images of the 1991 Gulf war – a pre-networked conflict, still bound to a geographical and temporal continuity: six months, occupation of Kuwait, liberation of Kuwait – have evolved into the post-2011 networked images in which multiple time-space continua are at work, from the boundary-less digital to the materialized virtuality of the caliphate in Raqqa or Mosul, to the fragmentation of Syria into an ever fluctuating and in-the-making territorial entity (central Damascus held by regime forces, its periphery partially controlled by rebel factions: a piece of land conquered, another piece lost[16]). Finally, the networked image gets rid of any residual representational feature to become fully operational; combining human and algorithmic attributes, embracing the multiplicity of times and spaces, pushing towards the ultimate disruption of meaning.

I am interested in Daesh's visual production not so much for the content in itself, but precisely for its understanding of this operational nature of the networked image, and its capacity to exploit the dynamics of participation, peer-production and diffuse distribution that the latter thrives upon. Although over-exposed by international media, violent content does not represent the bulk of the group's production,[17] which is rather dedicated to features on 'civil society' (Stern and Berger, quoted by Kraidy 2018: 40) and issues of daily life under the caliphate, such as governance, healthcare and commerce. Visual features on 'the good life' – *al-Hayat al-tayiba* is the title of a glossy documentary film à la *National Geographic*, highlighting the values of living under the caliphate, from fishing and cooking together to singing around the campfire[18] – are often underestimated in the scholarship (Farwell 2014; Kepel 2015; Napoleoni 2015; Adida et al. 2016; Hamid 2016; Power 2016; Rudner 2016), although some recent work has emphasized relevant aspects of jihadi everyday culture, such as poetry, singing, interpretation of dreams, and weeping (Semati and Szpunar 2018; Hegghammer 2017; Degerald 2017; Creswell and Haykel 2015; Leander 2017).

My focus on the metaphor of the camera as a weapon does not offer yet another reading of Daesh's violent, out-of-the ordinary production. Rather, reflecting on this trope – as shaped in the 2015 'Media Man You Are a Fighter, Too' video and in an Arabic document with the same title released the following year (Winter 2017; Kraidy 2017) – helps us to understand how the group crafts its 'visual projectiles' (Kraidy 2017), the operational images aimed at strengthening the process of digital, participatory state-building, and its viral spread *through* and *on* networked communications technologies.

At a first peer-production level, Daesh encourages everyone to take part in the jihad of the 'word', which 'can be more devastating than nuclear weapons'.[19] The 2016 Arabic document explicitly constructs a parallel between cameraman and gunman: 'Don't you see the photographer/cameraman carrying his camera in lieu of the Kalashnikov and running ahead of the soldier in our conquests, welcoming bullets with his breast?'; 'the media worker is a martyr-operator without a belt' (quoted by Kraidy 2017: 10–11). Everybody is welcome to participate in Daesh's fight in the media domain, no matter where they live, or whatever kind of family, work or life constraints they have: the virtual jihad is joinable whenever, and from wherever. This decentralized media-making process corresponds to the administrative structure of the caliphate, which is based on a regrouping of autonomous provinces (*wilayat*)[20] dispersed in several countries (e.g. Mosul in Iraq, Tripoli in Libya) yet linked to its capital, Raqqa.[21] At a media level, this is mirrored by an organizing principle articulated around an official production house including,

among others, the flagship companies al-Hayat and al-Furqan,[22] together
with a plethora of smaller production units corresponding to the caliphate's *wilayat* that are free to produce their own visuals, to which the
infamous Daesh black and white logo will later be added.[23] On top of
this already decentralized structure, another element is added that marks
Daesh's grassroots appeal to wannabe affiliates or sympathizers: the fact
that the latter can become cultural producers on behalf of the group just
by adding their own media creations, without needing formal approval
or membership. The 2015 'Media Man' video calls the media man an
'unknown soldier': unknown like those killed fighting for their country's
honour, and unknown like the anonymous crowds who turn themselves
into Daesh's dispersed gunmen on the networks, a peer-produced army
of avatar fighters.

This strategy of participatory, peer-produced state-building is
extremely well suited to the techno-human infrastructure of networked
communications technologies, revealing how participatory and sharing
cultures might be turned into amplifiers of violence and terror strategies,
and can actively contribute to a project of authoritarianism, as much as
opening to democratic paths. The state institution resulting from this
participatory process is everybody's state, a peer-produced entity to the
making of which any anonymous citizen – whether on the ground in
Daesh's controlled territory, or virtually from wherever on the planet –
can contribute even with the smallest act, such as tweeting or posting a
GIF. To paraphrase Clay Shirky's celebration of participatory cultures in
'Cognitive Surplus' – 'the stupidest possible creative act is still a creative
act' (Shirky 2010): *the stupidest possible creative act is still a jihadi act*.
As much as for the over-celebrated collective intelligence of Shirky's
crowds, for Daesh's anonymous sympathizers the manufacturing of
LOL cats plays a fundamental role in strengthening not only grassroots
creativity, but also feelings of enjoyment, commonality and belonging to
an inclusive group of people.

Fear and fun, as Kraidy (2018) observes, equally contribute to the
construction of Daesh's spectacle. And no matter how insignificant
this might seem to those of us accustomed to thinking about Daesh
as makers of extremely snuff visual media, the 'fun' side of the coin is
as relevant as the terror one. Even something as 'stupid' as LOL cats
provides affect, a trigger to move and achieve more: that 'something
extra' which is not an emerging new meaning, but rather refers to the
'intensity ... the excitement or thrill of more' (Dean 2015: 95) granted

by endless repetition, the excitement of the loops of communication for communication's sake. This viral circulation process thrives on both the fun-and-fear-inspired content around which Daesh has built its signature strategy, with networked communications technologies playing the leading role:

a drum roll and curtain raising (chatter about imminent offering), a performance (video posting on YouTube, anonymous messaging boards, and jihadi forums, with links circulated widely via 'open' platforms like Twitter, later via encrypted apps like WhatsApp and Telegram), and an intermission where the performance is commented widely ('mainstream' media coverage amplified by social media), before the cycle re-occurs. (Kraidy 2017: 6)

This mechanism has been indifferently tested with infamous brutal videos – such as the burning of the Jordanian air force pilot Muath al-Kasasbeh, which surfaced online in 2015 under the title 'Healing the Believers' Chests' (Kraidy 2017: 7–10) – and with 'light' content, like when CNN was mocked by the group after reporting of women being lured into Daesh's trap through the use of Nutella and kitten emojis on social media. The group's militants massively responded to this report by posting pictures of cute cats and chocolate and making comments like 'Yeh ... so this is how I heard we get married ... lol ... Why am I still single?' (Hall 2015), resulting in the mobilization of an online crowd outside the jihadi community, who in their turn created memes and hashtags about the massively lampooned story – 'Reports: mothers will stop buying Nutella afraid of their kids getting radicalised', one Twitter user wrote (Hall 2015). A massive wave of comments and more reports on international mainstream media, from Russia Today (RT.com 2015) to al-Arabiya (al-Arabiya 2015), were generated by these images and posts, in a perfect storm of infectious, hybrid forms of user and professionally generated content that circulated in a global glut to Daesh's ultimate benefit.

The way Daesh has cleverly orchestrated the 'virtuous' circle between mainstream and grassroots media, and used it to co-opt more sympathizers and strengthen its online unknown army, is far more sophisticated than any strategy previously adopted by other terror groups. Even al-Qaeda, who created the most infamous spectacle of contemporary visual culture – the real-time collapse of the Twin Towers on 9/11 – was in fact still working in the domain of pre-networked, broadcast media. In 2001 the techno-human infrastructure of the participatory web was just taking its baby steps, and massive social networking platforms like Facebook and YouTube did not yet exist. Al-Qaeda's leader Osama bin Laden needed al-Jazeera, a broadcast media, to spread his audio-visual messages to Arab and international audiences: messages crafted in a traditional style, filmed in a static shot, with little or no editing, and given in a long speech in classical Arabic, full of Quranic references that most people, even within the Muslim community, could probably not fully decode (Kovacs 2015). Conversely, the astonishing first appearance of Daesh's caliph al-Baghdadi at the al-Nuri mosque in Mosul, after the city was conquered by the terrorist group in June 2014, was an amazingly dynamic, well-orchestrated multi-media event which, in Kraidy's words, 'epitomizes the logic of display at the heart of I.S.'s spectacle' (Kraidy 2018: 42), providing terrorized global audiences with a typical made-in-Daesh show, in which networked communications technologies played the lion's share. Al-Baghdadi's sermon at the mosque – the official birth of the newly named 'Islamic State' (IS, a shorter and more social media friendly hashtag-name compared to ISIS) – dynamically shot with multiple camera angles (Kraidy 2018: 42–4), was in fact preceded in spring 2014 by a social media storm, carefully crafted as a Twitter grassroots initiative (Berger 2014): 'We demand Sheikh al Baghdady declare the caliphate [*sic*]' (Stern and Berger 2015: 69). This was later followed by commander Abu Muhammad al-Adnani's audio recording announcing the 'birth of "The Islamic State", calling al-Baghdadi "the sheikh, the fighter, the scholar"' (Kraidy 2018: 42), and by another Twitterstorm with the cleverly branded hashtag #AllEyesOnISIS',[24] which not only attracted the attention of wannabe media jihadis, but also of regular users who virally commented on the news of the takeover of Mosul by Daesh, expressed concern, or lampooned the group.

When al-Baghdadi surfaced from the pulpit of the famous mosque, dressed like 'the famous Muslim ruler sultan Salah ad-Din in the Hollywood movie *The Kingdom of Heaven* (Ridley Scott, 2005)' (Kovacs 2015: 59), it was indeed a spectacular appearance; or, better, an '*apparition*' (Kraidy 2018: 44). Yet the caliph disappeared as quickly and mysteriously as he had appeared. Al-Baghdadi, in fact, has never enjoyed a media presence like that of Osama bin Laden, who was the commander in chief and spokesperson for al-Qaeda, the only authority entitled to talk on behalf of the organization. Unlike the al-Qaeda-like jihadi elitism,

Daesh has instead democratized the figure of the fighter. What Cecile Boëx calls 'the banalization of jihad' (Boëx 2016), designed to make it appealing and accessible to anyone, is Daesh's unique strength, turning the group into a truly peer-produced organization perfectly suited to the networked environment. Fighters, whether on the ground or in the online domain, are ordinary people who are offered easy access to the glory of jihad and martyrdom via a language that appeals to millennials and largely builds on video games, memes, emojis, remixes and mash-ups, all prominent features of contemporary networked media culture.[25] Even Daesh's infamous flag, its trademark in the group's visual media creation, is designed to be networked-culture-friendly, and suitable for non-stop circulation on social media: the white letters emerging from an all-black background – composing the *shahada* (Islamic creed) 'There is no god but God, Mohammed is His messenger' – are clumsily cut. They look as if they were badly photoshopped, the work of a non-professional graphic designer, a triumph of amateur, remix culture. They build a bond with the web 2.0's anonymous crowds, reminding us of 'poor images' (Steyerl 2009), i.e. clips that have been uploaded, downloaded, cut, photo-shopped, pasted, compressed, reproduced and remixed endlessly: a sort of 'lumpen proletarian in the class society of appearances' (Steyerl 2009), yet perfectly suited to the non-stop circulation and enticing feedback loops of the networks' drive.

The black and white logo that comes embedded in all made-in-Daesh productions – whether packaged by its flagship media companies or by the *wilayat*, or generated by its online soldiers – and that circulates virally with every post, tweet or upload, triumphantly appears to open the doors of the organization to DIY cultures, strengthening the message of inclusiveness at the core of its media strategy. Yet Daesh-made images are not at all 'poor'. They aim at building a state, an aesthetic of the state; therefore they are authoritative, high-resolution, glossy and sophisti-cated. Even when conveying an impression of naturalness and familiarity – like in the 'Mujatweets' series (Leander 2017; Della Ratta 2015d), a name that combines *mujahidin* and *tweets* – they do so by visually con-structing a carefully orchestrated aesthetic. The one-two minute pills of daily life in the caliphate that have been virally circulating on Twitter and other social media platforms[26] feature cheerful scenes of crowds shopping in markets filled with good-looking vegetables; kebab sellers talking about food quality control; boys breaking the Ramadan fast together, cheerfully joking and singing Islamic *anashed* (a cappella hymns);

children playing and eating ice creams while they scream *Allahu akbar* ('God is the greatest'[27]). These snapshots of mundane, non-military life under Daesh hint at the aesthetic form of the selfie[28] and its popularity and viral spread on social networking sites.

By employing highly recognizable 'commercial tropes (shopping, markets, and branding)' that convey an 'unspectacular normality' (Leander 2017: 11) – and yet at the same time very spectacular, as Kraidy observes (2017) – Mujatweets help construct Daesh's claims to state-hood, and frame them within an ideology of 'the good life' (Wedeen 2013; Kraidy 2017). As the high-production-value documentary titled *al-Hayat al-tayiba* ('The Good Life', 2016) highlights with its well-shot images of daily fishing and cooking in Aleppo province, Daesh attempts to build its claims to statehood both through the content of its visual media, focusing on non-violent, ordinary aspects of daily life in the cali-phate, and through its authoritative aesthetics, reminding us of Osama Mohammed's words on the 'cinema of the murderer' quoted earlier: 'Only those who commit a crime, in fact, have the time to look for the most spectacular angle, fix the camera, and finally render their violence into an aesthetic performance that can be reproduced and re-enacted for the sake of the camera-eye' (Della Ratta 2017c: 115).[29]

Needless to say, the claims of statehood are also manifest in the extremely violent visual productions for which the organization has become known globally. Here, the choreography of the carefully orches-trated movements of both the jihadis and their victims, their costumes (all-black uniforms and orange jumpsuits à la Guantanamo) and props (knives, ropes), and the symbolic settings of the beheading scenes (a beach; the Roman theatre in Palmyra) all remind the viewer of a 'large, disciplined, and powerful organization with coordinated military and media departments' (Kraidy 2017: 9). The 'reverse shot' of such pro-ductions are the plethora of visual media portraying the caliphate's administrative power, such as the documentary 'ISHS' (Islamic State Healthcare Service) – whose title paraphrases the UK's NHS (National Health Service) – promoting welfare-state-like free medical assistance (Leander 2017: 10), or the 55-minute video focusing on Daesh's own currency, the gold dinar, launched in 2015, 'The Rise of Khilafah: Return of the Gold Dinar', cross-advertised on the organization's former online magazine Dabiq[30] and on social media with the hashtag #return_of_the_gold_dinar.[31]

Together, the gory visual productions and the state-building, ordinary life, feel-good media contribute to constructing Daesh as an empire on the ground as much as an empire of images, and help spread its ideology of terror and savagery, as well as the values of camaraderie, brotherhood and solidarity connecting its followers and sympathizers. Compared to this sophisticated apparatus, the counter-propaganda efforts initiated by the US government – like the video parody 'Welcome to the "Islamic State" Land'[32] (Miller and Higman 2015) or the 'Think Again, Turn Away' online campaign (Katz 2014a) – or those promoted by Arabic speaking, Saudi-owned media, such as MBC's *musalsalat* 'Selfie' (Della Ratta 2015b) or *Gharabeeb al-sud* ('Black Crows') (Della Ratta 2017d),[33] look extremely naive in their attempts to dismiss the enemy's discourse through insult, contempt and derision, in the hope of discouraging its wannabe supporters. These counter-propaganda media belong to a pre-networked era, in the sense that they enact a carefully orchestrated and centralized top-down strategy, failing to engage the anonymous crowds of the networks, and ending up being patronizing and ultimately boring.

This connects with the second level of Daesh's media strategy, which I identify as a viral distribution step. This step is successfully achieved through a viral mechanism that can be initiated, indifferently, by any of the group's official media companies, by the *wilayat*, or by its loosely affiliated wannabe supporters. It is a capillary distribution system that includes advertising billboards and media points physically placed on Daesh-controlled territory (Engel 2015), as well as virtual diffusion in every corner of the web. When major social networking platforms such as YouTube redact or sanction made-in-Daesh visual production, or when mainstream media stop talking about it, it is the architecture of the open web that redistributes it through open source archiving projects, mirror sites, paste bins, imageboards and the like.

Unlike al-Qaeda, Daesh does not need al-Jazeera or any other broadcast media. Unlike Syrian non-violent activists, it is indifferent to image-keepers and their claims to ownership and copyrights. No matter if state surveillance and platform capitalism are jointly trying to erase Daesh from the online domain, as much as the international anti-terror coalition thinks it has already done in Raqqa and Mosul: it keeps resurrecting in the digital commons, just as it will – sadly but surely – resurface on physical land. Terrorism despises authorship, being the quintessential form of anonymity and collective action. Again, in the words of Don

DeLillo: 'The artist is absorbed, the madman in the street is absorbed and processed and incorporated ... Only the terrorist stands outside' – Daesh is the anonymous, amateur, web 2.0 terrorist 'as *auteur*' (Ignatieff 2004, my emphasis).

From commons to commodities:
Notes on the political economy of the Syrian image

In 1970 the Dziga Vertov Group, co-founded by French filmmakers Jean-Luc Godard and Jean-Pierre Gorin, was invited by the Palestine Liberation Organization (PLO) to document the achievements of Palestinian *fida'yyin* in a film that would have celebrated their uprising's imminent victory ('Until Victory' was supposed to be the film's title). Yet only a few months after the filming ended, the *fida'yyin* were defeated and their revolution repressed in blood. 'Poor revolutionary fools, millionaires in images' (*Ici et ailleurs*) was Godard's bitter comment on the rich visual footage produced with the aim of paying tribute to the revolutionary moment. In the end, not only had the Palestinian revolutionaries lost their lives *shooting*, they had also lost control over their own visual production, which meant losing control over memory and the making of the past. Similarly, the Vertov collective – born in the midst of France's own revolutionary moment of 1968, with the aim of making militant films rejecting the idea of individual authorship – was also eventually dissolved. *Ici et ailleurs*, released in 1976 as a film signed individually by Godard, Gorin and Anne-Marie Miéville, was not only a bitter reflection on the inner violence performed by the 'here' – the place of consumption – over images generated 'elsewhere', and on the exploitation of the image-makers who were no longer the keepers of those images. The film itself represented a living memento of the filmmakers' own inability to dissolve authorship and individuality into a collective 'we', once the revolutionary moment was forever lost – in Palestine as much as in France.

Several decades later, another uprising, and another wave of excitement accompanied by the restless activity of filming at all cost. Syria's 2011 bears more than a passing resemblance to the failed Palestinian revolution of 1970 in regard to its visual production and the irremediable split between the makers and keepers of the revolutionary images. In the context of contemporary Syria this split is, however, dramatically accelerated by the seemingly endless circulating, manipulating, copying, storing, and sharing of whatever content produced by anonymous users made possible by networked communications technologies.

If a politically engaged collectivity has tirelessly filmed, not quite 'to produce an image' but as a way to 'constitute themselves as the people' (Snowdon 2016: 187), claim their sovereignty and shape their shared demands – 'the people want...' (*al-sha'ab yurid...*) – what happens to this visual production once the collective 'we' is dissolved in the fading of the revolutionary moment? If the filming was not meant to be an individual or narcissistic gesture but rather the joint endeavour of a politically aware collective entity, where does this common property end up once the revolutionary struggle seems to have been defeated by a civil war that fosters hatred and fragmentation within the population? The conflict unfolding on the ground coincides, at the level of cultural production, with the restoration of ideas of individual ownership, intellectual property and authorship in the domain previously inhabited by the commons. This implies, firstly, a wave of controversies and arguments over property rights among the revolutionary image-makers. In recent years, in fact, a number of Syrian documentary films have been prevented from being shown in public, or have had to undergo a long re-editing and repackaging process before their official release, because of copyright and ownership disputes.[34] Secondly, Silicon Valley-based platforms have become the de facto gatekeepers of Syrian-made images and, overall, of the country's post-2011 visual history which activists have narrated frame by frame, and struggled to upload on social networking sites in order to gain international visibility (El Deeb 2017). Ironically, these very platforms have been responsible for removing a dramatic amount of Syrian-generated content without notice. While sharing sites like YouTube claim that the redacted material did not comply with the platform's terms of service and community standards regarding violence and graphic images, activists insist that 'crucial evidence of human rights violations risks being lost' (El Deeb 2017).

The separation between those who have made the Syrian image, and those who have the power to preserve and control it, could not be more marked. The once revolutionary commons seems to have turned into a commodity in the hands of internet platform capitalists and former activists seduced by the global market. Once in demand from international media outlets and NGOs attempting to collect grassroots documentation and visual evidence of the violence on the ground, Syrian images are now mostly sought after by film and art exhibitions as expressions of an *auteur* perspective to be packaged, marketed and sold in elite venues. The increasing number of international film festivals and art gatherings that have paid attention to Syrian visual media in the past years – and celebrated the latter through awards, fellowships, special mentions, etc.[35] – testify of this commodification process in the making. On the one hand, this has triggered an increasing professionalisation of the sector by raising the production standards of Syria's growing image-making business,[36] injecting more cash and financial support and resulting in a number of quality *auteur* products that have scored success in terms of critical reviews and international market distribution. On the other hand, it has led to a take-over of the revolutionary visual commons by some of its anonymous makers now claiming back their intellectual property rights over what were once common goods. This has prevented an important part of the 'anarchive' from being made publicly available, concealing an entire side of contemporary Syrian history from public knowledge. Yet critics have argued that leaving the anarchive completely open and accessible to all runs the risk of it being looted by Syrian and international subjects who feel free to exploit other people's anonymous work – and their suffering – for their own material benefit.[37]

Ici et ailleurs placed this overall commodification mechanism at the centre of contemporary visual production, as its inherent and inevitable feature. 'There is nothing that cannot be captured as an image, given a value, circulated and exchanged' (Morrey 2005: 112): such is the film's bitter conclusion on the visuals produced by Palestine's defeated revolutionaries, visuals re-animated after being injected into a global circuit of distribution to be consumed and digested in the 'elsewhere'. And yet, how can one blame revolutionaries from Palestine, Syria or elsewhere, if they were obliged, at some point, to face the post-uprising dilemma of choosing between a digital commons of free-to-all images and images preserved and commodified as exclusive, immaterial properties? How can we pretend that, at some point, they would not have to submit to capital's global imperative of accumulation, commodification and circulation, in order to ensure their material survival and the possibility of carrying on their struggle in some way?

For the very idea of the digital commons, as Geert Lovink has rightly observed, brings to the surface a paradox. It implies a 'rational and egalitarian environment, built and maintained by well-paid engineers [and] tenured academics' (Lovink 2009: 40), materializing the early digital utopia of the networks as a free, common and open-to-all space for exchanging ideas and resources independently of market greediness and state control. The degradation of this idealized space began after the coming into play of 'individuals and corporations that drew on the value, produced by the commons, which they then consumed privately' (Lovink 2009: 41). Paradoxically, it was this shift from an elite-driven digital commons to the latter's appropriation by the general public, when it eventually gained mass access to networked communications technologies, that determined its progressive takeover and exploitation by '"dirty" market forces and even more "evil" government regulators' (Lovink 2009: 40).

Scholarly works, such as Lawrence Lessig's essay *The Future of Ideas* (2001), have traditionally looked at the so-called 'tragedy'[38] of the digital commons with a focus on its legal and regulatory aspects. Lessig argues that the 'ephemeral information space' (Lessig 1999) of the digital commons should be kept out of private ownership and remain freely accessible to the wider public, as it plays a key role in inspiring future generations' creativity and innovation. This would be a battle 'between *old* and *new*' (Lessig 2001: 6), the latter being the domain of the 'Read/ Write culture' (Lessig 2008) largely built on non-professional, amateur creativity, and empowered by networked communications technologies. In order not to limit this creativity, and not to prevent future inventions that, according to Lessig, always have to build on past knowledge, the digital commons should be kept free from market or state interference.

There are two aspects of the tragedy of the digital commons that Lessig's legally centred argument, because it was developed in the context of a Western neoliberal democracy, does not address, but that are indeed relevant in reflecting on Syria's post-2011 collectively produced images. Firstly, the labour element that, sooner or later, will dramatically infiltrate the commons. Lessig's own idea of a 'hybrid economy' (Lessig 2008), in which market and sharing economies coexist, does not hold in a crisis context such as Syria, any more than does Benkler's framework of a 'commons-based peer production' that is 'radically decentralized, collaborative, and non-proprietary' (Benkler 2006). In a situation of civil war, daily violence and the struggle for material survival, Syrian image-makers have been obliged, at some point, to rely on the commodification of visual media subtracted from the domain of the commons, in order to secure themselves a financial subsistence. In doing so, their survival has become dramatically intertwined with the demands of external subjects, such as media outlets and NGOs, whether international or regional. As

Khaled Abdulwahed's film *Jellyfish* bitterly shows, Syrian image-makers had to move 'to another level' when medical associations who sponsored field hospitals and distributed aid, or newly formed military battalions of the Free Syrian Army, started to commission visual media.[39] 'When a human tragedy takes place, all sorts of picture-arts take place' is *Jelly-fish*'s bitter conclusion. Framing the digital commons as a 'harmonious picture of a consensual society, freed of conflicts' ends up orientalizing the Syrian image-makers, turning them into 'intermediate buffers with the aim to create the illusion of "civil society"', or implicitly portraying them as '"useful idiots" that have to soften up the harsh sides of global capitalism' (Lovink 2009: 41–2).

Secondly, as Molly Sauter argues, the networked space that we experience today has a profoundly anti-commons nature: 'public spaces, as they are understood to exist in the physical world under the guise of parks, sidewalks and roadways, do not exist online' (Sauter 2014: 94). The civilized fantasy of a digital commons conceived as a sort of Habermasian public sphere does not take into account the fact that the commons has turned into a 'privately held public sphere' controlled by platform capital-ists and submitted to 'the norms of private property' (Sauter 2014: 94–5). Here terms of service and community standards count for more than freedom of speech and the right to preserve a country's digital history or to produce evidence of human rights violations. The ambiguity of the digital commons utopia lies in its ignoring or minimizing the corporate, commercially oriented nature of the online platforms providing the techno-human infrastructure for sharing and circulating immaterial goods. Even if in principle, as in the case of Syria, images are conceived as common goods, it is the inner structure of these sharing platforms, besides the conditions of emergency and instability inherently generated by an armed conflict, that dramatically pushes the commons towards commodification.

No matter if these platforms publicly commit themselves to entering into a dialogue with the image-makers whose visual media have become their de facto property, or pledge to find a solution whereby material that has been redacted can be restored and future uploads preserved. In the end, these image-keepers will not be liable, as they act within a framework that protects their private property rights, according to community rules that they have legally set, and with which the image-makers have complied when uploading and agreeing to their terms of service. Ironically, as we have seen, a better *onlife* is granted to Daesh and other armed groups' visual media that, even if constantly taken down by corporate platforms and sharing sites, are resurrected in the domain of the open web. Internet Archive – the brainchild of the internet's early settlers and an offspring of the 'Californian ideology' (Barbrook and Cameron 1995) with its libertarian dream of openness at all costs – is the non-profit repository of the digital commons where the majority of Daesh's compelling visual creations can still be found, watched, downloaded and shared.

War-torn, information-overloaded Syria reveals the fragility of the digital commons, originated as a collective practice, later expropriated and appropriated by the very few. At the time of writing, however, there are still some grassroots initiatives fighting to preserve the remnants of the post-2011 digital commons, and partially subtract them from the commodification logic dominating Syrian contemporary visual media.[40] Syria's anarchive should be defended and kept alive beyond the proprietary logic of internet platform capitalism, as it represents the most precious living testimony to a time when the 'commons' was not understood as a marketing tool for web 2.0 user-generated content or a feature of sharing economies, but as an integral part of the revolutionary practice of co-building and co-authoring a collective subject, in the very moment in which visibility is granted to it.

SNAPSHOT #8

A fragment of a documentary film that will likely not be screened in public inspires my reflection on the visualization of violence and the violence inherent to visuality, in a moment where everything – including human life and death – is indifferently rendered into an image, reproduced, shared and remixed. This is the 'sociality' of the Syrian image, no longer carrying references to the social collective once engaged in the political struggle, or committed to generating communicative acts aimed at a shared meaning and a common interpretative framework.

The Syrian image is 'social' in the mere fact of its being circulated: it spreads, in spite of the death it carries, or perhaps because of it. All the factions involved in the production of warfare on the ground act, at the same time, as digital labourers engaged in the (re)production of violence for the sake of circulation on the networks. In the hands of these multiple subjects, meaning is disrupted into clashing, multi-layered and cross-referenced contributions mirroring the fragmentation of the civil conflict and, in a feedback loop, further impacting on the chaos, sectarian divisions and the performance of violence. These 'me'-versions of identity and nationhood matching the clashing subjectivities active in the civil war suggest a new mode of the visual shaped by what I call 'networked images', emerging from the rubbles of Syria, from al-Ghouta to Palmyra.

Networked images no longer aim at advancing evidentiary or truth claims, nor at representing, mirroring or interpreting the real, but rather at *making* it. They take a distance from fake news, as truthfulness or falseness are no longer parameters or ways of assessing the visual. Circulation is what counts, as the sociality of networked images, which is their exchange value, unfolds in the process of spreading and establishing relations with the whole infrastructure of the web 2.0, indifferently humans or data.

These multiple subjectivities, whether global or local, professional or amateur, profit or non-profit, armed or peaceful, human or algorithmic, all shape Syria's media ecosystem, creating a complex visual (and political) formation incestuously imbricated with the warfare on the ground, and defined by a combination of the utmost violence and visibility, both thriving in a permanent state of hyper-stimulation, speed and acceleration, and heading towards disjunction, disaggregation and ultimate disruption.

8

Notes on a Theory of Violence and the Visual in the Networked Age

'Hypersociality' of the Syrian image

The sequence features a dialogue between two men. The first one, whom we don't get to see as he is hidden behind the camera, questions the other, a young man with an ironic smile and big, clear eyes. 'This is a picture of Ghiath', the latter explains, pointing at a frame of a dead body covered with flowers that has been frozen on a big screen behind the young man's back. 'One day before [dying] he told me: *I feel I'm going to die. I want you to make a film about me.* I told him: "OK, deal! You die and I'll make a film about you..."' Suddenly, the young man turns his eyes away from the dead pixels, and looks straight into the camera, addressing the filmmaker: 'I was joking', he says, as if seeking for a justification. 'You won't take him seriously ... this is what he told me one day in the street ... the next day he died.'

This is the final scene of *Jellyfish*, Khaled Abdulwahed's documentary film on Syrian image-mediated activism which was never screened in public. By showing activist-produced footage of the Syrian uprising, and asking its makers to comment on and critically assess it, Abdulwahed offers a deep and visually compelling reflection on the process of non-stop documentation that has relentlessly accompanied the different phases of the revolt. *Jellyfish* provides the viewer with a close-up of a generation of Syrian image-makers who, in the excitement of the revolutionary moment, enthusiastically filmed the 2011 protest movement, only to be forced quite soon into documenting its violent crackdown, the torture and human rights abuses, the bombings and airstrikes on besieged cities, and eventually the formation of the Free Syrian Army and other rebel factions that have dramatically contributed to transforming the peaceful uprising into a brutal armed conflict.

As the film's narration proceeds, we are drawn together with an entire country and its people into a painful descent into chaos and violence: something to which the act of filming is not immune either. Image-making is invested with the same process of decay going on in parallel with the loss of hope for peaceful change. With the degradation of the once non-violent struggle, it slowly abandons its faith in the evidence-image, its representational function and its moral claims, in order to fully embrace the dynamics of aestheticization and commodification. Military defections, Hollywood-like rescue operations under heavy shelling, surgical procedures in makeshift hospitals, newly formed battalions looking for crowdsourced funding and the support of *likes* and *shares*: all aspects of life are recorded on camera, edited, packaged, uploaded and shared. Likewise, death also is to be properly rendered into digital bits. *I feel I'm going to die. I want you to make a film about me*, says Ghiath to his activist friend; as if owning a digital copy of the self, one's extended algorithmic version, could preserve one's vitality together with the data. Yet the activist knows that image-making is not only a symbolic process of granting perpetual life, but also a material process of commodifying the latter by giving it an exchange value within a capitalistic system of circulating goods. Even as he jokes, he is well aware that, once his friend dies *for real*, his filmed version will surely be transformed into a news item and become a commodity – yet another product that he himself, as an underpaid digital labourer, will likely inject into the data stream of the war's immaterial economy.

In the 1960s, at the time of another revolution, the French philosopher Guy Debord anticipated the dramatic implications of this restless visual accumulation process which he called the 'spectacle', defining it not as 'a collection of images', but rather as 'a social relationship between people that is mediated by images' (Debord 1994: 12). Although produced in an era in which the commodification dynamic was markedly nurtured by advertising and commercial broadcast media, Debord's reflection does not seem to invest a specific medium, or even mediated content in general. Rather, it concerns the overall process of mediation, and the context shaped by the latter: a context where the logic of the spectacle has dramatically moved far beyond images to invest social beings. More precisely, social beings have become image-defined and image-determined; and even more so now that networked media have come into play, shaping an environment marked by what Jodi Dean calls 'secondary visuality', or 'the primacy of the image in technologically mediated mass personal communication' (Dean 2016: 4). Like in the story narrated by *Jellyfish*, we are all increasingly socially determined by images and, exactly like them, we wish to become 'common and reproducible': 'a realization we enact with every selfie and hashtag, even when we may not be fully aware' (Dean 2016: 8). Unlike Ghiath, who was probably well aware of this when he asked his activist friend to render him into digital bits in order to go beyond physical death, to remain shareable and reproducible *forever*.

As we shift from a broadcast to a networked context in reflecting on the transformations of the spectacle and its implications in contemporary Syria, there is something else to be noticed together with the sheer acceleration of the mediation process – which has itself evolved into a process of remediation, where the logic of immediacy and hypermediacy have dramatically melded (Bolter and Grusin 1999). In line with McKenzie Wark's remarks, contemporary spectacle seems in fact to have taken on a more sophisticated appearance than the overtly authoritarian power of the 'concentrated' spectacle, or the morbidly seductive commodity form of the 'diffuse' spectacle described by Debord. Moving even further away from the upgraded concept of the 'integrated spectacle' – introduced by the French philosopher twenty years after the publication of his seminal essay to define a process of mediatization now permeating 'all reality' (Debord 1990: 9) – Wark highlights the paradoxes of what he calls, in opposition (but also as a tribute) to Debord, '*the disintegrating spectacle*' (Wark 2013). In the environment of participatory networks, where we produce the communicative exchanges that become its actual content, 'our lives function both as the mediated object and the mediating subject' (Briziarelli and Armano 2017: 37). Far away from Debord's preoccupation with the spectacle being a matter 'of top-down control, of actors and spectators' (Dean 2015: 91), Wark notices that, instead, contemporary spectacle is being peer-produced and reproduced by the spectators themselves. Spectators in 'the spectacle 2.0' (Briziarelli and Armano 2017) are not, in fact, the passive recipients of spectacular content: rather, they are compelled to obey the peer-production and sharing imperatives of the web 2.0, becoming proactive makers of their own subjugation disguised as free choice and creative expression. The latter relies on a combination of paid, unpaid, semi-paid and voluntary work hiding beneath the 'cognitive surplus'[1] that defines the sharing economies and 'the wealth of the networks'[2] in neoliberal democracies where users have an extra amount of free time to devote to collaborative activities. And, as Wark notes, 'while the production of goods is outsourced to various cheap labor countries, the production of images is *in-sourced* to unpaid labor, offered up in what was once leisure time' (Wark 2013: 6). Users are now co-creators of the (disintegrating) spectacle that has replaced 'the monologue of appearances with the appearance of dialogue' (Wark 2013: 6) that serves only to extract a surplus exchange value for the sake of communicative capitalism, leaving users commodified *to death*, and voluntarily, as in Ghiath's case.

Spectacular power in the age of the networks is diffuse, decentralized and fragmented; sophisticated and pervasive, it is difficult to identify and eradicate. In the very moment when, giving the illusion of connectedness, it disjoints people, rendering them into shareable commodities and disintegrating everything but itself,[3] it paradoxically becomes more 'social'. By dissolving sociability,[4] it creates a new form of sociality that accomplishes its original project within the techno-human environment of networked communications technologies. What are the implications of incubating and performing this emerging form of sociality in a context of warfare where the range of fragmented political subjectivities involved merges with a range of material, productive relations – unpaid, underpaid, voluntary digital labour? If the revolutionary moment has been choked and the 'social' emptied of any politically dangerous implications for the status quo, then what is the new *social* about?

Naturally, this discussion about the new sociality is not exclusively related to a context of violence and warfare such as in Syria, but has been framed within wider reflections on networked media and sociality. 'What is the Social in Social Media?', asks Geert Lovink in his 2016 essay with the telling title: *Social Media Abyss*. The early 1990s' techno-utopian dream of turning the internet into the ideal free and creative place to develop relationships outside the market and as an alternative to it has dissolved – long before being shot down in Syria – in the Silicon Valley doctrine of sharing economies and the 'social web' (O'Reilly 2005). Here sociality is already understood as a set of productive relationships of unpaid social labour that should develop free of charge and free of rights for user-generated content, which has to circulate for free through crowdsourced marketing tools such as ranking, hashtagging, liking and retweeting, and which must offer itself to the self-immolation of data mining. Far from connoting angry mobs expressing political potential, or from carrying the very twentieth-century burden of class struggle, the *social* in social media has become 'a placeholder of something resembling interpersonal rubble, the leftovers after the neoliberal destruction of "society", a loose collection of "weak ties"' (Lovink 2016:

16). There's nothing left of the *social* in networked (social) media besides what they actually conceal behind the illusion of sociality: the pleasure of repetition, of circulation, of watching and surveilling others, of being watched and surveilled by others, which might constitute a powerful antidote against 'boredom, isolation, depression' (Lovink 2016: 15) or, conversely, its very origin and essence.

But how and why did social networking platforms become today's quintessential model for the new sociality, its actual shape, its material embodiment? Following Lovink's suggestion, it is perhaps precisely from the rubbles of the social emerging in the contemporary networked environment that an answer should be sought, i.e. from the social's very disappearance. *The End of the Social*, as Jean Baudrillard prophetically called it back in the 1970s – not by chance in the midst of another revolutionary period. Discussing the progressive withdrawal of the social into an endless simulation voided of any possible material referent – 'simulation by precipitation of every lost referential', a 'black box of every referential' (Baudrillard 1983: 6) – the French philosopher connected its tragic disappearance to two elements that in today's networked age have come to play a role more central than ever: the mass and the media. Both are, in their turn, inherently linked to a process of the loss of meaning: the same 'strike against understanding' (Kracauer 2005: 58) that Kracauer associated with the rise of the 'mass ornament'.

What Baudrillard calls the 'mass' carries a deeply fascinating allusion, in the original French, to both a sociological dimension and a physical layer of 'matter', of 'substance'.[5] This quality of the mass of being indistinguishable, of lacking clear borders, of being hazy, is what renders the claim of representativeness hidden behind its political and social meaning into a mere statistical and theoretical abstraction for the sake of sociological measurability and predictability in the hands of 'political demagogy' (Baudrillard 1983: 4). In Baudrillard's system of simulacra, the mass is a sign that does not correspond to a material existence but belongs to the domain of statistics, to the domain of simulation. Having 'nothing to do with any *real* population, body, or specific social aggregate' (Baudrillard 1983: 5), it cannot be represented, but only surveyed, tested, polled, guessed at. It is in this loss of whatever possible referent (the class, the proletariat, etc.) that the mass also annihilates the social. Because of its indistinctness, its lack of materiality, its nebulous, hazy, constellation-like shape, the mass disperses all possible meanings: it 'absorbs all the social energy, but no longer refracts it … It is happy to be a good conductor of flows, but of *any flows*, a good conductor of information, but of *any information*, a good conductor of norms, but of *any norm*, and thereby to reflect the social in its absolute transparency' (Baudrillard 1983: 28, my emphasis). That is why, no matter how hard power (whether political or religious) has tried to indoctrinate the (allegedly ignorant) masses in the name of a given *meaning* – whether dialogue, education, social or political progress – everything has been swallowed and digested by them without leaving a track. All assumptions made in the name of the possibility of rational communication, premised on the existence of a Habermasian public sphere, have in fact failed to understand that, while the masses 'are given meaning', they actually 'want spectacle'; while they are provided with messages, 'they only want some sign' (Baudrillard 1983: 10).

Furthermore, a parallel process is at work to choke and annihilate the social in the domain of the quintessentially spectacular, the media.[6] Like the mass that describes a floating, nebulous entity, Baudrillard's understanding of information also resonates more with a mode of ever circulating, 'constant emulsion' in the domain of physics than with a mode of 'communication or meaning' in the domain of semantics (Baudrillard 1983: 24–5). Information is an entropic process that triggers the annihilation of the social, at the same time seemingly enhancing it through the transmission of messages directed at creating a shared meaning. Instead, it merely generates a space for the entropic circulation of those very messages, a space 'of total dissemination, of a ventilation of individuals' (Baudrillard 1983: 83), where the latter become reflectors of data that circulate and combine endlessly. A 'space of connection' in which 'the rational sociality of the contract, dialectical sociality (that of the State and of civil society, of public and private, of the social and the individual)' has finally succumbed to the (spectacular) '*sociality of contact*' (Baudrillard 1983: 83, my emphasis).

This sociality of contact prophetically prefigures the fading of the modern social into the contemporary structure of the social networking site that has now taken centre stage to define sociality in terms of making visible – and therefore commercially exploitable – the once hidden patterns of individual connections, on which marketing predictions in terms of choices, preferences and future purchases can be based. In the networked environment the social has finally been rendered into a matter of individual consumption which is only visually presented in the 'collective' form of a network; yet it has been turned into a custom service to be enjoyed by loosely connected individuals, whose use is free of charge at a mere surface level. This 'technosociality of the hyper-social',[7] as Tiziana Terranova calls it (in opposition to Baudrillard, the French philosopher, contemplating the possibility of it containing some residual social energy), seems to be the perfect accomplishment of the suicidal disintegration of the social in the physical circuits of communication: Baudrillard's end of the social finally being fully realized in the techno-human infrastructure of networked communications technologies. Baudrillard's conclusion that the intensity of communication – its circulatory, entropic nature – ultimately causes indifference, collapse, and the repudiation of signification in favour of 'imploding the sign in fascination'[8] also resonates with Jodi Dean's description of the networks' circuits of affect and drive, where messages become mere contributions, and meaning is dispersed into 'whatever' content.

Yet contemporary Syria seems to add to the suicide of meaning – and of the social – in the structure of social networking sites a further, dramatic dimension: that of violence. Firstly, in the context of the current civil war, all the different factions involved on the ground – from the national army's soldiers to FSA battalions to jihadi groups – are also a social workforce engaged in its reproduction on the networks. When military factions involved in a civil conflict become digital labourers, they accelerate the disruption of meaning into multi-layered and cross-referenced messages that end up further impacting on chaos, sectarian and political divisions, and ultimately on the very performance of violence on the ground, as the tragic story of the Damascene Village will show.

All these actors are image-makers, whether victims or perpetrators, or victims and perpetrators at the same time. They talk to one another through the images they produce, they kill each other through the images they produce. They materialize the visually mediated social relationships described in Debord's spectacle, shaping an image-mediated sociality: a social mode of the image, and a visual mode of society. The social mode of images in the era of the networks is manifest in their desire to spread and be reproducible (Mitchell's 'What do pictures want?' is a timely question to ask here). Their 'vitality' expresses itself in the 'reproductive potency' (Mitchell 2005: 90) of 'spreadability' (Jenkins 2009; Jenkins et al. 2013) on and through networked communications technologies. An image that does not circulate in the networks' circuits of drive and affection is condemned to extinction. The a-social image quickly fades away. The 'social' image has to reproduce itself infinitely,[9] to circulate, to be used, copied, downloaded, re-uploaded, manipulated, indifferent to the content, no matter what message it carries.[10] As Henry Jenkins famously stated with regard to the functioning mechanism of the networks: 'If it doesn't spread, it's dead' (Jenkins 2009). Instead Syria's networked environment seems to tragically suggest: *If it's dead, it spreads.*

The visual mode of this emerging sociality is what Gilles Deleuze called 'langue III', i.e. a language that no longer relates 'to objects that can be enumerated and combined, nor to transmitting voices, but to immanent limits that never cease to move about – hiatuses, holes or tears you couldn't account for' (Deleuze 1995: 8). Langue III is the language that comes after that of names and voices, of rationality and memory, of objects and representation: it's the language of images, where the latter are dynamic entities, moving around, ever-changing, filled with a sort of self-destructive, ready-to-explode energy. These images are a process rather than a content; they disconnect from the thing represented, disengaging and transforming themselves into 'a possible event that doesn't even have to realize itself in the body of an object any longer: something like the Cheshire Cat's disembodied smile in Lewis Carroll' (Deleuze 1995: 43). Like the latter, they appear and disappear in thin air, they dissolve into space – the other component of langue III,[11] a space that can be 'any-space-whatever' (Deleuze 1995: 10). And because of their disembodiment, their disconnection from the object and from representation, they express all possibilities, and always allow new connections, new combinations to be done and undone.

Paradoxically, this combinatory possibility that images carry is also what, to use Deleuze's term, 'exhausts' them.[12] Exhaustion stands at the opposite of tiredness: 'the tired has only exhausted realization, while the exhausted exhausts all the possible' (Deleuze 1995: 3), as it can be made and remade in endless connections. Exhaustion is about combining all sets of variables and possibilities, playing with them, trying them out infinitely, renouncing 'all order of preference and all organization of goals, all *signification*' (Deleuze 1995: 3–4, my emphasis). Nothing materializes this combinatorial, algorithmic logic better than the networks: a logic that, like in Borges' 'Library of Babel' (1962), contains every association of words that could be written, every phrase that could be uttered, every item that could be fabricated, in a space that bears no space (the any-space-whatever), which leaves its users in shock and awe, in a state of paralysis before the infinitude and arbitrariness of all the combinations possible. Exhaustion speaks langue III, the language that swallows words and memory, and forces 'speech to become image, movement' (Deleuze 1995: 12), like the networks' secondary visuality that 'blends together speech, writing and image into something irreducible to its components, something new' (Dean 2016).

For Deleuze, 'making the image' means to produce something 'that is nothing but image', that appears in 'all its singularity' but is neither rational nor personal (Deleuze 1995: 8–9), that is disjunct from its object – like in the networks' secondary visuality where even faces, reduced to selfies, filters and hashtags, 'lose their individuating quality and become generic' in order to be common, reproducible (Dean 2016: 2). When the image is done, this signals that time is over, all possibilities have dried up, all combinations have been tried. The time of langue III, the time of images, is 'a moment very near to the end, an hour close to the last', Deleuze reminds us. Make the image, then die. Ghiath knew this when he told his friend: *I feel I'm going to die. I want you to make a film about me.* Ghiath, Syria, is the exhausted.

Expansion: Violence and visibility in the age of the networks

In early 2010 I was conducting ethnographic research work on Syrian TV drama in a place called the Damascene Village (*al-qariyya al-shamiyya*), located on the outskirts of Damascus.[13] The Village was a theme park reproducing the old city centre of Syria's capital, with its tiny alleys and magnificent Ottoman houses opening onto astonishing courtyards filled with orange trees and fountains: a *One Thousand and One Nights* setting, built with the aim of offering a commodified experience free from the hassles of Damascene urban life and for the sake of wealthy tourism from the Gulf. A whole section of this replica was devoted to filming the Syrian TV hit *Bab al-hara* ('The Gate of the Neighbourhood'). Surprisingly, but perhaps not by chance, the park was located in the urban suburb of al-Ghouta, the greenbelt surrounding Damascus which evokes vivid memories in Syria's collective imagination, as it was there that, in the 1920s, the local resistance movement against French occupation was organized – which is precisely the main theme of *Bab al-hara*'s saga.[14]

At a symbolic level, al-Ghouta is ideally linked with ideas of nationhood, national unity and resistance widely celebrated by domestic cultural production – and, more recently, on a larger, Pan Arab scale, by *Bab al-hara*, a TV fiction that has come to embody the quintessential image of Syria in the eyes of regional publics. In a spiral of overlapping

Figure 8.1   The Damascene Village, May 2010 (photo: Donatella Della Ratta).

times and spaces, fiction and history, the Damascene Village became the spatial replica of the 1920s rebel stronghold, conceived as a TV set for a re-enactment drama of the historical anti-French resistance which took place exactly in the location where the fictional copy had been rebuilt for the sake of media consumption. Finally, the Damascene suburb had been occupied, physically and metaphorically, by capital which reshaped the symbolic geography of al-Ghouta, turning it into a mass-mediated reproduction of itself as re-enacted by *Bab al-hara*. The latter, however, was not merely a commodity successfully packaged, distributed and consumed on the Pan Arab market, as it represented Bashar al-Asad's political vision of a seemingly inclusive and multicultural *watan* ('homeland') whose integrity and unity would have to be guarded and preserved under the guidance of an enlightened minority leadership. Yet the 'Syrian exception' (Donati 2009), jointly supported by cultural and political elites and promoted via *tanwir*-inspired TV drama, was called into question in March 2011, with the protest movement bringing to the surface the fact that a shared understanding of the *watan* and a joint political vision of its future were widely contentious issues. The people were challenging Bashar al-Asad and his seemingly multicultural and reformist approach, asking for genuine political reforms rather than the neoliberal ones promoted by his government, for civil rights and freedoms rather than market freedoms.

In August 2012, with the uprising already descending into the abyss of civil war, the Damascene Village was taken by an armed faction of rebels, then immediately retaken by the Syrian army. Fighting not only on the ground, both the rebels and the army produced their own mediated versions of the seizure of the park, and spread them on the networks. These contrasting video accounts did, however, have a common feature: whether narrating the 'liberation' of a territory occupied by a regime they deemed illegitimate, or celebrating the rescue of a symbolic location from opposition groups considered 'terrorists', they both borrowed themes, symbols and characters from *Bab al-hara*, and re-enacted entire sequences from the TV series, attaching their preferred meanings to them. To add a further layer to these already multi-layered accounts, where the symbolic and the fictional universe of the TV drama melded with the historical events that occurred with the French occupation in al-Ghouta and with the actual military occupation unfolding on the ground, Pan Arab channels remixed the rebel and army videos with archive footage taken from *Bab al-hara*, using the series' soundtrack to package their news items reporting on the Damascene Village. After being circulated online, these media were once more re-manipulated and remixed by anonymous users cross-referencing between the fictional Damascus of the 1920s portrayed by *Bab al-hara*, the theme park formerly known as the Damascene Village, and the 2012 news reports on the events in al-Ghouta.

The spiral of these multi-layered media, indifferently produced by grassroots users and industry subjects, whether with the aim of self-amusement or of generating a narrative capable of hitting both symbolically and at an armed level on the ground, finally disintegrated the fantasy of a united, inclusive and multicultural *watan* – promoted, through *Bab al-hara*, by the country's political and cultural elites – into multiple contradictory visions of Syria's political future. In the hands of both military and non-military subjects, all involved in the civil war and all engaged in peer-producing, remixing and sharing content, the seemingly innocent re-manipulated clips fragmented the conflict into a plethora of media versions, blurring the lines between fictional and factual, history and fantasy, symbolic and armed clashes. The fight over meaning on the web and on the ground abruptly stopped one year later, in August 2013, when a chemical attack was allegedly launched by the

Syrian regime on al-Ghouta with the goal of annihilating the armed opposition occupying the entire area.

At this point, a group of rebels who had barricaded themselves in the Damascene Village killed the lion in the theme park zoo, and ate his meat in a highly symbolic gesture, since the Arabic word for 'lion' is *asad*. Everything was caught on camera and uploaded online, probably with the aim of defying al-Asad's brutality with such an act of savagery. Yet, shortly after, the clip was removed by YouTube, its gratuitous violence likely being considered a violation of the platform's terms of service. No copies of the video could be found at the time of writing, only a snapshot taken from it, freezing the glorious moment before the consumption of the symbolic meal.[15] In the end, the overlapping of meanings, places, times and subjects initiated and nurtured by the ever-circulating data stream on the networks was halted by platform capitalism on the basis 'of a corporate principle establishing what ought to be remembered and what to be forgotten, sentencing violent images either to endless regeneration, or to disappearance and eternal oblivion' (Della Ratta 2017a: 3).

The incredible story of the rise and fall of the Damascene Village, which I first admired in its fake magnificence on the ground and then watched from a distance as it was violated and disrupted, pushed me to start reflecting on the zones of intersection between violence and visibility, when a physically destroyed place is resurrected in multiple re-manipulated versions on the networks, and when modes of (peer-)production meet and merge with modes of destruction. I have named 'expansion' (Della Ratta 2017a, 2015c) this double-sided dynamic of annihilation and regeneration which is initiated when places that have been degraded by physical violence 'find a new online after-life – an *onlife* – by virtue of their multiple mediated versions being constantly produced, manipulated, and shared through networked communication technologies' (Della Ratta 2017a: 4). Central to the process of expansion is the techno-human infrastructure of the web 2.0, understood both as the technical framework supporting practices of sharing and remixing, and as the human network actively engaged in this reproduction and re-manipulation process.

Paradoxically, this human network of social remixers boosting the *onlife* of the Damascene Village mirrors the fragmented network of divided subjectivities that has destroyed it on the ground and that makes up the infrastructure of the Syrian civil war. While television, and particularly TV drama, had played a key role in facilitating processes of nation-building and national identity-formation in Syria as in the wider Arab region, now the networks concur in undoing and fragmenting the idea of nationhood into a plethora of personal and clashing visions. The *musalsal* is no longer the symbolic loci of unity, the repository of a shared identity and a common past history; it has turned into a highly contentious space where those very concepts are redefined in light of political beliefs and affiliations that have emerged post-2011. In the clashing video accounts of the seizure of the Damascene Village, the reference to Syria's glorious anti-colonial resistance is used either to support a pro-regime message or, on the contrary, to defy it. In the case of the former, the historical resistance in al-Ghouta as narrated in the fictional universe of *Bab al-hara* is symbolically exploited to emphasize the 'Syriannness' of the national army in its fight against those who are deemed 'occupiers', i.e. the anti-regime groups. For the latter, the same historical reference is employed to compare Bashar al-Asad to the foreign oppressors of the 1920s. Finally, in the universe of tailor-made, self-packaged meanings boosted by the networks, the message of unity and shared identity once promoted by the TV series is disrupted, as *Bab al-hara* itself is transformed into, at the same time, a pro-regime and an anti-regime work (with all due nuances, from the non-violent to the jihadist versions).

Beside the key role played by remixers known (the Syrian army, the rebels, the Pan Arab TV channels) and unknown (random users, sympathizers, wannabee revolutionaries or jihadis) in attaching new meanings to *Bab al-hara* and donating extra *onlife* to the Damascene Village, yet expansion is not merely a process of remixing: 'Expansion is not inherent in the form of remixing just because they have in common the falling away from referentiality. Expansion is based upon remixing practices, yet it does not merely unfold in the latter. It takes place with the remixing, cross-layering and hyperlinking of data; but it does not emerge as a mere result of a remix' (Della Ratta 2017a: 6). It is a highly contentious event that triggers the process of expansion; an event that comes to add yet another layer to an already layered situation, where different times and spaces and their mediated versions intertwine; e.g. the 1920s of the anti-colonial resistance remediated by a 2000s TV series shot in that very physical location, and reconfigured by Pan Arab capital. It is the 2011 uprising that expands, unpacking all these layered meanings and strata of time and confounding them, finally opening up the possibility for *whatever* being – armed, unarmed, peaceful, jihadi – to build new (potentially endless) personalized versions of Syria's past and, therefore, of its future. It is the 2011 uprising that expands al-Ghouta into *Bab al-hara* into the Damascene Village, and back again, post-chemical attack, into a desolate al-Ghouta. It thereby fragments the unidimensional, phony TV version of the *watan* generated by the once-virtuous circle of whispers between an authoritarian regime, cultural elites and the Pan Arab market into a myriad personalized, 'me' versions of it that tragically also produces the multiplicity of subjectivities active in the civil war.

These clashing versions are all equally *real*; they enjoy the same power of creating 'fictions' à la Rancière (2013), i.e. symbolic universes that take material forms in the empirical world. They re-divide the sensible by attaching a novel sense to the pre-existing universes of al-Ghouta and *Bab al-hara*, undoing the 'old' meanings. On a semantic level, these re-manipulated accounts are all the same. All the meanings they propose are equal, they are all true; as there is no meaning left in the Damascene Village, all meanings are possible. Everything has been lost in the multi-layered process of expansion. And yet the catastrophe does not lie only in this dynamic of disrupting meaning that goes on in parallel with the proliferation of versions and subjectivities, online as much as on the ground.

If the disruption of meaning is, in fact, a process generally at work on networked communications technologies – even in very ordinary and mundane situations[16] – expansion has combined it with a markedly violent component, which itself becomes 'ordinary' and 'mundane' in a civil war context. Violence is the added value of expansion, the dark side of visibility. A new relationship between violence and visibility is forged by blending the disruptive potential granted by the networked environment, thriving on circulation and reflexivity of content and on the diffused ownership and decentralized authorship of content-makers (Della Ratta 2017a), together with another disruptive potential which is the outbreak of the 2011 uprising. The Damascene Village expands after being physically violated by clashing factions in the uprising turned civil war, but also once it has been symbolically occupied and re-occupied by their self-produced video accounts – something that can only happen in the domain of the networks, where everybody has the right to remix, to be an author, to 'read' *and* 'write culture' (Lessig 2008).

Violence activates expansion. Expansion replicates violence. The more self-produced accounts are generated by a given armed faction and uploaded online, the more the rival faction responds with violent acts that are, in their turn, filmed and re-injected into the data stream. However, as much as violence can generate violent images, it can also prevent them from circulating, as the removal of the video of the lion being eaten shows. 'Finally, violence is performed through the image and, at the same time, inflicted on the image' (Della Ratta 2017a: 7).

Expansion needs violence to fully unfold as a process. Yet it is not merely violence, nor the presence of a networked context, that activate expansion, but their combination: their intertwinement in the presence of a physical site that carries a strong symbolic potential and is attached to a plethora of meanings, spaces and times. Like the 1920s al-Ghouta that gets remediated by *Bab al-hara*, by the Damascene Village and, once more, by the 2013 al-Ghouta attacked with chemical weapons and isolated by the siege. Or like Palmyra, another highly symbolic and very controversial site in Syria's collective imagination. Officially embodying the country's heritage and its richness in terms of a multicultural past that reflects on a multicultural present guarded by enlightened minorities, Palmyra has always – but much more obscurely – represented the latter's political brutality, as the site is (in)famously known for hosting an underground prison where dissidents are brutally tortured and sometimes also killed.[17] When Daesh first occupied it in 2015, their immediate symbolic action was to turn the ancient Roman theatre, once devoted to secular pleasures such as opera and ballet, into a space for public executions (Hutcherson 2015). As a response to this brutal act, and to the blowing up of several ancient sites in the old Roman city, al-Asad's Russian allies, once they had regained control of Palmyra in March 2016, organized a symphonic orchestra concert on the very same stage that had previously hosted the barbaric mass killings (BBC News 2016). However, Palmyra was then retaken by Daesh in December of the same year (McKirdy and Dewan 2016), and the mass executions on the theatre stage were resumed (Dearden 2017), until the Syrian regime regained control over the site once again in March 2017, with the help of Russian and Iranian armed forces (Chulov 2017).

Exactly like the Damascene Village, Palmyra was not only violated as a physical site; it was also re-manipulated as a symbolic entity by all the political and armed subjectivities that occupied it, each of them producing its own mediated version of it. Self-generated accounts and visual media have been circulated on the networks, expanding the *onlife* of the site and causing it to explode in a multitude of meanings and references to times and spaces – the ancient Roman Palmyra, the jihadi

Figure 8.2   Palmyra remix (anonymous).

Palmyra, the prison Palmyra, the cultural elites' Palmyra – such that it is no longer possible to restore any sense of symbolic unity, albeit phony, as in the pre-uprising times.

The 'disintegrated spectacles' (Dean 2009: 173) generated from the disruption of signification on networked communications technologies, and the failure to restore meaning resulting from the networking of meanings,[18] combined with the violence of the process of expansion, hint at 'the dark side of peer-production, sharing economies, remixing and participation' (Della Ratta 2017a: 8), suggesting that these practices at the core of the web 2.0. can enable creativity and self-empowerment yet also multiply violence, anxiety, terror and fear. Expansion brings to light the participatory dimension of violence in the networked age. Unlike previous highly mediated wars which lacked a networked component – such as Iraq in 2003 – Syria is in fact the first conflict of our networked age clearly revealing 'how sharing platforms, and the network of people involved in that very practice of sharing, have become dramatically entangled with modes of producing and reproducing violence' (Della

Ratta 2017a: 9). This network of people is made up of the celebrated, anonymous users and remixers of participatory cultures, yet also of the political and armed subjectivities active in the civil war, the two types probably overlapping with one another. They claim their right to create and re-manipulate on the networks, as much as they claim their freedom to conquer, occupy and destroy on the ground. They are active makers, empowered subjects, both at the level of creation and at the level of destruction. They kill and annihilate, then they give *onlife* back.

In this networked mode of production where visibility and violence intertwine, knowledge has been reduced to a mere matter of visibility – which also means, in the era of the networks, a matter of reproducibility and accessibility. In his seminal essay on photography, Siegfried Kracauer pointed to the latter as generating a misleading form of knowledge, since it preserves and recognizes as true only those time-space continuums that gain visibility (Kracauer 2005: 51), ignoring other forms, other time-space continuums. For Kracauer this meant that visibility had become knowledge voided of meaning. He bitterly concluded: 'never before has an age been so informed about itself, if being informed means having an image of objects that resembles them ... Never before has a period known so little about itself' (Kracauer 2005: 58).

Never before has a period resonated with Kracauer's description more than our networked age. Images of the Damascene Village, of Palmyra, of al-Ghouta, emerging all together, all of a sudden, expanding physical sites and exploding meanings, do not even attempt to declare a truth or establish a signification. They simply aim at making their own worlds, their own 'me'-meanings, appealing to fragmented subjectivities in a situation of mounting chaos. They aim at existing which, in the networks' jargon, means circulating, being exchanged, uploaded, downloaded, re-uploaded, posted, shared. Consumed.[19]

Epilogue: The rise of the networked image

'Poor images': this is how digital media artist Hito Steyerl (2009) defines images whose aesthetic value has been corrupted by the endless sharing and re-manipulation on the networks' circuits of drive. Yet this very process has, at the same time, enriched them in terms of their exchange value, the core element in today's networked communications technologies' political economy. Circulation and shareability have replaced values of authenticity and truthfulness that were once central in shaping and animating the ethical regime of images. The new visual regime is indifferent to meaning and representation, and does not aim at achieving semantic or indexical truth.

Expanded places inhabit this new visual regime defined by networked images. Although infused by some sort of surreal touch, these images should not shock us for their 'unreality' – *Bab al-hara* taking over both the historical and the chemical al-Ghouta; Daesh's executions taking over from ballet and opera in Palmyra, while at the same time reconnecting to the cruel reality of 'legal' tortures and killings perpetrated in the Syrian regime's jail. Rather, they should be understood for their 'operational reality' (Mitchell 2011: xviii), for what they do push to act and accomplish. Killing the lion, eating the lion: 'the metaphoric becomes literal, and the image becomes actual' (Mitchell 2011: xviii).

We are far from the evidence-images produced in the first phase of the uprising, from their ethical commitment and their willingness to inform and unveil the 'truth'. We are also far from pre-networked images of horror, such as Abu Ghraib. The tortures, the pictures, come one after another, like in a linear scheme, in accumulation. Expanded versions of the Damascene Village and of Palmyra grow in a circulatory dynamic, adding layers of time and space; they establish conversations across data, across the living archive of the networks – *living* as it never stops being produced by anonymous users, remixers, the web 2.0's participatory cultures. Networked images move beyond the relationship between image-makers and publics to construct a multilateral dialogue with the networked environment inhabited by human and non-human subjectivities (data, algorithms, automats and bots, AIs). If, as W. J. T. Mitchell (2011) has written, the image is feminine while the bearer of the look, the public, is masculine, then what happens when this bilateral relation disintegrates into a multilateral one? When the look is multiplied, fragmented into a multiplicity of bearers (remixers, manipulators and the like) that are not necessarily gendered, or even human? What happens to the reassuring, bilateral, heteronormative relation between the image and its consumer in a pre-networked form? Are networked images immersed in a post-human orgy contemplating a multitude of mutant, non-human and post-human, trans-gender encounters?

For networked images have to be looked at in their *social* mode of being. The networked image is social and performative, it acquires 'meaning' (understood here as value) through its surrounding environment, produced not only by 'human interactions but also by the technical infrastructure supporting this very interaction – the interface, the database, the algorithm' (Della Ratta 2017a: 12). It is as if Jacques Lacan's sardine can could finally talk back. While the French psychoanalyst was out fishing, the can glittered in the sun. His fisherman friend asked him: 'You see that can? Do you see it? Well, it doesn't see you!' (Lacan 1981: 95), laughing at him. In the networked environment, the sardine can strike back: it is the algorithmic eye of smart technologies, the gaze of the object finally accomplished in the artificial intelligence. Things *do* in fact look back in the age of networks, and the human act of seeing is indeed oriented by algorithmic savviness. And, as Lacan points out, 'the subject in question is not that of the reflexive consciousness, but that of desire' (Lacan 1981: 89). Under the complex post-human eye of the networked image, we are all '*photo-graphed*' (Lacan 1977: 106) by sardine cans.

Networked images are affirmative and world-making: they are the offspring of remix and participatory cultures where everyone and anyone can create and manipulate meaning. They do not want to bear witness or convey truth or represent; they want to make their own realities, to grow and prosper not because of their content but '*in spite of* it' (Della Ratta 2017a: 12). To this extent, as we have seen, the visual media explosion – or expansion – corresponds to the explosion of political and armed subjects on the ground; the media proliferation mirrors the fragmentation of the civil war. For, as much as the uprising turned civil war is a matter that no longer concerns only Syria but, rather, a plethora of regional and international subjects, so is the Syrian image no longer the exclusive domain of Syrian image-makers. For, as much as we cannot, and will not, find a solution to Syria's endless pain and bloodshed except through the involvement of all those players who have made it the quintessential twenty-first-century war, so we cannot, and will not, find our bearings in the country's troubled visual landscape unless we consider the question of the image in Syria as something that no longer concerns truthfulness and representation. The question of the Syrian image is not a question of true or fake news, not a question of ethical images, as it has for the most part been rendered in international venues. It is rather a question of how networked images have become operational – by virtue of what process, for example, each of the expanded versions of al-Ghouta or Palmyra can claim back the same reality with full rights.

Syria's networked images are the most perfectly accomplished visual (and political) formation of our time, a formation to the making of which everybody contributes, from Silicon Valley platform capitalists, to non-violent activists and casual remixers, to regime soldiers and Daesh jihadis, to the YouTube and Facebook algorithms. A formation which can no longer be separated from its own contradictions, and from its inner violence. A violence essentially linked to its inherent character of full spreadability and visibility, *in spite of all.*

Notes

Introduction

1. The video was uploaded on 29 April 2011 and is still available at this link: www.youtube.com/watch?v=DsOjUgdMDjE (last accessed 20 June 2018).
2. Mroue 2013.
3. *Ma'a al-fidda* ('Silvered Water: Syria's Self-Portrait', 2014). Film. France/ Syria: Osama Mohammed and Wiam Simav Bedirxan.
4. Jünger and Nassar 1993: 24–5.
5. Sontag 1977.
6. Keenan 2012: 32.
7. Baudrillard 1995.
8. Mirzoeff 2006.
9. O'Reilly 2005; Jenkins 2006a.
10. Mirzoeff 2009: 1-20.
11. Della Ratta 2015c; 2017.
12. Jenkins 2006a; Lessig 2008.
13. Jenkins 2009.
14. Della Ratta 2015a.
15. Baudrillard 1983: 24.
16. DeLillo 1991: 157.
17. Ignatieff 2004.
18. Snowdon 2016: 18.
19. Debord 1994.
20. Wark 2013.
21. Della Ratta 2017a.
22. Didi-Huberman 2008: 90.
23. Deleuze 1995.
24. Deleuze 1995.
25. Mitchell 2005.
26. Lessig 2008.
27. Giroux 2002: 61.
28. Baudrillard 1994: 49.

1 Making Media, Making the Nation: Syria's Tanwir *in Neoliberal Times*

1. This is a recurrent expression used by my director friend in our personal communications.
2. Syrian drama producers often use the word *tanwir* to describe their work. As Najeeb Nseir, author of many successful *musalsalat* – his TV series

Zaman al-'ar ('Time of Disgrace', 2009) won the Shaikh Maktoum drama award at Dubai Film Festival in 2009 – puts it: 'I would say I have a mission of *tanwir*. My works don't aim to hold a mirror up to society. I want society to discuss issues that are dealt with in my *musalsalat* and progress through this discussion. I don't want to describe; I want to provoke debates and drive social change.' Personal interview, November 2010, Damascus.

3. This expression is often repeated by Syrian drama makers, whether writers, directors or producers. Bashar al-Asad himself is reported to have hinted at TV drama being a way to heal the 'backwardness of the society'. Quoted by TV director Laith Hajjo, personal communication, Damascus, November 2010.

4. I have extensively discussed the *tanwir* ideology and its application to TV series in Della Ratta 2014a; 2015a.

5. To quote just two titles: *Ma malakat aymanukum* ('Those Whom Your Right Hand Possesses', 2010), on religious extremism and jihadism in Syrian society with a focus on women; and *La'nat al-thin* ('The Curse of the Mud', 2010), on the rise of the Muslim Brotherhood in the 1980s and the destabilization of the country. For an extensive discussion of this topic, see the following chapters.

6. For further discussions on this issue see Chapters 2 and 3.

7. For a thorough analysis of the connection between the post-colonial state and the *tanwir* project in Egypt, see Abu-Lughod 2005.

8. On Syria's troubled political history see van Dam 2011.

9. For a further reading, see Boëx 2011.

10. In her analysis of the National Cinema Organization in Syria, Boëx (2011) has described these several different phases where, alternately, either state institutions or the secret services became the main interlocutor in negotiations with cultural producers over public-funded film production.

11. See Kawakibi 2003: 186–7.

12. This episode was publicly reported by Hakki himself during the PhD school on Arab TV Fiction and Entertainment Industries, hosted by The Danish Institute in Damascus, 30 November 2010.

13. Fuad Ballat, speech given at the PhD school on Arab TV Fiction and Entertainment Industries.

14. Riad Nasaan Agha, at the time Syrian TV's director of programmes in charge of the drama production unit, explains this in slightly different terms: 'The state had a huge and talented creative class made up of people who were sent to study abroad – mostly to Moscow – with government-sponsored scholarships. Once they returned to the country, these people should have been entitled to become state employees, although often the state lacked positions and the resources to employ them, and that is why we encouraged them to open private businesses.' Personal communication, Damascus, November 2010. Nasaan Agha's version, though, does not take into account that many of these producers kept their public sector jobs while working for their private companies.

15. 'At that time, the Gulf had started to launch national TV channels, so it was the right moment to push Syrians to produce programmes to feed their TV schedules. The state would take advantage of this situation by letting private producers invest in drama production to cater to a regional market and eventually share the benefit of a fast-growing national industry.' Haytham Hakki, personal communication, Paris, February 2012.

16. Talking about the fascination of Syrian cultural producers for the ideology of *tanwir*, Salam Kawakibi, a Syrian intellectual and head of the Arab Reform Initiative in Paris, has emphasized that 'at the time the party had an intellectual project (*mashru' fikri*) which later evolved into a security project (*mashru' amni*)'. Personal communication, Paris, February 2012.

17. For a further reading, see Salamandra 2016.

18. According to Kawakibi (1997: 48), Pan Arab channels like Orbit or MBC operating from Europe at the time needed to fill their schedules with TV programmes that could be less strict (*moin severes*) than those from TV channels based in the Middle East. This would have eventually pushed market demand towards programmes dealing with social issues, which Syrians were ready to provide.

19. This practice of discussing taboo issues in public through *musalsalat* plots was also well established in Egypt. See Armbrust 1996: 16.

20. Riad Nasaan Agha, personal communication, Damascus, November 2010.

21. Riad Nasaan Agha, personal communication, Damascus, November 2010.

22. See Boëx 2011.

23. A good example of this intermediary figure is described by Boëx (2011: 122–3), quoting former minister of culture Najah al-'Attar who, enjoying Hafiz al-Asad's personal trust, was able to bypass the secret services and managed to keep filmmakers' creativity – and also defiance, to some extent – alive. Confrontational films were produced but generally distributed only abroad. This was a compromise solution that, while relegating criticism to the elite sphere, did manage to keep it going.

24. Haddad recalls the first '"troika" of men who, under the state's watchful eye, were allowed to launch the first large-scale private business ventures in the Ba'athist era. The troika was composed of Sa'ib Nahhas, Uthman al-'Aidi and 'Abd al-Rahman al-'Attar. Their deal with the regime became the model for state-business partnerships' (Haddad 2012).

25. Perthes estimates the core of this new class to be around a hundred people who 'made most of their big deals by virtue of their connections, in "partner-ship" with influential bureaucratic or political figures with whom they had to share their cuts or under whose auspices other non-legal or semi-legal practices like smuggling and marketing of smuggled goods could take place' (Perthes 1991: 3).

26. As TV drama writer Najeeb Nseir has commented: 'Many things in Syria just happen informally before happening formally. That is the case in sectors like cars, for example: people started to buy licences to open local branches of international big brands, like Mercedes, long before they were formally allowed into the country. When the law finally permitted this, some people

had already bought the authorizations. TV is no exception to this way of thinking.' Najeeb Nseir, personal communication, Damascus, November 2010.

27. 'It is the new commercial bourgeoisie, and especially its top group or "new class," who, having profited the most both from the state-led opening of the 1970s and the privatization of the 1980s, supports the regime and cooperates with it most actively' (Perthes 1992: 226).

28. As Haddad emphasizes: 'Badr al-Din al-Shallah, then president of the Union of the Syrian Chambers of Commerce, assured Assad in a historic 1982 meeting that the big businesses whose loyalty he commanded would stand by the regime. The regime proceeded to beat back the uprising in the northwestern city of Hama, where at least 15,000 residents were killed. The brutal tank and artillery assault on Hama proved to be a lasting defeat for the Brothers. It also welded the future of Shallah and his peers to the fate of the regime' (Haddad 2012).

29. 'Contrary to conventional wisdom, the Syrian regime cannot be narrowly explained as an Alawi regime ruled by the Assad dynasty. During the reign of the late Syrian president Hafiz al-Assad, the security of the regime rested on a military-merchant complex at the centre of which had been a symbiotic relationship between Alawi military officers and Sunni merchants. The elder Assad steadied this relationship by checking and balancing the power of Alawi security officers against the patronage his state offered to Sunni merchants. In other words, Assad's infamous iron fist rule was in no small measure predicated on preventing divergent interests among and between his officers and his Sunni merchant class base of support' (Rabil 2015).

30. An average of two per year. Data obtained from the Industry Commission for Cinema and Television, Damascus, May 2010.

31. As Boëx notes when discussing similar changes taking place in the cinema sector, this is a relevant difference with the previous generation, when public officials such as former minister of culture Najah al-'Attar or Antoun Maqdissi, responsible for publications and translations at the same ministry, were acting as true intermediaries negotiating between state powers and cultural producers. Theoretically, they never opposed censorship as a tool for ensuring state control over cultural production; practically, they were able to invent new ways to circumvent it and let the message pass within 'a certain margin of manoeuvre' (Boëx 2011: 92).

32. Personal communication, Damascus, February 2011.

33. Haytham Hakki's *Al-Dughri* ('The Straight', 1992) and Najdat Anzour's *Nihayat rajul shuja'* ('The End of a Brave Man', 1993) are among the most successful *musalsalat* produced by Sham International.

34. The Syrian regime was suspected of being involved in the assassination, however this was never proved in court.

35. According to Mazen Rifka, who was at the time vice-president of the company. Personal communication, Doha, April 2010.

36. See Landis 2006.

37. Including the multi-season satirical drama *Buq'at al-daw* ('Spotlight', 2001–17); see Chapters 2 and 3.
38. Including Akram Jundi (Landis 2006).
39. On paper, well-known Syrian businessmen from different religious sects were part of the venture, such as Suleiman Maarouf and Omar Karkour. However, according to many Syrian industry insiders, Mohamed Hamsho takes all executive and editorial decisions. According to Mahir Ramadan, from the Industry Commission for Cinema and Television (personal communication, Damascus, May 2010), the law states that any private channel in Syria should be co-owned in a partnership of at least six businessmen 'reflecting all the different religious backgrounds of the country' who have proved 'their loyalty to the nation (*wataniyya*) by investing within the country, not abroad'. However, all attempts to obtain a written copy of the text of the law have been unsuccessful.
40. This principle was reaffirmed during a meeting of TV producers, which I personally attended, hosted on 2 March 2011 by the Industry Commission for Cinema and Television at Sham Palace Hotel in Damascus. On that occasion, Imad al-Rifae, head of the Industry Commission for Cinema and Television, said: 'It is forbidden to work with Orient TV. Today we got something on this which is more than just advice. I do hope that nobody here will work with those who want to destroy Syria.'
41. As reported at the beginning of this chapter, the official rhetoric spread by regime-backed media has employed expressions such as 'events' or 'crisis' to define the March 2011 political unrest.
42. Among the most prominent signatories from the TV drama were writers Rima Fleihan and Khaled Khalifa, actors Mona Wassef, Karis Bashar and Yara Sabri, and director Rasha Shurbatji.
43. The text of the statement and the list of signatories were posted on Facebook, *Bayan sharikat al-intaj al-fanni al-suriyya raddan 'ala ma sami nida' atfal Dara'a* (2011).
44. Actors Abbas Nouri, Bassem Yakhour and Abed Fahd, actress Amal Arafa, and director Seif Eddine Sbei joined the TV debate from Addounia TV studios on 6 May 2011.
45. 'The first seed of Syria's civil society movement (*harakat al mujtama' al madani*) was planted even earlier, at a 28 May 2000 meeting at the Damascus home of film director Nabil al Maleh … The subject of the meeting was: How could we revive the cultural and democratic movement in Syria?' (George 2003: 33).
46. It is worth remembering that the civil rights movement and public debates on civil society were already active in Syria in a first 'spring' which occurred in the late 1970s and which was crushed by Hafiz al-Asad along with the Muslim Brotherhood-led uprising in the early 1980s (George 2003: 34). At the time, cultural producers, and especially filmmakers like Omar Amiralay and Mohammad Malas, were leading many public debates as part of the cine-clubs movement (Boëx 2011: 206–7).

204 · SHOOTING A REVOLUTION

47. 'Bashar, whose only formal title before 2000 was chairman of the Syrian Computer Society (like his late brother Basil when he was being prepared to take over from his father) was fully identified with the new mood, bringing forward younger, more dynamic individuals and spearheading an (admittedly somewhat cynical) anti-corruption campaign, again as Basil had done' (George 2003: 31).

48. 'We took advantage of the occasion. It seemed the time was right for us to build a civil movement and start discussing issues publicly, so we immediately did it.' TV director Haytham Hakki, personal communication, Paris, February 2012.

49. 'I will quickly review the reform process since 2000. It is true that we talked about this at the time but only in headlines. The picture was not very clear about the shape of that reform' (al-Asad 2011a).

50. Haytham Hakki, personal communication, Paris, February 2012.

51. '[The president] said he wanted to learn from us and from Syrian drama about how to move the country forward.' Laith Hajjo, personal communication, Damascus, December 2010.

52. As TV director Ma'moun al-Bunni noted: 'We used to have an enlightening message (*risala tanwiriyya*) that the *musalsalat* industry has now taken away from us.' Personal communication, May 2010, Damascus.

53. For a further reading see cooke 2007.

54. I am grateful to Lisa Wedeen for recalling an anecdote that portrayed Hafiz al-Asad himself suffering from a shortage of bananas at home.

55. 'On Friday, the Muslim day of rest, Asma al-Assad opens the door herself in jeans and old suede stiletto boots, hair in a ponytail, the word happiness spelled out across the back of her T-shirt' (Buck 2011).

56. Bashar al-Asad and his spouse made an official visit to France in December 2010. Angelina Jolie and Brad Pitt visited Syria in 2009, and were warmly welcomed by the presidential couple.

57. Honey al-Sayed, radio host of the programme *Ana suri*. Personal communication, Damascus, March 2011.

2   The Whisper Strategy

1. On the Damascus Spring, see Chapter 1. For further readings on 'Spotlight', see Dick 2007; Salamandra 2011b, 2012; Della Ratta 2012a.

2. Wedeen (1999: 88–91) describes the safety-valve arguments and criticizes them, offering a four-pronged alternative to interpret some tolerated criticism in Syrian artistic and TV products.

3. E.g. Bashar al-Asad's brother Mahir, commander-in-chief of the Fourth Armoured Division, the core of the country's security forces.

4. Mahir Azzam, Head of Censorship at the Organization for Radio and Television Production (the unit that produced the *musalsal*), quoting the words of Sami Moubayed in his interview with Ibrahim al-Jabin. Ibrahim al-Jabin, talk given at the University of Copenhagen, 9 September 2011, during the seminar 'Where Are Arab TV Serials Heading? The uprisings

and political unrest challenging TV drama industries in Syria: an evaluation after Ramadan 2011'.

5. At the time, Moubayed occupied a prominent position among the Syrian cultural, reform-minded elite: he used to teach political science at the private Kalamoon University in Damascus and at the SIA, a prominent school of PR and International Affairs in the upscale district of Mezzeh that I have personally attended for some years (Moubayed being one of my professors). Moubayed was also the editor-in-chief of *Forward Magazine*, a monthly publication from the powerful media group Haykal, which promoted the idea of a progressive, liberal Syria under the al-Asad family's leadership. Reading any of Moubayed's articles on the Syrian uprising – some of them published in American outlets such as the *Huffington Post* – gives one a sense of his diplomatic skills in eschewing regime rhetoric while at the same time embracing some of the arguments on which al-Asad bases his claims for the legitimacy of his leadership, e.g. the fight against Islamism and religious extremism (Moubayed 2011).

6. Mahir Azzam interviewed by Ibrahim al-Jabin. Talk given at the University of Copenhagen.

7. The roof also serves as the platform where different – and divergent – opinions can come together and be discussed, as suggested by Baraqawi, the *musalsal* director, in an interview with web-magazine '*Aks al-sirr*. When asked about the ambiguity of the series, which seemingly supported both the regime's point of view and the protesters' requests, Baraqawi replied that: 'We nurtured a form of civilized dialogue. We don't have to present works that feature one side without the other, or entertainment works. My goal is to invite the viewer, whatever his political orientation, to see himself and the other in the series' (Halabi 2011).

8. In May 2011, Bashar al-Asad called for reconciliation 'under a national platform' (*taht saqf al-watan*), underlining the key role that artists play in reforming society and the 'need' (*darura*) for their works to reflect reality as it is in order to help in solving problems. On their side, the artists re-confirmed their support for the reform process that had progressed 'under the leadership of president al-Asad' (*bi-qiyadat al-ra'is al-Asad*, Sana 2011). Bashar al-Asad also employed the same metaphor in an interview he gave to Syrian state TV on 21 August 2011.

9. Sami Moubayed and Mahir Azzam were appointed consultants to the project, while Diana Jabbour became its executive producer in her capacity as head of the Radio and TV Production Organization, but she was soon replaced by Firas Dahni. Each episode was drafted by the group of writers and sent directly to Moubayed and Azzam, bypassing the control of the *lajnat al-qira'a*, the committee that gives the green light to drama scripts, and edits or censors them. This exception was made because of the Palace's direct involvement in the *musalsal*, as it is required that every production submit a written script for prior approval. Only 30 episodes were approved by the two consultants, Azzam and Moubayed, out of the 100 presented, and 20 days before Ramadan just eight episodes were ready to be aired.

10. Ibrahim al-Jabin, talk given at Copenhagen University.
11. Mahir Azzam interviewed by Ibrahim al-Jabin. Talk given at Copenhagen University.
12. Quoted by Ibrahim al-Jabin, talk given at Copenhagen University.
13. See for example the 'I am with the law' campaign, discussed in Chapter 4.
14. Nabil Maleh, personal communication, Dubai, May 2012.
15. Ibrahim al-Jabin, talk given at Copenhagen University.
16. Adib Kheir, personal communication, Beirut, August 2011.
17. 'Things that are not allowed to be said in one way can be said in another. My belief is that you can always negotiate on controversial topics if you know how to deliver the message to the right people.' TV writer Adnan al-Aouda, personal communication, Damascus, December 2010.
18. I have reiterated the idea of a bilateral relationship between political powers and cultural producers, stressing the latter's agency in the whisper strategy, in Esber 2014.
19. Already a few years after his seemingly reformist strategy had begun, the changes made by the new president did not indicate that 'the new generation necessarily had an alternative agenda to that of their predecessors or those they sought to replace' (Perthes 2004: 96–7).
20. These meetings are usually attended by producers, directors, actors, representatives of state-owned media and representatives of the Industry Commission for Cinema and Television. During the meetings, many practical issues related to the industrial aspect of the TV drama production are discussed, such as how to improve productivity, raise exports, waive taxes, etc. 'All these measures show the interest of the president in – and his personal support for – the growth of Syrian TV drama as a sector of strategic and national interest.' TV director Najdat Anzour, personal communication, Damascus, November 2010.
21. According to a report filed in English by the state-owned news agency Sana, in the 2010 post-Ramadan meeting with the president 'the discussion focused on the importance of drama and the human and noble goal it could achieve to serve the national and pan-Arab issue' (DP News Sana 2010a).
22. Taysir Khalat, Head of Culture Section at Sham Press website, personal communication, Damascus, January 2011.
23. Personal communication, Damascus, February 2011.
24. Personal communication, Damascus, February 2011.
25. Here a parallel emerges with Khoury's analysis of Egyptian anti-terrorism *musalsalat*. According to her, Egyptian TV series are constructed as 'events' (*evenements*) narrated in a 'language code shared by the educated and the politicians' (Khoury 1996: 266). This offers them the opportunity to reiterate their positions vis-à-vis a topic of their interest and to generate a debate around it through the emotional language of the *musalsalat*.
26. Speaking about *Wara' al-Shams*, Taysir Khalat has remarked that 'the *musalsal* has been produced to please the First Lady and her public awareness efforts on the topic. Producers gather information about what the

sulta will like before doing anything.' Personal communication, Damascus, January 2011.

27. For an in-depth analysis of these TV series in relation to the whisper strategy theory see Della Ratta (2015a).

28. His producer being Mohamed Hamsho, the Syrian MP and businessman who owns the SAPI production company. See Chapter 1.

29. In director Laith Hajjo's words: '*Buq'at al-daw* was born in the atmosphere of the Damascus Spring. It is the direct expression of Bashar al-Asad's first phase.' Personal communication, Damascus, December 2010.

30. See Chapter 1.

31. Despite the large number of existing free-to-air Arabic channels – around 600 stations counted in 2010 – very few of them have any market value. According to estimates, 15 channels account for 64% of the audience share and earn 80% of the Pan Arab TV ad revenues (Dubai Press Club 2010: 43–5).

32. Industry reports consider the MBC group, owned by Saudi Sheikh Walid al-Ibrahim, to be the dominant broadcasting player in the region, collecting 50% of total advertising revenues in the Arab world, and over 40% of the viewing share – mostly concentrated on its flagship station, MBC1 (Dubai Press Club 2010: 47). For a detailed description of the group's channel offering, see Kraidy and Khalil 2009: 35–41. For a profile of Sheikh Walid al-Ibrahim, see al-Saied 2015.

33. For further readings about the ownership of top Pan Arab satellite channels and their links with the Saudi royal family, see Della Ratta 2000; Sakr 2001; Della Ratta et al. 2015.

34. Despite the lack of reliable and independent audience studies, and several other structural problems related to audience measurement (Sakr 2007: 4–5; Dubai Press Club 2010: 21), TV buyers and advertisers de facto concentrate their financial efforts in this period of the year. 'Ramadan is the most important time of the year for regional TV channels, with a boost in advertising as families gather in the evenings to watch big-budget dramas and comedies on television. The leading broadcasters typically earn about 30 per cent of their annual advertising income during the Holy Month' (Flanagan 2010).

35. TV drama series represent 'one of the most attractive ways for broadcasters to differentiate themselves in a competitive market'. They are 'among the most popular types of programming in the Middle East, as reflected by their high share of total rating points' (Booz Allen Hamilton 2007: 3).

36. According to several buyers from Gulf-backed Pan Arab channels, in the first five years of the 2000s Syrian *musalsalat* had many competitive advantages over their Egyptian equivalents: along with high production quality at cost effective prices, they featured strong characters and storylines (as opposed to the Egyptian equivalents which exclusively revolved around the performance of an actor or an actress), and employed highly professional directors. Badih Fattouh, MBC Group Director of Content, personal communication, Dubai, October 2009; Abdallah al-Ejla, Head of Drama

Production, Dubai Media Incorporated, personal communication, June 2011; Mohamed Abdulrahman al-Kuwari, Director General, Qatar TV, personal communication, Doha, June 2011.

37. According to Abdallah al-Ejla, Head of Drama Production at Dubai Media Incorporated, in Gulf or Pan Arab channels (including the Lebanese station LBC), '50% of the drama purchased for Ramadan comes from the Gulf itself, the other 50% is divided between Syrian and Egyptian productions. A standard Ramadan schedule in a Pan Arab TV station would be divided into 50% of TV drama acquired from the Gulf (four *musalsalat*), the other 50% (two plus two) acquired from Syria and Egypt.' Personal communication, Dubai, June 2011. Ramzi Baramki, Head of Arabic Service at Orbit Network, has confirmed those data: 'With the only exception of Ramadan 2011, before we used to have 50% Syrian *musalsalat* and 50% Egyptian in our Ramadan schedule.' Personal communication, Beirut, August 2011. In exceptional cases, the amount of TV hours purchased from Syrian producers for Ramadan has overtaken the quantity purchased from Egypt. Mohamed Abdulrahman al-Kuwari, Director General, Qatar TV, personal communication, Doha, June 2011.

38. Badih Fattouh, MBC Group Director of Content at the time, affirms this but declines to disclose the exact ratings. Personal communication, Dubai, October 2009.

39. *Bab al-hara* is still being broadcast on MBC. In Ramadan 2017 it reached its ninth season, after being interrupted for some years following the beginning of the uprising. On its audience success see Nammari 2007; Omer 2008; Ma'an News Agency 2009.

40. Scriptwriter Kamal al-Murra, personal communication, Damascus, May 2010.

41. Producer Hani al-'Ashi, personal communication, Damascus, June 2010.

42. Journalist and TV drama critic Maher Mansour, personal communication, Damascus, June 2010.

43. Badih Fattouh, personal communication, April 2011.

44. Director Mou'min al-Malla has lamented that the commissioning agreement between Maysaloon (Bassam al-Malla's company) and MBC was an 'unfair one'. Mou'min al-Malla, *Bab al-hara* press conference, Damascus, November 2010.

45. In several interviews I have conducted on the topic, this opinion was largely shared both by Pan Arab and Syrian industry informants and journalists. I have experienced this myself, during my fieldwork on the filming of season 5 of *Bab al-hara* in 2010. No MBC executive producer was on set in Damascus; the only influence exercised by the network on the production was at a marketing and promotion level. Photo-shoots and articles about the filming were strictly controlled by MBC. Sometimes the channel would send its crew to shoot a backstage programme to promote the upcoming season, or to interview the *musalsal*'s leading actors for the group's website.

46. Ali al-Zein, Regional Director of Content at Impact BBDO, personal communication, Beirut, June 2010.

47. Kamal al-Murra, personal communication, Damascus, May 2010.

48. Personal communication, Damascus, June 2010.

49. After 2011, this offered the clashing factions in the Syrian conflict the opportunity of appropriating the *musalsal*'s idea of resistance and turning it to their own advantage (see Chapter 8).

50. On minorities and the sectarian argument in Syria, see van Dam 2011.

51. The 'Real Syrian Image', promoted by the ministry of tourism to attract more tourism and investment in Syria, has been built around the idea of the country being the 'cradle of religions' (*Mahd al-Adyan*), a place of 'religious tolerance and coexistence' (*al-Tasamuh al-Dini wa al-Ta'aish al-Silmi*), and a setting for 'dialogue among civilizations and religions' (*al-Hiwar bayna al-Hadarat wa al-Adyan)* (Yasuda n.d.).

52. Maher Mansour, personal communication, Damascus, June 2010.

53. Maher Mansour, personal communication, Damascus, June 2010.

54. This is the image at the basis of a documentary sponsored by the First Lady's office and the Syrian ministry of culture, *Nawafidh al-ruh* ('The Windows of the Soul'), produced in early 2011, just before the uprising. The promo, dubbed in English (like the entire documentary), addresses a foreign audience, potential tourists or investors, stressing Syria's cultural and religious diversity. It can be retrieved here www.youtube.com/watch?v=_FyGnP8WnUs (last accessed 4 April 2018).

55. 'Bashar al-Asad has given us reforms that we have wanted for many years … Now is the time to support him and to encourage his reform project to move forward' (quoted in Davis 2007).

56. Mohamed Mansour, personal communication, Damascus, June 2010.

57. 'Sometimes we are so involved in the *musalsal* storyline that we cannot see its faults; when constructive critics made us aware, we happily welcomed them.' Kamal Murra, personal communication, Damascus, May 2010.

58. Samer al-Masri, interview with al-Arabiya, 16 June 2017, at www.youtube.com/watch?v=W9UfP32IDCo (Arabic, last accessed 4 April 2018). Also reported in Aksalser.com 2017.

59. The show is named *Tash ma Tash* after a Saudi game similar to the coin-tossing 'heads or tails'. It has been on air since 1992 on Saudi Arabia TV; from Ramadan 2005 it was broadcast by MBC.

60. The episode is called 'My Uncle Butros' and features two Saudi brothers traveling to Lebanon to meet some distant uncles, only to find that they are Christian. 'After a long dialogue between the Muslim men from Saudi Arabia – which bans the practice of any other religion on its soil – and their Lebanese Christian uncles, all finally conclude that all monotheist religions carry a similar message' (Agence France Press 2010).

61. According to its website, MBC1 is 'the number one family entertainment channel in the region'; www.mbc.net/en/corporate/channels/mbc1.html (last accessed 4 April 2018).

62. Marissa Argent, MBC's Product Development Executive for Merchandising and Licensing, explained that the group usually selects the characters for the *musalsal*'s official merchandising according to their 'presence/appearance

and impact in the series'. Marissa Argent, personal communication, April 2011.

63. As the anthropologist Lila Abu-Lughod has remarked in the case of Egypt: 'By drawing attention to the religious identities of characters and representing the religions in terms of the obvious formalities of dress or action, they contribute to the objectification of religion itself as a kind of cultural element. This rewrites religious distinctions as *cultural differences*, which leads the way for multicultural conceptions of religions as national sub-cultures, not opposing truths or political antagonists' (Abu-Lughod 2006: 14–15, my emphasis).

64. *Bab al-hara*, season 4, episode 16.

65. For example, a Muslim character who is given the opportunity to seek revenge for his dead father, chooses to forgive the son of his murderer, freeing him from a French prison. Shortly afterwards, they are featured united in the fight against the French occupation. Forgiving the enemy is acceptable but only when it concerns fellow Syrians. At the end of season 5, the character of Ma'moun Bek, a Syrian turned spy on behalf of the French, is shot at by his wife in a square, then finally killed by the neighbourhood men. Here the rhetoric of national unity is able to overcome not only religious differences but also gender differences. Umm Joseph is the one who encourages Ma'moun Bek's wife to seek revenge by putting a gun in her hands. She then invites all the *hara* to celebrate, praising the unity between men and women, a metaphor for the entire country.

66. Since the beginning of the uprising the main outdoor location of the show, a theme park in the outskirts of Damascus, was occupied by armed forces and later bombed (see Chapter 8). Other indoor locations inside the city have been threatened by bombings. In 2012 one of the actors, Mohammed Rafeh, a staunch supporter of the Syrian president, was kidnapped and then reportedly killed by anti-government gunmen.

67. Its ninth season was broadcast during Ramadan 2017.

68. For example, attacking Turkey for a historical controversy over the ownership of Alexandretta (something that reconnects to the current troubled diplomatic relations between the two countries due to the Turkish support for the Syrian opposition). Samer al-Masri, interview with al-Arabiya, 16 June 2017, at www.youtube.com/watch?v=W9UfP32IDC0 (Arabic, last accessed 4 April 2018).

69. Although this trend has been slowly reversing over the past couple of years.

70. Syrian drama makers claimed that there was an ongoing boycott of Syrian media products (see Hatahet 2011; Albawaba 2011). In a public move to support the local drama industry Bashar al-Asad pushed government-owned TV channels 'to buy 28 Syrian-produced series to support the industry', which was mostly a PR move to reiterate the president's support for local cultural producers (Faek 2012).

71. This was also confirmed in the interviews I conducted in June 2011 with some of the major Gulf-backed Pan Arab players, such as MBC, Dubai TV, Qatar TV, Orbit and Rotana. None of them spoke of boycotting Syrian

drama, and in their Ramadan schedules the slight decrease in the number of Syrian *musalsalat* was rather due to the deteriorating security situation in the country, which prevented some producers from completing their products in time for the Ramadan season.

3   The Death of Tanwir in Real-Time Drama

1. Personal communication on Skype, January 2015.
2. I have extensively dealt with *Wilada min al-khasira* part three in Della Ratta 2014a.
3. The sequence is available with English subtitles at www.youtube.com/ watch?v=DJg-wYkjafA&feature=em-upload_owner (last accessed 4 April 2018).
4. Personal communication, Beirut, January 2014.
5. On anti-corruption campaigns designed to pave the way for the new leadership, see George 2003: 31; Boëx 2011: 209, n. 559; Haddad 1999; Bar 2006: 19–21.
6. Even after the outbreak of the uprising, in an interview aired on Syrian TV on 21 August 2011, the president reiterated the idea that his government was engaged in a fierce fight against corruption (the YouTube video has since been removed).
7. This the title of a seminal book by Imad Fawzi Shoaibi, a professor of philosophy at Damascus University and chairman of the Syrian think-tank Data & Strategic Studies Centre (Shoaibi 2007).
8. There are many valuable examples, such as *Yawmiyyat mudir 'am* ('Diaries of a Director General', 1997) or various scenes in *Maraya* ('Mirrors', 1982–2011). An extensive analysis can be found in Wedeen 1999.
9. The eleventh five-year plan, which started in 2011, listed as one of its main objectives: 'to reduce corruption by introducing performance related pay and decentralizing responsibility'. 'In the 2010 Corruption Perceptions Index, produced by the anti-corruption organization Transparency International, Syria ranks 127 out of 178 countries' (de Blois 2011).
10. Syrian prime minister from 1987 to 2000, al-Zoubi allegedly committed suicide in 2000 after being involved in a major corruption scandal. Having served Hafiz al-Asad for decades, he was seemingly considered an impediment to Bashar's rising power, a member of the old guard who had to be eliminated in order to readjust the power balance within the regime's inner circle and modify its support base. The BBC reported at the time that 'Mr Zohbi [*sic*] was the most senior official to be targeted by an anti-corruption campaign led by President al-Asad's son and heir apparent, Bashar' (BBC News 2000).
11. On Abdul Halim Khaddam, see also Chapter 2.
12. On the metaphor of the roof and *Fawq as-saqf*, see Chapter 2.
13. This echoes in Bashar al-Asad's words: 'however, when you punish a corrupt individual, society might produce tens of other corrupt and more devious

individuals skilled at evading the law in a manner that cannot be detected or punished' (al-Asad 2014).

14. As an example see 'Top Goon. Diaries of a Little Dictator', a successful web-satire of Bashar al-Asad in person (Batty 2013).

15. Personal communication, February 2016, Beirut.

16. Ali confirms that this occurred to him with season one of 'The Godfather', when Abu Dhabi TV censored several scenes in which the comparison with a Syrian minister was made explicit. Personal communication, February 2016, Beirut.

17. Mohamed Abdulrahman al-Kuwari, personal communication, Doha, June 2011.

18. Unless there is an official diplomatic break, as in the ongoing crisis at the time of writing, between a Saudi-led coalition of mostly Gulf countries and Qatar, which has resulted in blocking Qatari-owned media such as al-Jazeera (Alkhalisi 2017).

19. Interview with Jamal Suleiman, Orient TV, 21 July 2012, at www.youtube.com/watch?v=zZSpMXTWwfs&feature=youtu.be (last accessed 4 April 2018).

20. Najdat Anzour is a well-known Syrian director who has authored the 'trilogy of terrorism' in TV drama: Al-Hurr al-'ayn ('The Beautiful Maidens', 2005); Al-Mariqun ('The Renegades', 2006); and Saqf al-'alam ('The Roof of the World', 2007).

21. 'Najdat Anzour, the drama producer – long considered critical of Syria's autocratic regime – was among those outraged by what he derisively called the "milk statement". In response, he and 21 production companies issued a notice of their own, announcing they would never again work with anyone who had signed the petition, saying they had "offended both the Syrian nation and its government". "The milk statement lied about the situation in Deraa", Mr Anzour, now viewed as firmly pro-regime, said in an interview. "There was never any shortage of food or milk. It was a political statement. The authorities were dealing with armed terrorist groups in Deraa"' (Sands 2011).

22. '"Syrian government policy is to terminate the existence of ISIS and all the terrorist groups that are fighting in Syria," say Anzour and Kamaleddin, using the regime's preferred terms for describing their enemies, "and in this we fully support the government"' (Georgi 2016).

23. Haddad also claims that, since his first speech, Bashar al-Asad has talked about a 'conspiracy' against Syria which proved to be right. The YouTube video, which was available here www.youtube.com/watch?v=Sh2MAxXsi-s, has been now removed.

24. Ibid.

25. Ibid.

26. Ibid.

27. Rafi Wahbi, personal communication, Beirut, February 2015.

28. This is what Rafi Wahbi declared to be his goal when writing the *musalsal*. Personal communication, Beirut, February 2015.

29. Salam Kawakibi has noted that 'Wannous and his generation of intellectuals were much more free than those from Bashar al-Asad's era. A process of progressive destruction of the engaged intellectual à la Gramsci was started under Hafiz al-Asad but took an institutional form only under Bashar.' Salam Kawakibi, personal communication, Paris, February 2012.

30. It has to be noted here that Hafiz al-Asad's generation of intellectuals described by cooke (2007) mostly came from literature and filmmaking, whereas the cultural producers described here are mostly engaged in the TV business. However, these drama makers include actors who have worked mainly in the theatre domain, and writers that have also worked for cinema. Many of them come from a background of confrontation with the Syrian powers; yet they softened their critique after Bashar al-Asad became president and committed himself to a seemingly reformist project for the country.

31. There are two different committees in charge of evaluating a TV work submitted to state television: *lajnat al-qira'*, a committee that evaluates the script; and *lajnat al-mushahada*, which judges the final product before airing it.

32. According to Ibrahim al-Jabin, whose job at Syrian state TV was to supervise the scripts and give his opinion regarding final approval, the only *musalsal* that was not approved in 2010 was one related to Shi'ism. It was rejected because of the great sensitivity of the topic given the delicate balance between religious minorities in the country. All the other proposed *musalsalat* got the green light. Personal communication, Damascus, May 2010.

33. 'I would speak of an artistic evaluation of the scripts rather than censorship.' Najeeb Nseir, personal communication, Damascus, November 2010. Many other Syrian writers, directors and producers of *musalsalat* have used the same expression to refer to the parameters used by Syrian censorship to judge their works.

34. Like director and producer Haytham Hakki.

35. 'There is something in the way the *musalsalat* are written which does not harm the system: even if a *musalsal* talks about corruption, it never mentions the process which produced corruption. It talks about the people who became corrupt, not about the system which forced them into corruption.' Najeeb Nseir, personal communication, Damascus, November 2010.

36. In particular, the term *fitna* (a Quranic word evoking sectarian divisions) has been used by the government to raise fears and anxieties in the population at a time of unrest. In the first months of the uprising, an advertisement campaign appeared in public spaces linking the street protests to *fitna*.

37. A BBC report filed in October 2007 already spoke of more than 200 women murdered every year in the country by their brothers, fathers or cousins. 'The Syrian authorities are trying to crack down on the practice of "honour killing", and they have widespread support', the BBC noted (Sinjab 2007).

38. This happened in July 2009. In October 2008, the Syrian council for family affairs had hosted the largest meeting in the history of Syria to publicly discuss the phenomenon of killing in the name of honour.

39. Although still allowing mitigated punishment for honour killing crimes, the new article required a sentence of at least two years instead of the previous one-year sentence (Human Rights Watch 2009).
40. This is my own understanding of 'reformist' and not Dick's (2007).
41. See Chapter 4 on internet memes.
42. Personal communication, Damascus, April 2011. 'Jamil', an alias for the director of the same web-series, is himself an actor who has performed in different Syrian *musalsalat*. He has also taken a strong distance from Syrian TV drama in crafting his work. Personal communication, Beirut, October 2011.
43. Wedeen's analysis focuses particularly on the works of Laith Hajjo, the director of the first season of 'Spotlight'.
44. 'To be complicit is to allow oneself to be made an accomplice, to become bound up in the actions and practices that the regime promotes' (Wedeen 1999: 74).
45. This is Joubin's main argument against the whisper strategy; see Esber 2014.

4   The People's 'Raised Hands'

1. This paragraph builds on Della Ratta 2012f.
2. The project under the name of *Kull muwatin masu'ul* was planned by a group of media professionals in agreement with Bashar al-Asad's entourage at the Palace. Personal communication with one of the designers of the campaign who still lives in Syria and wishes to remain anonymous, October 2011.
3. Although this expression might be interpreted as slightly racist, 'I am not Indian' uses the reference to a distant national, cultural and linguistic belonging to underline that being Syrian means being able to understand a common cultural and linguistic code. The regime cannot fool the Syrian people because they understand this code; unlike Indians (or any other distant culture). We have a similar expression in Italian that underlines how those born in a given country understand the cultural, linguistic, unwritten codes in a way that foreigners usually do not.
4. Personal communication with one of the campaigners who still lives in Syria and wishes to remain anonymous, April 2012.
5. The term 'web 2.0' was popularized by Tim O'Reilly in late 2004 at the O'Reilly Media web 2.0. conference. In his understanding, the web was conceived as 'a platform' linking people and information (O'Reilly 2005). This idea was also stressed by the anthropologist Michael Wesch in the popular video 'Web 2.0 ... The Machine is Us/ing Us', www.youtube.com/watch?v=6gmP4nkoEOE (last accessed 4 April 2018).
6. I have myself curated and co-curated several art exhibitions on Syria's grassroots creativity, such as 'Culture in Defiance. Continuing Traditions of Satire, Art and the Struggle for Freedom in Syria' (Amsterdam 2012), and 'Syria's Art of Resistance' (Copenhagen 2013).
7. For a critical review of the literature using this approach, see Schäfer 2011.

8. Henry Jenkins first used the expression 'participatory culture' to stress users' active role in shaping digital cultural production and challenging corporate media texts and official politics using internet-enabled platforms (see Jenkins 1991, 2006a; Jenkins et al. 2013).

9. 'In countries that lack opportunity for democratic process, the use of memes to express dissent is akin to a public protest assembly' (Mina quoted by Huntington 2013: 1).

10. See Dawkins 2006. However, it has since been debated in the literature whether this definition derived from genetics best describes the process of manipulating, re-framing and sharing cultural ideas which lies behind the production and reproduction of memes. A discussion of this literature can be found in Shifman 2014.

11. I am grateful to Jodi Dean for suggesting this image.

12. Personal communication with one of the campaigners, October 2011.

13. A Facebook page was set up for 'I am with Syria' in May 2011, and is still operational at www.facebook.com/pages/I-am-with-Syria/15888678 4177416 (last accessed 4 April 2018).

14. The head of a prominent Syrian advertising agency defined Syria 'a failed national brand' during a public talk at the Hermitage Museum, Amsterdam, 18 October 2012. For security reasons, he presented his paper under the pen name of 'Dado Midani'.

15. The slogan chanted at the first demonstration in Damascus, 15 March 2011, was: 'one, one, one, the Syrian people are one' (Sinjab 2013).

16. Another advertising campaign that mushroomed in the streets of Syria in the second half of March 2011 featured coloured posters stating 'no to division', 'no to sectarianism'.

17. On ideas of failed nationalism interpreted through Syrian TV drama, see Della Ratta 2014a.

18. Ryan Milner introduced this expression, talking about Occupy Wall Street and the 'we are the 99%' meme (Shifman 2014: 136).

19. For an ideology critique of the idea of 'empowerment' see Della Ratta (2017b).

20. Habermas himself has suggested this link in claiming that 'the phenomenon of a world public sphere' is 'becoming a political reality for the first time in a cosmopolitan matrix of communication' (Habermas 1996: 514).

21. '...otherwise unrelated people', i.e. strangers, those who actively contribute to the making of a public through the activities they generate around a given text (Warner 2002: 68).

22. Warner defines the public as 'a space of discourse organized by nothing other than discourse itself', which exists only 'by virtue of being addressed' (Warner 2002: 67).

23. '...the use of words, the understanding of abstract concepts, and the enactment of everyday practices produce specific logics and generate observable political effects' (Wedeen 2008: 14–15).

24. This is the definition originally given by Simondon and used by Goriunova.

25. Goriunova (2013) refers to it as 'aesthetics'.

5   Fear and Loathing on the Internet: The Paradoxes of Arab Networked Activism

1. His real name was Bassel Khartabil but he liked to call himself 'Safadi' to underline his Palestinian origins, coming as he did from the village of al-Safad, now part of the occupied Northern District in Israel.
2. Information about Aikilab is still available at https://wiki.hackerspaces.org/ Aiki_lab (last accessed 4 April 2018).
3. Information about the event can be found at https://openclipart.org/ detail/180586/mitchell-baker-from-mozilla-at-aiki-lab-damascus (last accessed 4 April 2018).
4. An entire district in Damascus, al-Bahtha, was devoted to selling cheap electronics and all sorts of pirated software, content and devices.
5. Information about the event can be found at www.mail-archive.com/cc-arab-world@googlegroups.com/msg00216.html (last accessed 4 April 2018).
6. See the discussion of the smartphone campaign in Chapter 6.
7. Personal communication, Damascus, December 2009.
8. 'Syria went from being an information black hole to one of the biggest YouTube video producers in the world.' Reuters, 14 November 2013, at https://twitter.com/ReutersAgency/status/400955732902019072/photo/1 (last accessed 3 July 2018).
9. Syrian Emerging Media report, March 2014 (unpublished). Also see De Angelis et al. 2014.
10. For a critique of the neoliberal expression 'Arab Spring', and the use of technology in the framework of the Arab uprisings see Della Ratta 2017b.
11. Both Bassel and myself are visible in this video account of the sit-in which has recently resurfaced on YouTube: www.youtube.com/ watch?v=IKH5b1Ai6UM (last accessed 4 April 2018).
12. Like bloggers Hussein Ghrer and Razan Ghazzawi, and filmmaker Orwa al-Mokdad.
13. At the time of writing the coalition has officially 'liberated' Raqqa, the capital of the self-proclaimed 'Islamic State'.
14. I officially held this position from 2008 until 2013. A farewell blogpost can be found here: https://creativecommons.org/2014/02/18/thank-you-donatella-della-ratta (last accessed 4 April 2018).
15. A collective book under the name *Cost of Freedom* was produced in a book sprint in November 2015 by friends, artists and activists (VvAa 2015). At the time, we did not know that Bassel had been already executed. His wife got confirmation only two years later (Qiblawi 2017).
16. Not by chance, 'Revolution 2.0: the power of the people is greater than the people in power' is the title of a book authored by Wael Ghonim (2012), the Google executive behind the We are all Khaled Said Facebook page that became the poster boy of the Egyptian uprising. Rami Nakhle, formerly known under the pen name of 'Malath Aumran', was one of the cyber dissidents that international media highlighted as a powerful force behind the Syrian uprising (Blanford 2011; Macleod 2011; Shadid 2011).

17. https://twitter.com/basselsafadi, 31 January 2012 (last accessed 3 July 2018).

18. https://twitter.com/basselsafadi, 31 January 2012, my emphasis (last accessed 3 July 2018).

19. 'Post-truth' was named 'word of the year 2016' by Oxford Dictionaries, https://en.oxforddictionaries.com/word-of-the-year/word-of-the-year-2016 (last accessed 3 July 2018).

20. 'On Uncertainty: Fake-News, Post-Truth, and the Problem of Judgment in Syria' is the title of a recent lecture by Lisa Wedeen at Central European University, Budapest, https://spp.ceu.edu/events/2017–02–16/uncertainty-fake-news-post-truth-and-problem-judgment-syria (last accessed 3 July 2018).

21. The third was held in Tunis in 2011.

22. For an overview of the Arab Techies and other tech-led groups see Della Ratta and Valeriani 2012, 2017.

23. See for example Bensaada 2015; Carapico 2013: 195.

24. To problematize concepts such as human rights and civil society, see Guilhot 2005; Carapico 2013.

25. 'In the aftermath of the 9/11 terrorist attacks and the growing concern of the international community of the alarm represented by "fragile states", democracy assistance received new incentive as a means of the international community to counterbalance the threat and push for democratic transitions. Military intervention in Afghanistan and Iraq had, once again, proved unsuccessful and, what was worse, counterproductive, nourishing more hatred towards the West and favouring the increase of terrorism. Therefore, the international community became more aware of the need to develop new strategies of democracy promotion, which could engage and build partnership with non-governmental Arab groups and local citizens, and build links across Middle Eastern countries' (Brownlee 2017: 5).

26. Some of these funding strategies are critically discussed in Ben Gharbia 2010.

27. This was the title of Obama's 2009 speech in Cairo.

28. Both are among the main sponsors of the Arab Bloggers' Meeting.

29. Also, as pointed out by Ben Gharbia, there is a whole political economy around the issue (see the section 'The hyped and ideological market of circumvention technology' in Ben Gharbia 2010).

30. A critical discussion of this study can be found in Ben Gharbia 2010.

31. I am grateful to Greet Lovink for having suggested this.

32. Pictures of the campaign are available here: www.facebook.com/freebassel/photos/a.780414958705239.1073741831.326127250800681/1000192930060773/?type=3&theater (last accessed 4 April 2018).

33. The confirmation of his execution came only two years later, in 2017. The official statement is available on the website of the FreeBassel campaign: http://freebassel.org/campaign/statements/2017/08/03/death-of-bassel-khartabil/ FreeBassel.org (last accessed 3 July 2018).

34. Mostly in Tunisia and Egypt. For a discussion of those activities see Della Ratta and Valeriani 2017.

35. Some of the pre-uprising initiatives in the domain of digital activism, whether carried out with the official approval of the government or under cover, and their donors, are described by Brownlee 2017: 7–12.

36. See www.sitesofconscience.org/en/membership/enab-baladi-syria (last accessed 4 April 2018).

37. Enab Baladi Weekly Newspaper, Enab Online News Service Website, the Syrian Print-Media Archive, and an English news website: http://english. enabbaladi.net/aboutus.

38. See https://english.enabbaladi.net/aboutus (last accessed 4 April 2018).

39. See www.syriauntold.com/en/about-syria-untold (last accessed 4 April 2018).

40. 'We' meaning myself and my friend and colleague Enrico De Angelis, who were co-founders of the project and actively involved in securing funds for its survival. As the only two non-Syrian members who also had daily paid jobs we worked on SyriaUntold as volunteers. Today we sit on the board of Untold Stories, the NGO running SyriaUntold, as president (De Angelis) and board member (myself), still on a volunteer basis.

41. Untold Stories was officially registered in 2016. At the time of writing, we are in the process of moving the organization to Berlin where most staff members now reside as political refugees.

42. I am grateful to Geert Lovink for suggesting this.

43. Even the non-violent component of the movement, which was often attributed to the influence of Gene Sharp's work through Western NGOs was in fact locally grown and inspired by the work of Syrian Islamic scholar Jawdat Said (2002, 2017).

44. See www.youtube.com/watch?v=TvlRgL7tbXU&feature=youtu.be (last accessed 4 April 2018).

45. 'They invoked detestable sectarian discourse which we have never endorsed and in which we only see an expression of a hateful ideology which has never been part of our religion, history or traditions and which has been an anathema and a sacrilege to our national, pan-Arab and moral identity' (al-Asad 2011b).

46. 'In some cases, peaceful demonstrations were used as a pretext under which armed men took cover; in other cases, they attacked civilians, policemen and soldiers by attacking military sites and positions or used assassinations. Schools, shops and highways were closed by the use of force, and public property was destroyed, ransacked and put to fire deliberately. Cities were cut off from each other by blocking highways. All of this has posed a direct threat to the normal daily life of the citizens and undermined their security, education, economic activity, and communication with their families. They distorted the country's image in the outside world and opened the way, and even called for, foreign intervention' (al-Asad 2011b).

47. The commercial is available at www.youtube.com/watch?v=axSnW-ygU5g (last accessed 4 April 2018).

48. The remix is available at www.youtube.com/watch?v=GsF8qQmLYoo (last accessed 4 April 2018).

49. SyriaUntold is in this category, see Issa 2016.
50. A poster was also created with the slogan 'Borders mean nothing when you have wings, free Amina Arraf'. See www.avaaz.org/en/free_amina_arraf/?twi (last accessed 4 April 2018).
51. Or Syria Civil Defence, nominated twice for the Nobel Peace Prize 2016 and 2017; see www.whitehelmets.org/en (last accessed 4 April 2018).
52. A violent, armed, jihadi group.
53. A video recording of the interview is available here: www.youtube.com/watch?v=GI_FMKpW9mE (last accessed 4 April 2018).
54. On the proliferation of blurred videos see Chapter 6.
55. 'Rebel Rocket Attack', at www.youtube.com/watch?v=FsF3HspQY6A (last accessed 4 April 2018).

6   Screen Fighters: Filming and Killing in Contemporary Syria

1. This video is part of a private archive assembled by Bassel Safadi. According to Orwa al-Mokdad, a close friend of Bassel, the person in the video is Amjad Sioufi, a prominent civil activist in his twenties who was known as 'the button man' for always carrying a hidden camera inside his shirt. Amjad was killed during a shelling in 2013. Personal communication with Orwa al-Mokdad, August 2017. Also see al-Mokdad 2017a.
2. The Free Syrian Army was officially founded on 29 July 2011 by officers who had defected from the national army. Its importance on the ground had started to grow by the end of 2011 (Landis 2011b).
3. A video of the market protest can be found here: www.youtube.com/watch?v=qDHLsU-ik_Y (last accessed 4 April 2018).
4. The only exception being the revolt of the Kurds in 2004–5 (Fattah 2005); however, this was ethnically marked, unlike the 2011 movement that, from the beginning, claimed to be non-sectarian, with slogans such as 'the Syrian people are one'.
5. I personally witnessed this first-hand during the sit-ins in front of the Libyan embassy in February 2011. While on the first day of the sit-in we just experienced an incredible tension between protesters and police, during the second day the police attacked the crowd, and arrested some of the youth gathered there.
6. *Muzahara al-fannaniyyn* was held on 13 July 2011. Actors Khaled Taja and Fares al-Helou, filmmaker Nabil Maleh, and journalist Mazen Darwish were among the protesters. During the demonstration the security forces arrested the actors the Malas twins, the actress May Skaf, and the writer Rima Fleihan, who were later all released. A video of the event can be found here: www.youtube.com/watch?v=nv7NLkcc6Ho (last accessed 4 April 2018).
7. Fares al-Helou was severely beaten and his office raided by security forces. He soon had to leave the country for exile. Skaf and Fleihan have also lived in exile since. Khalifa, a prominent writer whose novels are internationally known (his latest being *No Knives in the Kitchen of this City*), was also severely beaten in a demonstration, yet he decided to stay in Syria and,

despite his overtly anti-regime position, continues to live in Damascus at the time of writing.

8. Suleiman, an Alawite actress who several times addressed the crowds through YouTube videos (e.g. www.youtube.com/watch?v=auHoFV9jvNk) that have become iconic of the first phase of the uprising, recently died of cancer while in exile in Paris (Roberts 2017).

9. Resulting in the tradition of naming the Fridays of protest (Friedman 2011).

10. Every public cultural event in Syria needs authorization from the ministry of culture and the informal yet mandatory approval (*mu'aqafa*) of the *mukhabarat*, who have the power to withdraw the authorization at any time without giving a reason.

11. 'The filmer feels that the camera is *stronger* than the gun ... by not only capturing the sniper's image, but by imitating his gesture as she does so, and turning it back against him, she feels that she is acquiring and exercising a kind of *mimetic power* over him' (Snowdon 2016: 92).

12. In March 2015, 4-year-old refugee girl Hudea surrendered to photographer Omar Sagirli's camera, thinking that he was about to shoot at her (BBC Trending 2015). A video can be found here: www.youtube.com/watch?v=HZtU8io82Vg (last accessed 4 April 2018).

13. The Sonderkommando was a work unit composed of Jewish prisoners who were forced under the threat of death to aid in the disposal of gas-chamber victims in the Nazi death camps.

14. Which she calls 'cyber[riotal]space' (Hamadeh 2016: 13).

15. Calling fellow citizens 'germs' or 'insects' is a quite common trope in Arab authoritarian regimes: Qaddafi used the same expression in his speech after the outbreak of the Libyan uprising in 2011.

16. On the connection between national identity and obedience to the rules set up by the regime, see Chapter 4.

17. Things changed once the uprising became militarized, as we will see throughout the next chapters.

18. 'Nation-wide protests did not "diffuse" as much as they occurred in parallel' (Leenders 2013: 282).

19. This chant was traditionally used to hail Hafiz al-Asad (*bi ruh, bi damm, nafdik ya Hafiz*).

20. The Arabic word *shahid*, 'martyr', is used here to refer to a person killed during the demonstrations.

21. Even if other sparks had manifested throughout February 2011. The video of the 15 March 2011 protest is available here: www.youtube.com/watch?v=kwjzm9uMpzw (last accessed 4 April 2018).

22. For example, the 'clock square' sit-in, 18 April 2011, available at www.youtube.com/watch?v=4xiidCjnb7s (last accessed 4 April 2018).

23. An idea that is constantly reiterated in *tanwir*-inspired TV drama; see Chapter 3.

24. Under what Donati 2009 calls the 'Syrian exception'; see Chapter 2.

25. Regime-backed advertising campaigns that mushroomed in the streets of Syria in the second half of March 2011 featured coloured posters stating 'no

to division', 'no to sectarianism', as a way of reminding citizens not to protest. See Chapter 4.

26. The video is available at www.youtube.com/watch?v=kuit6PegrlU (last accessed 4 April 2018).

27. In the original: 'nouvelle culture protestataire qui s'élabore aussi dans les images et les sons' (my translation).

28. I am grateful to Chadi Elias and Zaheer Omareen (2014) for directing me to Espinosa's manifesto.

29. 'Imperfect cinema is no longer interested in quality or technique. It can be created equally well with a Mitchell or with an 8mm camera, in a studio or in a guerrilla camp in the middle of the jungle. Imperfect cinema is no longer interested in predetermined taste, and much less in "good taste". It is not quality which it seeks in an artist's work' (Espinosa 1979).

30. Osama Mohammed is a prominent Syrian filmmaker, living since mid-2011 in exile in Paris. For background information on his cinema see Boëx 2014; Wedeen 1999.

31. The film premiered at Cannes Film Festival 2014.

32. Referring to the perpetrators in the Indonesian genocide.

33. Orwa al-Mokdad, personal communication, October 2012.

34. The first film of the history of cinema. During its first public screening the audience was reportedly in a state of panic because of the realism of the images.

35. On the politics of aesthetics, see Rancière 2013.

36. On the global circulation of violence, torture and the imagination of terror, see Austin 2016, 2017, forthcoming.

37. Many have reflected on this sort of 'filming one's own death' genre. See Mroué 2013; Hamadeh 2016; Snowdon 2016.

38. 'The Pixelated Revolution' (2012) is the telling title of Lebanese artist Rabih Mroué's lecture-performance on the Syrian user-generated videos.

39. 'This is perhaps why the Syrian images did not proliferate, as did those of the Egyptian revolution, for it becomes very difficult to say, "we are all Syrians," as some would say we are all Palestinians or Egyptians' (Rich 2011).

40. As an example of a fake pixelated clip, see 'Syrian Hero Boy', quoted in Tarnowski 2017. See also Chapter 5.

41. The film was scheduled to premiere at the Berlin film festival in 2016, but a few weeks before the event the director decided to cancel the public screening due to security concerns regarding one of the activists featured in the film. However, other controversies seem to have later emerged and prevented the film from being shown in public, such as questions of ownership and copyright concerning some of the activists' footage included in the documentary. The director prefers not to address the issue in public. I wish to thank Khaled for the opportunity to screen the film multiple times and discuss it with him.

42. For a problematization of the concept of empowerment behind networked technologies, see Della Ratta 2017b.

43. On this point see the debate generated by the film collective Abounaddara around creating a 'dignified image' of the Syrian people (Abounaddara 2016,

2017, 2018; Kiwan 2014; Elias 2017; Boëx 2012). Although the collective itself claims to have taken inspiration from Vertov's approach to filmmaking, their visual production presents multiple, very sophisticated layers of storytelling and filmmaking that do not entirely reflect the idea of documenting reality 'as it is'.
44. His debut feature *300 Miles* premiered at Locarno Film Festival in 2016, and won the prize as best first feature film at DocLisboa 2016.
45. 'Television, your pacifying newspapers...' (Pasolini 1975).
46. 'Until victory' (*Jusqu'à la victoire*) was the original title of the film when the shooting took place in 1970. Six years later, the film was released with the title of *Ici et ailleurs*.

7   Syria's Image-Makers: Daesh Militants and Non-Violent Activists

1. 'The Management of Savagery' is the title of a book by an alleged Daesh ideologue. It talks about the establishment of the caliphate passing through a phase of widespread chaos and terror. An English translation is available online at https://azelin.files.wordpress.com/2010/08/abu-bakr-naji-the-management-of-savagery-the-most-critical-stage-through-which-the-umma-will-pass.pdf (accessed 3 July 2018).
2. Many of its leaders, like Ghiath al-Matar, are all youths under the age of 35.
3. This is also suggested by my personal experience as co-founder of a 'hacker-space' in Damascus, which I witnessed spontaneously turning into a youth activism space after March 2011. See Chapter 5.
4. For example, in Bassel Safadi's archive (see Chapter 6).
5. This is the case with 'The Good Life' video discussed in the next sections.
6. Orwa al-Mokdad is a personal friend and was also one of the first visitors to Aikilab. See Chapter 5.
7. These thoughts are reflected in 'Little Dictator', a 2012 documentary by Annasofie Flamand and Hugh Macleod, available here: www.aljazeera.com/programmes/witness/2012/08/2012820111648774405.html (last accessed 4 April 2018).
8. Orwa al-Mokdad, personal communication, October 2017.
9. See the case of Hamza al-Khateeb, a 13-year-old boy who was mutilated and killed (Macleod and Flamand 2011), whose extremely graphic live autopsy is still available at www.youtube.com/watch?v=MOv95E_vi_U (last accessed 4 April 2018).
10. For suggestions on further reading on the role of emotions in conflict escalation see Wessels (forthcoming).
11. 'The collective's aim is not to shock international viewers into action but rather empower local, civil society to independently produce its own images about itself' (Lensculture n.d.).
12. 'The Syrian People Know Their Way' is the name of a Syrian grassroots art collective; see Halasa et al. 2014.

13. At the time of writing, both Mosul and the capital of the self-declared caliphate, Raqqa, have been officially reconquered by the US-led international anti-terror coalition.

14. The essay was first published in the *Frankfurter Zeitung*, on 28 October 1927, under the title 'Die Photographie'. It was later reprinted in Kracauer's collection of essays, *Das Ornament der Masse* (1963), which appeared in English as *The Mass Ornament* (1993).

15. The definition has been elaborated in relation to the artist's work 'Eye/Machine' (2001). Later, for 'Eye/Machine III', he changed 'operative' into 'operational images'.

16. This situation is in constant evolution at the time of writing, since the regime is slowly reconquering pieces of land, such as the area of al-Ghouta which was previously controlled by oppositional armed forces.

17. For example, of the 9,000 official images Daesh released in 2015 and 2016, less than half (48%) have a military theme, the others depicting governance, commercial, religious, lifestyle and other themes (Milton 2016, quoted by Kraidy 2018: 46).

18. The video's original title is *al-hayat al-tayyba*; it was released in February 2016 by Daesh's media branch in Aleppo. I have discussed the video in Della Ratta 2016b (Italian).

19. 'O Media Worker, You are a Mujahid' is a document released by Daesh in 2016 (second edition), quoted and translated from Arabic by Kraidy (2017).

20. On the military and administrative 'territorial methodology', see Zelin 2016.

21. Al-Tamimi (2016) has collected and translated a large number of documents that are helpful in understanding the administrative structure of the caliphate.

22. They are responsible for most of the ground-breaking, glossy-looking Daesh productions, including also terror videos. For an overall review of the Daesh media structure, see Milton 2016. For a first-hand account of the media men working for Daesh, see Miller and Mekhennet 2015.

23. As an example, 'The Good Life' is a video produced by Daesh's Aleppo province media branch.

24. The hashtag is still available on Twitter at the time of writing: https://twitter.com/hashtag/alleyesonisis (last accessed 4 April 2018). For an analysis of the campaign, see Maher and Carter 2014. On Daesh's use of Twitter, see Katz 2014a; Berger and Morgan 2015.

25. Comparing Daesh and al-Qaeda media strategies: 'which do you think is more likely to attract the attention of an 18-year-old boy dreaming of adventure and glory: a badass video with CGI flames and explosions, or a two-hour lecture on the Koran from a gray-haired old man?' (Byman and Williams 2015).

26. At the time of writing some episodes of the series are still available, among others, on several Pinterest pages, e.g. www.pinterest.com.au/pin/853361829362579835; www.pinterest.co.uk/mijetniyomdecha/mujatweets; www.pinterest.com.au/pin/853361829365558120; and on YouTube: www.youtube.com/watch?v=i2fAofF39Eg (last accessed 4 April 2018).

27. For example, Mujatweet #4 is called 'Life in Mosul prospers under DAESH' (as per Leander's transcription, however Daesh is never used in the groups' official productions, where it is always self-labelled as 'Islamic State') (Leander 2017: 10).

28. On the aesthetics of the selfie, see Peraica 2017; Wendt 2014.

29. See also Chapter 6.

30. For background information on *Dabiq* and *Rumiyah*, Daesh's online magazines, see The Carter Center 2015; Wignell et al. 2017.

31. See Kraidy 2018; see also the short video at http://jihadology.net/2017/07/28/new-video-message-from-the-islamic-state-inside-the-caliphate (last accessed 4 April 2018).

32. The video can be seen here: www.dailymail.co.uk/embed/video/1118502.html (last accessed 4 April 2018).

33. The series can be watched with English subtitles at www.youtube.com/watch?v=aRNHwyHBKno (last accessed 4 April 2018).

34. *Jellyfish* by Khaled Abdulwahed is one of these (see Chapters 4 and 8).

35. For example: *Coma* ('Coma') by Sarah Fattahi, awarded at Visions du réel, Festival of Nyon, 2015; *Manazil bila abuwab* ('Houses Without Doors') by Avo Kaprealian, awarded at Torino Film Festival 2016; *Akhar al-rijjal fi Halab* ('Last Men in Aleppo') by Feras Fayyad, nominated as best documentary at the Oscars 2018; *Ta'm al-ismint* ('Taste of Cement') by Ziad Khaltum, winner of several international awards, among which Visions du réel, Festival of Nyon, 2017.

36. Exemplary of this trend is the production company Bidayyat, led by Syrian filmmaker Ali al-Atassi.

37. As an example, see the controversies surrounding Osama Mohammed's 'Silvered Water' in Zabunyan 2014: 160–4; Abounaddara 2017.

38. In 1968, the US ecologist and philosopher Garrett Hardin (1968) coined the expression 'the tragedy of the commons', hinting at a situation in which shared natural resources that are not privately owned but remain accessible to all members of society would soon be extinguished or seriously damaged if left to be self-regulated according to the personal interests of their individual users, rather than through a careful management of the common good.

39. 'the media, same as the medical, same as the military issues … they all share the same concept of converting us into a media product that has their names on it' (*Jellyfish*, 2015).

40. See, for example, SyriaUntold, The Creative Memory of the Syrian Revolution, The Syrian Archive.

8 Notes on a Theory of Violence and the Visual in the Networked Age

1. The title of a famous 2010 book by Clay Shirky, with the telling subtitle *How Technology Makes Consumers into Collaborators*.

2. The title of a famous book by Benkler (2006) that became the bible of the sharing economies.

3. The disintegrating spectacle 'can countenance the end of everything except the end of itself' (Wark 2013: 3).

4. 'The idea of the Spectacle re-proposes a grand narrative of modernity as a loss of people's sociability' (Briziarelli and Armano 2017: 25).

5. See Baudrillard 1983: 1, translator's note.

6. 'The mass and the media are one single process. Mass(age) is the message' (Baudrillard 1983: 44).

7. I wish to thank Tiziana Terranova for allowing me to read an excerpt of her forthcoming manuscript where she focuses on developing this idea of the technosociality of the hypersocial, exploring whether it has the potential to resurrect the *social* within a kind of new sociality where a dialectic between subsumption and liberation could still be envisaged.

8. 'For it is not meaning or the increase of meaning which gives tremendous pleasure, but its neutralization' (Baudrillard 1983: 36).

9. Mitchell also talks about the sociality of the image: 'the life of images is not a private or individual matter. It is a *social* life.' 'They form a social collective' (Mitchell 2005: 93).

10. See also Dean: 'An image's circulatory capacity, its power to repeat, multiply and acquire a kind of force, has triumphed over its meaning' (2016: 4).

11. That is, 'the language of images and space' (Deleuze 1995: 12).

12. The title of the essay is 'The Exhausted' (Deleuze 1995).

13. This paragraph builds on my previous analyses of the Damascene Village in Della Ratta 2017a; Della Ratta 2015c. I have also reflected on the fate of the Damascene Village in my video ethnography *Images in Spite of All*, which can be seen here: https://vimeo.com/133892234.

14. Al-Ghouta is the same area where, in February 2018, regime-led troops began carrying out a cleansing operation of what are described as terrorist groups. Humanitarian organizations claim that the majority of the population is made up of civilians. A UN resolution has called for a ceasefire, however activists on the ground claim that the heavy bombings have not stopped. At the time of writing the fate of the people of al-Ghouta is yet to be determined.

15. I have used this snapshot in *Images in Spite of All*, at https://vimeo.com/133892234.

16. See, for example, the discussion of selfies in Dean 2016.

17. For a discussion of the role of the Palmyra prison in Syria's literature and popular culture, see cooke 2017.

18. I am grateful to David Weinberger for suggesting this.

19. 'Consumed' is the title of the latest novel by David Cronenberg, exploring the (self)consuming, cannibalistic dimension of the networks.

Bibliography

Except where otherwise noted, all online references cited were last accessed 4 April 2018.

Abounaddara (2016) 'We Are Dying', Zeit Online, www.zeit.de/politik/ausland/2016–04/syria-victims-images-personal-rights-dignity-filmmakers-abounaddara.

Abounaddara (2017) 'Dignity Has Never Been Photographed', www.documenta14.de/en/notes-and-works/15348/dignity-has-never-been-photographed.

Abounaddara (2018) 'The Revolting Animals/La révolte des animaux', www.facebook.com/notes/abounaddara-films/the-revolting-animals-de-revolterande-djuren-la-r%C3%A9volte-des-animaux/1745373475523352.

Abu-Lughod, L. (2005) *Dramas of Nationhood: The Politics of Television in Egypt.* Chicago: University of Chicago Press.

Abu-Lughod, L. (2006) *Local Contexts of Islamism in Popular Media.* Leiden: Amsterdam University Press, ISIM paper 6, www.mafhoum.com/press9/282C37.pdf.

Adida, C., Laitin, D. and Valfort. M-A. (2016) *Why Muslim Integration Fails in Christian-Heritage Societies.* Cambridge, MA: Harvard University Press.

Agence France Press (2010) 'Popular Ramadan Series Still Provokes Religious Authorities in Saudi Arabia', *The Daily Star Lebanon*, www.dailystar.com.lb/Culture/Film/2010/Aug-27/119845-popular-ramadan-series-still-provokes-religious-authorities-in-saudi-arabia.ashx.

Ain News (2010) 'Bab al-hara: zawjat al-ra'is Bashar salhat al-hardaniyyn wa-shakhsiyya kabira iqirahat nihayat dramiyya dakhma yastashhad fiha jami' al-abtal!', http://ainnews.net/17440.html.

Aksalser.com (2017) 'Akid "Bab al-hara" ya'ri al-qai'miyyin 'aleyhi', https://tinyurl.com/yaguj87p.

Alabaster, O. (2016) 'Syrian Activists Languish in Government Jails', al-Jazeera, www.aljazeera.com/indepth/features/2016/12/syrian-activists-languish-government-jails-161226134131836.html.

Albawaba (2001) 'Thuraya Signs Distribution Agreement in Syria', www.albawaba.com/business/thuraya-signs-distribution-agreement-syria.

Albawaba (2011) 'Sulaf Fawakhirji and her Husband Boycotted for Supporting Bashar al Asad', www.albawaba.com/latest-news/sulaf-fawakhirji-and-her-husband-boycotted-supporting-bashar-al-asad-380637.

Alhamwi, M. K. (2017) 'Why Syria No Longer Plays a Leading Role in Ramadan TV Dramas', Syria Deeply, www.newsdeeply.com/syria/articles/2017/07/07/why-syria-no-longer-plays-a-leading-role-in-ramadan-tv-dramas.

Ali, N. (2011) 'Syrian Forces Beat Up Political Cartoonist Ali Ferzat', *Guardian*, www.theguardian.com/world/2011/aug/25/syria-cartoonist-ali-ferzat-beaten.

Alkhalisi, Z. (2017) 'Al Jazeera Blocked by Saudi Arabia, Qatar Blames Fake News', CNN, http://money.cnn.com/2017/05/24/media/al-jazeera-blocked-saudi-arabia-uae/index.html.

Allain, J. (2017) *International Law in the Middle East: Closer to Power Than Justice*, 2nd edition. New York: Routledge.

Andén-Papadopoulos, K. (2013) 'Media Witnessing and the "Crowd-Sourced Video Revolution"', *Visual Communication*, 12(3): 341–57.

Aouragh, M. (2014) 'Online and Offline Maneuvering in Syria's Counter-Revolution', Jadaliyya, www.jadaliyya.com/Details/30870/Online-and-Offline-Maneuverings-in-Syria%60s-Counter-Revolution.

Appadurai, A. (2013) *The Future as Cultural Fact*. London: Verso.

al-Arabiya (2015) 'ISIS Uses "Nutella, Kittens" to Lure Women Recruits', http://english.alarabiya.net/en/variety/2015/02/19/ISIS-uses-Nutella-kittens-to-lure-women-recruits.html.

Armbrust, W. (1996) *Mass Culture and Modernism in Egypt*. Cambridge: Cambridge University Press.

al-Asad, B. (2011a) 'Speech at Syrian People's Assembly', Voltaire Network, www.voltairenet.org/article169245.html.

al-Asad, B. (2011b) 'Speech at Damascus University on the Situation in Syria', Voltaire Network, www.voltairenet.org/article170602.html.

al-Asad, B. (2014) 'Inaugural Speech of President al-Assad', Voltaire Network, www.voltairenet.org/article184784.html.

Atassi, B. (2011) 'A Colourful Uprising in Damascus', al-Jazeera, www.aljazeera.com/indepth/features/2011/12/20111211105436823841.html.

Atran, S. (2015) 'ISIS is a Revolution', AEON, https://aeon.co/essays/why-isis-has-the-potential-to-be-a-world-altering-revolution.

Austin, J. (2016) 'Torture and the Material-Semiotic Networks of Violence Across Borders', *International Political Sociology*, 10(1): 3–21.

Austin, J. (2017) 'We Have Never Been Civilised: Torture and the Materiality of World Political Binaries', *European Journal of International Relations*, 23(1): 49–73.

Austin, J. (forthcoming) *Small Worlds of Violence: A Global Grammar for Torture*. MS in preparation for submission to University of Minnesota Press.

Austin, J. and Bocco, R. (2017) 'Becoming a Torturer: Towards a Global Ergonomics of Care', *International Review of the Red Cross*, 98(903): 859–88.

Badran, T. (2006) 'Syrian-Saudi Media Wars', Cedars Revolution, http://www.cedarsrevolution.net/jtphp/index2.php?option=com_content&do_pdf=1&id=748.

Badt, K. (2014) 'Filming Killing: "Silvered Water, Syria Self-Portrait" by Ossama Mohammed and Wiam Simav Bedirxan', Huffington Post, www.huffingtonpost.com/karin-badt/filming-killing-silvered_b_6203380.html.

Baiazy, A. (2012) 'Syria's Cyber Operations', Jadaliyya, www.jadaliyya.com/Details/25272/Syria%60s-Cyber-Operations.

Banet-Wiser, S. and Mukherjee, R., eds. (2012) *Commodity Activism: Cultural Resistance in Neoliberal Times.* New York: New York University Press.

Bar, S. (2006) 'Bashar's Syria: The Regime and its Strategic Worldview', The Interdisciplinary Center Herzliya, Lauder School of Government, Diplomacy and Strategy, Institute for Policy and Strategy, www.herzliyaconference.org/_Uploads/2590Bashars.pdf.

Baraniuk, C. (2016) 'Citizen Journalism is Playing a Crucial Role in Aleppo – But it Comes at a Cost', Wired, www.wired.co.uk/article/syrian-citizen-journalists.

Barbrook, R. and Cameron, A. (1995) 'The Californian Ideology', *Mute*, 1(3), www.comune.torino.it/gioart/big/bigguest/riflessioni/californian_engl.pdf.

Batty, D. (2013) 'Syrian Satirists Take Puppet Show Into War-Torn Towns to Mock Bashar al-Assad', *Guardian*, www.theguardian.com/world/2013/jun/22/satirical-puppet-show-syria-bashar-al-assad.

Baudrillard, J. (1983) *In the Shadow of the Silent Majorities ... or The End of the Social and Other Essays.* New York: Semiotext(e).

Baudrillard, J. (1994) *Simulacra and Simulation.* Ann Arbor: University of Michigan Press.

Baudrillard, J. (1995) *The Gulf War Did Not Take Place.* Bloomington and Indianapolis: Indiana University Press.

BBC News (2000) 'Former Syrian PM Commits Suicide', http://news.bbc.co.uk/2/hi/middle_east/757960.stm.

BBC News (2011) 'Syria Unrest: Government Pledges Political Reforms', www.bbc.com/news/world-middle-east-12853634.

BBC News (2016) 'Russia's Valeri Gergiev Conducts Concert in Palmyra Ruins', www.bbc.com/news/world-middle-east-36211449.

BBC News (2018) 'Syria Profile – Media', www.bbc.com/news/world-middle-east-14703914.

BBC Trending (2015) 'The Photographer Who Broke the Internet's Heart', www.bbc.com/news/blogs-trending-32121732.

Beeley, V. (2016) 'White Helmets: The "Mannequin Challenge", a Publicity Stunt that Backfired? Vanessa Beeley talks to RT', 21st Century Wire, https://21stcenturywire.com/2016/11/23/white-helmets-the-mannequin-challenge-a-publicity-stunt-that-backfired-vanessa-beeley-talks-to-rt.

Bell, M. and Flock, E. (2011) '"A Gay Girl in Damascus" Comes Clean', *Washington Post*, www.washingtonpost.com/lifestyle/style/a-gay-girl-in-damascus-comes-clean/2011/06/12/AGkyH0RH_story.html?utm_term=.3ef75bbbe550.

Ben Gharbia, S. (2009) '2nd Arab Bloggers Meeting', Global Voices Advox, https://advox.globalvoices.org/2009/12/05/2nd-arab-bloggers-meeting.

Ben Gharbia, S. (2010) 'The Internet Freedom Fallacy and the Arab Digital Activism', Nawaat, https://nawaat.org/portail/2010/09/17/the-internet-freedom-fallacy-and-the-arab-digital-activism.

Benkler, Y. (2006) *The Wealth of Networks: How Social Production Transforms Markets and Freedom.* New Haven: Yale University Press.

Bensaada, A. (2015) *Arabesque$: Enquête sur le rôle des États-Unis dans les révoltes arabes.* Bruxelles: Investig'Action.

Berg, A. (2011) '9/11 Attacks Seen by First-Person Footage', The Daily Beast, www.thedailybeast.com/911-attacks-seen-by-first-person-footage-video.

Berger, J. M. (2014) 'How ISIS Games Twitter', The Atlantic, www.theatlantic.com/international/archive/2014/06/isis-iraq-twitter-social-media-strategy/372856.

Berger, J. M. and Morgan, J. (2015) 'The ISIS Twitter Census: Defining and Describing the Population of ISIS Supporters on Twitter', The Brookings Project on US Relations with the Islamic World, Analysis Paper 20, www.brookings.edu/research/the-isis-twitter-census-defining-and-describing-the-population-of-isis-supporters-on-twitter.

Bertho, A. (2016) Les Enfants du Chaos: Essai sur le Temps des Martyrs. Paris: La Découverte.

Black, I. (2009) 'The Television Soap Opera That Has the Arab World Agog', Guardian, www.guardian.co.uk/world/2009/mar/16/bab-al-hara-arab-soap-opera.

Blanford, N. (2011) 'On Facebook and Twitter, Spreading Revolution in Syria', The Christian Science Monitor, www.csmonitor.com/World/Middle-East/2011/0408/On-Facebook-and-Twitter-spreading-revolution-in-Syria.

de Blois, M-A. (2011) 'Syria: Planning Ahead', Forward Magazine, 48.

Boëx, C. (2011) 'La contestation médiatisée par le monde de l'art en contexte autoritaire. L'expérience cinématographique en Syrie au sein de l'Organisme général du cinéma 1964–2010', PhD thesis, University of Aix en Marseille III.

Boëx, C. (2012) 'Emergency Cinema: An Interview with Syrian Collective Abounaddara', www.booksandideas.net/IMG/pdf/abounaddara_en.pdf.

Boëx, C. (2013) 'La grammaire iconographique de la révolte en Syrie: Usages, techniiques et supports', Cultures & Conflicts, 91/92: 65–80, https://journals.openedition.org/conflits/18789.

Boëx, C. (2014) Cinéma et politique en Syrie. Écritures cinématographiques de la contestation en régime autoritaire (1970–2010). Paris: L'Harmattan.

Boëx, C. (2016) 'Daesh: decryptage de la progagande visuelle' [video], www.youtube.com/watch?v=4HVJJGoAlt8.

Bolter, J. D. and Grusin, R. (1999) Remediation: Understanding New Media. Cambridge, MA: MIT Press.

Booz Allen Hamilton (2007) Trends in Middle Eastern Arabic Television Series Production: Opportunities for Broadcasters and Producers. Beirut: Booz Allen Hamilton.

Borges, J.L. (1962) Ficciones. New York: Grove Press.

ten Brink, J. and Oppenheimer, J., eds. (2012) Killer Images: Documentary Film, Memory and the Performance of Violence. London and New York: Wallflower Press.

Briziarelli. M. and Armano, E., eds. (2017) The Spectacle 2.0: Reading Debord in the Context of Digital Capitalism. London: University of Westminster Press.

Brownlee, B.J. (2017) 'Media Development in Syria: The Janus-faced Nature of Foreign Aid Assistance', Third World Quarterly, 38(10): 1–19.

Buck, J.J. (2011) 'Asma al-Assad: A Rose in the Desert', Vogue, http://gawker.com/asma-al-assad-a-rose-in-the-desert-1265002284.

Burgess, J. (2008) '"All Your Chocolate Rain Are Belong to Us?" Viral Video, YouTube and the Dynamics of Participatory Culture', in G. Lovink and S. Niederer, eds., *VideoVortex Reader: Responses to YouTube*. Amsterdam: Institute of Network Cultures, pp. 101–9.

Burgess, J. and Green, J. (2009) *YouTube: Online Video and Participatory Culture*. Cambridge: Polity Press.

Burris, G. (2011) 'Lawrence of E-rabia: Facebook and the New Arab Revolt', *Jadaliyya*, www.jadaliyya.com/Details/24512/Lawrence-of-E-rabia-Facebook-and-the-New-Arab-Revolt.

Byman, D. and Williams, J. (2015) 'Al-Qaeda vs. ISIS: The Battle for the Soul of Jihad', *Newsweek*, www.newsweek.com/al-qaeda-vs-isis-battle-soul-jihad-317414.

Cadava. E. (1997) *Words of Light: Theses on the Photography of History*. Princeton: Princeton University Press.

Calamur, K. (2016) 'The New Face of the Syrian Civil War', *The Atlantic*, www.theatlantic.com/news/archive/2016/08/syria-aleppo-omran-daqneesh/496442.

Carapico, S. (2013) *Political Aid and Arab Activism: Democracy Promotion, Justice, and Representation*. Cambridge: Cambridge University Press.

The Carter Center (2015) 'Overview of Daesh's Online Recruitment Propaganda Magazine, Dabiq', www.cartercenter.org/resources/pdfs/peace/conflict_resolution/countering-isis/dabiq-report-12–17–15.pdf.

Castells, M. (1997) *The Information Age: Economy, Society and Culture, vol. II: The Power of Identity*. Oxford: Blackwell.

Cham Press (2009) 'President al-Assad Awards actress Mona Wasef Syrian Order of Merits, Stresses Drama's Role in Embracing National and Pan Arab Principles'.

Christmann, A. (1996) 'An Invented Piety: Ramadan on Syrian TV', *Diskus* 4(2), http://jbasr.com/basr/diskus/diskus1–6/CHRISTMA.txt.

Chulov, M. (2017) 'Syrian Regime Recaptures Palmyra from Islamic State', *Guardian*, www.theguardian.com/world/2017/mar/02/syrian-regime-recaptures-palmyra-from-islamic-state.

Cohen, J.A. (2009) *Diverting the Radicalization Track*. Hoover Institution, www.hoover.org/research/diverting-radicalization-track.

cooke, m. (2007) *Dissident Syria: Making Oppositional Arts Official*. Durham, NC: Duke University Press.

cooke, m. (2017) *Dancing in Damascus: Creativity, Resilience, and the Syrian Revolution*. New York and London: Routledge.

Coker, M., Scheschner, S. and Flynn, A. (2015) 'How Islamic State Teaches Tech Savvy to Evade Detection', *The Wall Street Journal*, www.wsj.com/articles/islamic-state-teaches-tech-savvy-1447720824.

Creswell, R. and Haykel, B. (2015) 'Battle Lines', *The New Yorker*, www.newyorker.com/magazine/2015/06/08/battle-lines-jihad-creswell-and-haykel.

Cronenberg, D. (2014) *Consumed*. New York: Scribner.

van Dam, N. (2011) *The Struggle for Power in Syria: Politics and Society under Asad and the Ba'ath Party*, 4th edition. London and New York: I.B. Tauris.

Daney, S. (1976) 'Theorize/Terrorize (Godardian Pedagogy)', in Wilson, D., ed. , *Cahiers du Cinema – Volume 4: 1973–1978: History, Ideology, Cultural Struggle*. New York and London: Routledge/British Film Institute.

Davis, S.C. (2007) 'Colette Khoury: Come See Syria First, Then Judge', *Forward Magazine*, https://archive.li/IFr5f.

Dawkins, R. (2006) *The Selfish Gene*, 30th anniversary edition. New York: Oxford University Press.

Dean, J. (2003) 'Why the Net is not a Public Sphere', *Constellations*, 10(1): 95–112.

Dean, J. (2005) 'Communicative Capitalism: Circulation and the Foreclosure of Politics', *Cultural Politics*, 1(1): 51–74, https://commonconf.files.wordpress.com/2010/09/proofs-of-tech-fetish.pdf.

Dean, J. (2009) *Democracy and Other Neoliberal Fantasies: Communicative Capitalism and Left Politics*. Durham, NC: Duke University Press.

Dean, J. (2010) *Blog Theory: Feedback and Capture in the Circuits of Drive*. Cambridge: Polity Press.

Dean, J. (2015) 'Affect and Drive', in Hillis, K., Paasonen, S. and Petit, M., eds., *Networked Affect*. Cambridge, MA: MIT Press, pp. 89–102.

Dean, J. (2016) 'Faces as Commons: The Secondary Visuality of Communicative Capitalism', *Open! Platform for Art, Culture & the Public Domain*, www.onlineopen.org/faces-as-commons.

De Angelis, E. (2011) 'The State of Disarray of a Networked Revolution: The Syrian Uprising's Information Environment', *Sociologica*, 3: 1–24, www.sociologica.mulino.it/journal/article/index/Article/Journal:ARTICLE:508/Item/Journal:ARTICLE:508.

De Angelis, E., Della Ratta, D. and Badran, Y. (2014) 'Against the Odds: Syria's Flourishing Mediascape', *al-Jazeera*, www.aljazeera.com/indepth/opinion/2014/0/8/against-odds-syria-flourishing--201483094530782525.html.

Dearden, L. (2017) 'Isis Carries Out Mass Executions in Palmyra's Ancient Ruins After Retaking Syrian City', *Independent*, www.independent.co.uk/news/world/middle-east/isis-palmyra-syria-executions-islamic-state-retake-city-russia-assad-ruins-roman-theatre-civilians-a7535026.html.

Debord, G. (1990) *Comments on the Society of the Spectacle*. London and New York: Verso.

Debord, G. (1994) *The Society of the Spectacle*, 3rd edition. New York: Zone Books.

Degerald, M. (2017) 'Daesh Lives on … in Trap Music?', *Medium.com*, https://medium.com/@MENAhistorian/daesh-lives-on-8d3d685cfe1c.

Deleuze, G. (1995) 'The Exhausted', *SubStance* 24(3): 3–28, http://ghostprof.org/wp-content/uploads/2015/09/Gilles-Deleuze-The-Exhausted.pdf.

DeLillo, D. (1991) *Mao II*. New York: Penguin.

Della Ratta, D. (2000) *Media Oriente: Modelli, strategie e tecnologie nelle nuove televisioni arabe*. Roma: ed. Seam.

Della Ratta, D. (2011) 'Creative Resistance Challenges Syria's Regime', *al-Jazeera*, www.aljazeera.com/indepth/opinion/2011/12/20111222162349451619.html.

Della Ratta, D. (2012a) 'Syrian TV Drama Provides Ineffective Release Valve', al-Jazeera, www.aljazeera.com/indepth/opinion/2012/08/2012823956299674 41.html.

Della Ratta, D. (2012b) 'Syria: The Virtue of Civil Disobedience', al-Jazeera, www. aljazeera.com/indepth/opinion/2012/04/20124283638298672.html.

Della Ratta, D. (2012c) 'Dramas of the Authoritarian State', Middle East Research and Information Project, www.merip.org/mero/interventions/dramas-authoritarian-state.

Della Ratta, D. (2012d) 'Irony, Satire and Humor in the Battle for Syria', Muftah, https://muftah.org/irony-satire-and-humor-in-the-battle-for-syria/#. WvAuL9VuboA.

Della Ratta, D. (2012e) 'Towards Active Citizenship in Syria', in *Culture in Defiance: Continuing Traditions of Satire, Art and the Struggle for Freedom in Syria*. Prince Claus Fund Gallery, pp. 10–12, www.slideshare.net/donadr/culture-indefiance.

Della Ratta, D. (2012f) 'Syrian Hands Raised: User-generated Creativity Between Citizenship and Dissent', Jadaliyya, www.jadaliyya.com/Details/27307/Syrian-Hands-Raised-User-Generated-Creativity-Between-Citizenship-and-Dissent.

Della Ratta, D. (2014a) 'Making Real-Time Drama: The Political Economy of Cultural Production in Syria's Uprising', The Annenberg School for Communication, Pennsylvania University, PARGC Paper II, http://media.wix.com/ugd/86a19a_7aa1c99fd6c14105a2fe1f8ofc0a8300.pdf.

Della Ratta, D. (2014b) 'ISIL and Western Media: Accidental Allies?', al-Jazeera, www.aljazeera.com/indepth/opinion/2014/09/isil-western-media-allies-201492412181732913.html.

Della Ratta, D. (2015a) 'The Whisper Strategy: How Syrian Drama Makers Shape Television Fiction in the Context of Authoritarianism and Commodification', in Salamandra, C. and Stenberg, L., eds., *Syria from Reform to Revolt, Volume II: Culture, Society, and Religion*. Syracuse: Syracuse University Press, pp. 53–76.

Della Ratta, D. (2015b) 'La Tv araba prova a fare satira sullo Stato islamico', *Internazionale*, www.internazionale.it/opinione/donatella-della-ratta/2015 /07/08/selfie-serie-tv-arabia-saudita.

Della Ratta, D. (2015c) 'Violence and Visibility in Contemporary Syria: An Ethnography of the "Expanded Places"', *CyberOrient*, 9(1), www.cyberorient. net/article.do?articleId=9557.

Della Ratta, D. (2015d) 'Gli spot del califfato formato famiglia', *Internazionale*, https://www.internazionale.it/opinione/donatella-della-ratta/2015/02/25/video-isis-propaganda.

Della Ratta, D. (2016a) 'A Meme Returns, Crying for Justice in Syria', Hyperallergic, https://hyperallergic.com/313055/a-meme-returns-crying-for-justice-in-syria.

Della Ratta, D. (2016b) 'La dolce vita ai tempi dello Stato islamico', *Internazionale*, www.internazionale.it/opinione/donatella-della-ratta/2016/02/10/stato-islamico-aleppo-video.

Della Ratta, D. (2017a) 'Expanded Places: Redefining Media and Violence in the Networked Age', *International Journal of Cultural Studies* 21(1): 1–15.

Della Ratta, D. (2017b) 'On the Narrative of the Arab D.I.Y. Revolutions and How it Fits into Our Neoliberal Times', in Bennet, P. and McDougall, J., eds., *Popular Culture and the Austerity Myth: Hard Times Today*. London: Routledge, pp. 139–55.

Della Ratta, D. (2017c) 'The Unbearable Lightness of the Image: Unfinished Thoughts on Filming in Contemporary Syria', *Middle East Journal of Culture and Communication* 10(2–3): 109–32.

Della Ratta, D. (2017d) 'Fighting ISIL Through TV Drama: The Case of Black Crows', al-Jazeera, www.aljazeera.com/indepth/features/2017/06/fighting-isil-tv-drama-case-black-crows-170611101134470.html.

Della Ratta, D. and De Angelis, E. (2014) '"Mind the Gap": Bridging Knowledge and Practices of Activism at the Fourth Arab Bloggers Meeting', Jadaliyya, www.jadaliyya.com/Details/30786/%60Mind-the-Gap-Bridging-Knowledge-and-Practices-of-Activism%60-at-the-Fourth-Arab-Bloggers-Meeting.

Della Ratta, D. and Valeriani, A. (2012) 'Remixing the Spring! Connective Leadership and Read-Write Practices in the 2011 Arab Uprisings', *CyberOrient*, 6(1), www.cyberorient.net/article.do?articleId=7763.

Della Ratta, D. and Valeriani, A. (2017) 'Just a Bunch of (Arab) Geeks? How a "Techie" Elite Shaped a Digital Culture in the Arab Region and Contributed to the Making of the Arab Uprisings', in Sabry, T. and Ftouni, L., eds., *Arab Subcultures: Transformations in Theory and Practice*. London: I.B. Tauris, pp. 62–86.

Della Ratta, D., Sakr, N. and Skovgaard-Petersen, J., eds. (2015) *Arab Media Moguls*. London: I.B. Tauris.

Dick, M. (2007) 'Syria Under the Spotlight: Television Satire that is Revolutionary in Form, Reformist in Content', *Arab Media & Society*, www.arabmediasociety.com/syria-under-the-spotlight-television-satire-that-is-revolutionary-in-form-reformist-in-content.

Dickinson, Kay (2016) *Arab Cinema Travels: Transnational Syria, Palestine, Dubai and Beyond*. London: BFI/Palgrave Macmillan.

Didi-Huberman, G. (2008) *Images in Spite of All: Four Photographs from Auschwitz*. Chicago and London: University of Chicago Press.

Donati, C. (2009) *L'exception syrienne. Entre modernisation et resistance*. Paris: La Découverte.

DP News Sana (2010a) 'President al-Asad is Satisfied with the Syrian Drama', http://dp-news.com/pages/detail.aspx?articleId=54696.

DP News Sana (2010b) 'Under the Patronage Mrs. Asma al-Assad Torch of 7th Special Olympics Was Lit', www.dp-news.com/en/detail.aspx?articleid=55606.

Drabinski, J.E. (2008) *Godard Between Identity and Difference*. New York: Continuum, eBook.

Dubai Press Club (2010) *Arab Media Outlook 2009–2013. Inspiring Local Content: Forecasts and Analysis of Traditional and Digital Media in the Arab world*, www.fas.org/irp/eprint/arabmedia.pdf.

Elali, N. (2011) 'The Syrian Revolution in Sketches', Now Lebanon, www.nowlebanon.com/Arabic/NewsArchiveDetails.aspx?ID=292824.

El Deeb, S. (2017) 'History of Syria's War at Risk as YouTube Reins in Content', APNews, https://apnews.com/d9f1c4f1bf20445ab06cbdff566a2b70.

ElGohary, M. (2010) 'Syria: Tal al-Molouhi, a 19-year-old Female Blogger in Jail for Almost a Year', Global Voices Advox, https://advox.globalvoices. org/2010/09/15/syria-tal-al-molouhi-19-year-old-blogger-in-jail.

Elias, C. (2017) 'Emergency Cinema and the Dignified image: Cell Phone Activism and Filmmaking in Syria', *Film Quarterly*, 71(1), https://filmquarterly. org/2017/09/14/emergency-cinema-and-the-dignified-image-cell-phone-activism-and-filmmaking-in-syria.

Elias, C. and Omareen, Z. (2014) 'Syria's Imperfect Cinema', in Halasa, M., Omareen, Z. and Mafhoud, N., eds., *Syria Speaks: Art and Culture from the Frontline.* London: Saqi Books, pp. 257–68.

Ellis, C. (2004) *The Ethnographic I: A Methodological Novel About Autoethnography.* Walnut Creek: AltaMira Press.

Enab Baladi (2016) 'Syrian Drama ... Tashbih (Acts of pro-Assad), Looseness and Velvet Societies', http://english.enabbaladi.net/archives/2016/06/syrian-drama-tashbih-acts-pro-assad-looseness-velvet-societies.

Enab Baladi (2017) '"Abu Jawdat" is Lost Between the Artists Syndicate and the Position of Police Chief', http://english.enabbaladi.net/archives/2017/06/abu-jawdat-lost-artists-syndicate-position-police-chief.

Engel, P. (2015) '"It's Similar to North Korea": Inside ISIS' Sophisticated Strategy to Brainwash People in the "Caliphate"', Business Insider, www.businessinsider. com/isis-propaganda-strategy-2015–11?IR=T.

Esber, O. (2014) 'The Whisper Strategy (Drama and Power Relations in Syria): An Interview with Donatella Della Ratta', Jadaliyya, www.jadaliyya.com/ Details/30064/The-Whisper-Strategy-Drama-and-Power-Relations-in-Syria-An-Interview-with-Donatella-Della-Ratta.

Espinosa, J.G. (1979) 'For an Imperfect Cinema', *JumpCut*, 20: 24–6, www. ejumpcut.org/archive/onlinessays/JC20folder/ImperfectCinema.html.

Etling, B., Kelly, J., Faris, R. and Pulfrey, J. (2010) 'Mapping the Arabic Blogosphere: Politics and Dissent Online', *New Media & Society*, 12(8): 1225–43.

Faek, R. (2012) 'Pushed Offstage. Syrian Drama Production is Suffering from the Country's Growing Uprising', *Syria Today*, August.

Farocki, H. (2004) 'Phantom Images', *Public* 29, pp. 12–22, https://public.journals. yorku.ca/index.php/public/article/view/30354/27882.

Farwell, J.P. (2014) 'The Media Strategy of ISIS', *Survival* 56(6): 49–55.

Fattah, H.M. (2005) 'Kurds, Emboldened by Lebanon, Rise up in Tense Syria', *New York Times*, www.nytimes.com/2005/07/02/world/middleeast/kurds-emboldened-by-lebanon-rise-up-in-tense-syria.html.

Flanagan, B. (2010) 'Strong Advertising Forecast for Ramadan Programmes', *The National*, http://news-feed.artificial-flowers.com.au/article/30b17f04-b0bf-4ecb-9f40–300a48167481.html (last accessed April 2013).

Forward Magazine (2008) 'Muthanna Subh: My Dream Was to Become Martyr or Director', October.

Foucault, M. (1977) 'The Confession of the Flesh', in Gordon, C., ed., *Power/Knowledge: Selected Interviews and Other Writings 1972–1977*. New York: Pantheon Books, pp. 194–228.

Friedman, U. (2011) 'How Syrian Activists Name Their Friday Protests', *The Atlantic*, www.theatlantic.com/international/archive/2011/09/how-syrian-activists-name-their-friday-protests/337848.

Frisk, A. (2016) 'This Iconic Photo of Syrian Boy Pulled from Rubble in Aleppo is Fake, According to President Bashar Assad', Global News, https://globalnews.ca/news/3015545/this-iconic-photo-of-syrian-boy-pulled-from-rubble-in-aleppo-is-fake-according-to-president-bashar-assad.

Frosh, P. (2009) 'Telling Presences', in Frosh, P. and Pinchevsky, A., eds., *Media Witnessing: Testimony in the Age of Mass Communication*. London: Palgrave Macmillan, pp. 49–72.

George, A. (2003) *Syria: Neither Bread nor Freedom*. New York: Palgrave.

Georgi, D. (2016) 'War Porn and Barrel Bombs: Inside Assad's Propaganda Offensive', *Vanity Fair*, www.vanityfair.com/news/2016/02/syria-assad-anti-isis-film.

al-Ghazzi, O. (2014) '"Citizen Journalism" in the Syrian uprising: Problematizing Western Narratives in a Local Context', *Communication Theory*, 24(4): 435–54.

Ghonim, W. (2012) *Revolution 2.0: The Power of the People is Greater Than the People in Power: A Memoir*. Boston: Houghton Mifflin Harcourt.

Giroux, H.A. (2002) 'Rethinking Cultural Politics and Radical Pedagogy in the Work of Antonio Gramsci', in Borg, C., Buttigieg, J. and Mayo, P., eds., *Gramsci and Education*. Lanham: Rowman & Littlefield Publishers, pp. 41–66.

Gordon, A. (2017) 'Blood, Dust and Tears Wiped Away, New Pictures Show the Bloodied Little Boy Who Became a Symbol of Aleppo's Struggle After his House was Bombed', *Daily Mail*, www.dailymail.co.uk/news/article-4574234/Little-boy-symbol-Aleppo-s-struggle.html.

Goriunova, O. (2013) 'The Force of Digital Aesthetics: On Memes, Hacking, and Individuation', *Zeitschrift für Medienwissenschaft*, 8: 70–87.

Guilhot, N. (2005) *The Democracy Makers: Human Rights and the Politics of Global Order*. New York: Columbia University Press.

Gulf News (2010) 'Poems Come Alive: Ruler's Poetry is Subject of TV Series', www.pressreader.com/uae/gulf-news/20100315/284601713811351.

Haddad, B. (1999) 'Change and Stasis in Syria: One Step Forward', Middle East Research and Information Project, 213, www.merip.org/mer/mer213/change-stasis-syria-0.

Haddad, B. (2012) 'The Syrian Regime's Business Backbone', Middle East Research and Information Project, 262, www.merip.org/mer/mer262/syrian-regimes-business-backbone.

Habermas, J. (1989) *The Structural Transformation of the Public Sphere: An Inquiry into a Category of Bourgeois Society*. Cambridge, MA: MIT Press.

Habermas, J. (1996) *Citizenship and National Identity*. Cambridge, MA: MIT Press.

Halabi, Alaa (2011) 'Al-tilfiziun al-suri yuwaqif 'ard musalsal "Fawq al-saqf" alladhi yatahaddath 'an "al-ahdath" fi-Suriya', Aksalser.com, www.aksalser.

com/?page=view_news&id=23de57e4c35b3f297a6061e201d268a2
&ar=99211197#.

Halasa, M., Omareen, Z. and Mafhoud, N., eds. (2014) *Syria Speaks: Art and Culture from the Frontline*. London: Saqi Books.

Hall, J. (2015) '"They Have Learned Our Secrets": CNN Ridiculed After Ludicrous Claim that ISIS is Luring Women with Kittens and Nutella', *Daily Mail*, www.dailymail.co.uk/news/article-2961578/ISIS-supporters-Twitter-mock-claim-luring-women-Nutella-kittens.html.

Hamadeh, D. (2016) 'Syrians Revolting Against Immortality: The Politics of Filming One's Own Death', MA dissertation, University of Amsterdam.

Hamid, S. (2016) *Islamic Exceptionalism: How the Struggle Over Islam is Reshaping the World*. London: St. Martin's Press.

Hardin, G. (1968) 'The Tragedy of the Commons', *Science*, 162(3859): 1243–8.

Harding, L. (2012) 'Syria's Video Activists Give Revolution the Upper Hand in Media War', *Guardian*, www.theguardian.com/world/2012/aug/01/syria-video-activists-media-war.

Harkin, J., Anderson, K., Morgan, L. and Smith, B. (2012) 'Deciphering User-generated Content in Transitional societies: A Syria coverage Case Study', Internews Center for Innovation and Learning, www.internews.org/sites/default/files/resources/InternewsWPSyria_2012–06-web.pdf.

Hatahet, L. (2011) 'Syrian TV Dramas: Demonising GCC Bucks', *Variety Arabia*, 18 July.

Hegghammer T., ed (2017) *Jihadi Culture: The Art and Social Practice of Militant Islamists*. Cambridge: Cambridge University Press.

Heydemann, S. (1993) 'Taxation Without Representation: Authoritarianism and Economic Liberalization in Syria', in Goldberg E., Kasaba, R. and Migdal, J. S., eds., *Rules and Rights in the Middle East: Democracy, Law and Society*. Seattle: University of Washington Press.

Heydemann, S. (2007) *Upgrading Authoritarianism in the Arab World*. Washington DC: Saban Center for Middle East Policy at the Brookings Institution, www.brookings.edu/wp-content/uploads/2016/06/10arabworld.pdf.

Human Rights Watch (2009) 'Syria: No Exceptions for "Honor Killings"', www.hrw.org/print/news/2009/07/28/syria-no-exceptions-honor-killings.

Huntington, H.H. (2013) 'Subversive Memes: Internet Memes as a Form of Visual Rhetoric', *Selected Papers of Internet Research*, 3, https://spir.aoir.org/index.php/spir/article/view/785.

Hutcherson, K. (2015) 'ISIS Video Shows Execution of 25 Men in Ruins of Syria Amphitheater', CNN, https://edition.cnn.com/2015/07/04/middleeast/isis-execution-palmyra-syria/index.html.

IFAD (2011) 'Syrian Arab Republic', www.ifad.org/documents/10180/7c26bd8a-48b6-4beb-a78b-6f4760883bdc.

Ignatieff, D. (2004) 'The Terrorist as Auteur', *New York Times*, www.nytimes.com/2004/11/14/movies/the-terrorist-as-auteur.html.

Issa, A. (2016) 'Syria's New Media Landscape: Independent Media Born Out of War', Middle East Institute Policy Papers, www.mei.edu/sites/default/files/publications/PP9_Issa_Syrianmedia_web_0.pdf.

al-Jazeera (2011a) 'Assad Orders New Syrian Amnesty', www.aljazeera.com/news/middleeast/2011/06/2011621944198405.html.

al-Jazeera (2011b) 'Q&A: Syrian Activist Suhair Atassi', www.aljazeera.com/indepth/2011/02/201129135657367367.html.

Jenkins, H. (1991) *Textual Poachers: Television Fans and Participatory Culture*. London and New York: Routledge.

Jenkins, H. (2006a) *Convergence Culture: Where Old and New Media Collide*. New York: New York University Press.

Jenkins, H. (2006b) *Fans, Bloggers and Gamers: Exploring Participatory Culture*. New York: New York University Press.

Jenkins, H. (2009) 'If it Doesn't Spread, it's Dead (Part One): Media Viruses and Memes', Confessions of an Aca-fan (blog), http://henryjenkins.org/blog/2009/02/if_it_doesnt_spread_its_dead_p.html.

Jenkins, H., Ford, S. and Green, J. (2013) *Spreadable Media: Creating Value and Meaning in a Networked Culture*. New York: New York University Press.

Jihadology (2015) 'New Video Message from the Islamic State: "Media Man You Are a Mujahid Too – *Wilayat Salah al-Din*"', http://jihadology.net/2015/05/27/new-video-message-from-the-islamic-state-media-man-you-are-a-mujahid-too-wilayat-%E1%B9%A3ala%E1%B8%A5-al-din.

Joubin, R. (2013) *The Politics of Love: Sexuality, Gender, and Marriage in Syrian Television Drama*. Lanham: Lexington Press.

Joyce, M., ed. (2010) *Digital Activism Decoded: The New Mechanics of Change*. New York and Amsterdam: International Debate Education Association, http://sec.cs.ucl.ac.uk/users/smurdoch/papers/digiact1oall.pdf.

Jünger, E. and Nassar, A. (1993) 'War and Photography', *New German Critique*, 59: 24–6.

Kanaan, W. (2011) 'Actor Jamal Suleiman Will Not Return to Syria', Al Akhbar English, http://english.al-akhbar.com/node/1200.

Kandil, A. (2010) 'A Critical Review of the Literature About the Arab Civil Society', Paper presented at the Regional Conference on Research on Civil Society Organisations, Foundation for the Future.

Katz, A. (2016) '"This is a Forged Picture": Bashar Assad Disputes "Boy in the Ambulance" Account', *Time*, http://time.com/4538448/omran-daqneesh-bashar-assad-syria-aleppo.

Katz, R. (2014a) 'Follow ISIS on Twitter: A Special Report on the Use of Social Media by Jihadists', Insite Blog on Terrorism & Extremism, http://news.siteintelgroup.com/blog/index.php/categories/jihad/entry/192-follow-isis-on-twitter-a-special-report-on-the-use-of-social-media-by-jihadists.

Katz, R. (2014b) 'The State Department's Twitter War with ISIS is Embarrassing', *Time*, http://time.com/3387065/isis-twitter-war-state-department.

Kawakibi, S. (1997) 'Le role de la télévision dans la relecture de l'histoire', *Monde arabe Maghreb Machrek*, 158.

Kawakibi, S. (2003) 'Les usages politiques de la fiction télévisuelle: l'expérience syrienne', in Mermier, F., ed., *Mondialisation et nouveaux médias dans l'espace arabe*. Paris: Maisonneuve et Larose.

Keenan, T. (2012) 'Publicity and Indifference: Media, Surveillance, and "Humanitarian Intervention"', in ten Brink, J. and Oppenheimer, J., eds., *Killer Images: Documentary Film, Memory and the Performance of Violence*. London and New York: Wallflower Press, pp. 15–40.

Kepel, G. (2015) *Terreur dans l'Hexagone. Genèse du Djihad français*. Paris: Gallimard.

Khatib, L. (2012) *Image Politics in the Middle East: The Role of the Visual in Political Struggle*. London: I.B. Tauris.

Khito, H. (2014) 'Sallum Haddad...'awda al-ibn al-dal', *Al Araby*, https://tinyurl.com/ybmavek7.

Khoury, D. (2013) 'Losing the Syrian Grassroots: Local Governance Structures Urgently Need Support', German Institute for International and Security Affairs, SWP Comments 9, p. 8, www.swp-berlin.org/fileadmin/contents/products/comments/2013C09_kou.pdf.

Khoury, N. (1996) 'La politique antiterroriste de l'État égyptien à la télévision en 1994', *Revue Tiers-Monde*, 37(146).

Kiwan, C. (2014) 'Cellphone War Reporting Dumbs Down the Truth', *Newsweek*, www.newsweek.com/cellphone-war-reporting-dumbs-down-truth-289763.

Knobel, M. and Lankshear, C. (2007) 'Online Memes, Affinities and Cultural Production', in Knobel, M. and Lankshear, C., eds., *A New Literacies Sampler*. New York: Peter Lang, pp. 199–227.

Kovacs, A. (2015) 'The "New Jihadists" and the Visual Turn from al-Qa'ida to ISIL/ISIS/Da'ish', *Biztpol Affairs*, 2(3): 47–70, http://epa.oszk.hu/02400/02475/00004/pdf/EPA02475_BiztpolAffairs_2014_03.pdf.

Kracauer, S. (2005) *The Mass Ornament: Weimar Essays*. Cambridge, MA: Harvard University Press.

Kraidy, M. (2016) *The Naked Blogger of Cairo*. Cambridge, MA: Harvard University Press.

Kraidy, M. (2017) 'The Projectilic Image: Islamic State's Digital Visual Warfare and Global Networked Affect', *Media, Culture & Society*, 39(8): 1194–209.

Kraidy, M. (2018) 'Fun Against Fear in the Caliphate: Islamic State's Spectacle and Counter-spectacle', *Critical Studies in Media Communication*, 35(1): 40–56.

Kraidy, M. and Khalil, J. (2009) *Arab Television Industries*. London: Palgrave Macmillan.

Kuipers, G. (2005) '"Where Was King Kong When We Needed Him?" Public Discourse, Digital Disaster Jokes, and the Functions of Laughter After 9/11', *The Journal of American Culture* 28(1): 70–84.

Kuntsman, A. and Stein, R. (2011) 'Digital Suspicion, Politics, and the Middle East', *Critical Inquiry*, http://criticalinquiry.uchicago.edu/digital_suspicion_politics_and_the_middle_east.

Kuntsman, A. and Stein, R. (2015) *Digital Militarism: Israel's Occupation in the Social Media Age*. Stanford: Stanford University Press.

Kusa, M. (2008) 'Al-adabiyya Kulit Khury: musalsal "Bab al-hara" jamil..lakinnahu laysa Dimashq'. Syria News, www.syria-news.com/var/articlem.php?id=3060

Lacan, J. (1977) *Écrits: A Selection*, trans. Alan Sheridan. New York: W.W. Norton & Co.

Lacan, J. (1981) *The Four Fundamental Concepts of Psychoanalysis*, trans. Alan Sheridan. New York: W.W. Norton & Co.

Landis, J. (2006) 'Syrian Corruption Hits Prime Time', Syria Comment, www.joshualandis.com/blog/syrian-corruption-hits-prime-time.

Landis, J. (2011a) 'Assad Speech II (16 April 2011)', Syria Comment, www.joshualandis.com/blog/assad-speech-ii-16-april-2011.

Landis, J. (2011b) 'Free Syrian Army Founded by Seven Officers to Fight the Syrian Army', Syria Comment, www.joshualandis.com/blog/free-syrian-army-established-to-fight-the-syrian-army.

Leander, A. (2017) 'Digital/Commercial (In)visibility: The Politics of DAESH Recruitment Videos', *European Journal of Social Theory*, 20(3): 348–72.

Leenders, R. (2013) 'Social Movement Theory and the Onset of the Popular Uprising in Syria', *Arab Studies Quarterly*, 35(3): 273–89.

LensCulture (n.d.) 'Abounaddara: The Lives That Remain in Syria', www.lensculture.com/articles/abounaddara-collective-abounaddara-the-lives-that-remain-in-syria.

Lessig, L. (1999) *Reclaiming a Commons*. Cambridge, MA: The Berkman Center's 'Building a Digital Commons', https://dlc.dlib.indiana.edu/dlc/bitstream/handle/10535/8047/Reclaiming%20a%20Commons.pdf?sequence=1&is Allowed=y.

Lessig, L. (2001) *The Future of Ideas: The Fate of the Commons in a Connected World*. New York: Random House.

Lessig, L. (2008) *Remix: Making Art and Commerce Thrive in the Hybrid Economy*. London and New York: Bloomsbury.

Listening Post (2012) (TV programme) al-Jazeera English, www.aljazeera.com/programmes/listeningpost/2012/05/2012525141859285303.html.

Lovink, G. (2009) *Dynamics of Critical Internet Culture (1994–2001)*. Amsterdam: Theory on Demand, Institute of Network Cultures, http://networkcultures.org/_uploads/tod/TOD1_dynamicsofcriticalinternetculture.pdf.

Lovink, G. (2016) *Social Media Abyss: Critical Internet Cultures and the Force of Negation*. Cambridge: Polity Press.

Lynch, M., Freelon, D. and Aday, S. (2014) *Syria's Socially Mediated Civil War*. Washington DC: United States Institute of Peace, www.usip.org/sites/default/files/PW91-Syrias%20Socially%20Mediated%20Civil%20War.pdf.

Ma'an News Agency (2009) 'Syrian Soap Superstars Enter Gaza', www.maannews.com/Content.aspx?id=241764.

McKernan, B. (2017) 'Aleppo's "Boy in the Ambulance", Omran Daqneesh, Safe and Well in Newly Emerged Footage', *Independent*, www.independent.co.uk/news/world/middle-east/aleppo-omran-daqneesh-new-photos-syria-syrian-civil-war-white-helmets-bashar-al-assad-a7776026.html.

McKirdy, E. and Dewan, A. (2016) 'Reports: ISIS Retakes Ancient City of Palmyra', CNN, https://edition.cnn.com/2016/12/12/middleeast/palmyra-syria-isis-russia/index.html.

Macleod, H. (2011) 'Syria's Young Cyber Activists Keep Protests in View', *Guardian*, www.theguardian.com/world/2011/apr/15/syria-activists-protests-in-view.

Macleod, H. and Flamand, A. (2011) 'Tortured and Killed: Hamza al-Khateeb, Age 13', al-Jazeera, www.aljazeera.com/indepth/features/2011/05/201153185 927813389.html.

Maher, S. and Carter, J. (2014) 'Analyzing the ISIS "Twitter Storm"', War on the Rocks, https://warontherocks.com/2014/06/analyzing-the-isis-twitter-storm.

Mansour, M. (2008)). 'Ru'ya ikhrajiyya li-l-Muthanna Subh ... "Laysa saraban" ... drama a'n "nahnu wa hum"', *Baladna*, 27 September.

al-Marashi, I. (2011) 'The Strange Logic Behind Syria's Culture of Conspiracy', *The National*, www.pressreader.com/uae/the-national-news/20110421/ 282325381527020.

Marks, L. (2015) *Hanan al-Cinema: Affections for the Moving Image*. Cambridge, MA: MIT Press.

Marsh, K. (2011) 'Syria: Four Killed in Deraa as Protests Spread Across South', *Guardian*, www.theguardian.com/world/2011/mar/22/syrian-protests-troops-kill-deraa.

Merkley, R., Maher, K. and Surman, M. (2017) 'Honoring Our Friend Bassel: Announcing the Bassel Khartabil Free Culture Fellowship', Creative Commons, https://creativecommons.org/2017/08/11/bassel-free-culture-fellowship.

Miller, G. and Higman, S. (2015) 'In a Propaganda War Against ISIS, the U.S. Tried to Play by the Enemy's Rules', *Washington Post*, www.washingtonpost.com/ world/national-security/in-a-propaganda-war-us-tried-to-play-by-the-enemys-rules/2015/05/08/6eb6b732-e52f-11e4–81ea-0649268f729e_story. html?utm_term=.ea71cac48fbc.

Miller, G. and Mekhennet, S. (2015) 'Inside the Surreal World of the Islamic State's Propaganda Machine', *Washington Post*, www.washingtonpost.com/world/ national-security/inside-the-islamic-states-propaganda-machine/ 2015/11/20/051e997a-8ce6–11e5-acff-673ae92ddd2b_story.html?utm_ term=.6d0f157014f9.

Milton, D. (2016) *Communication Breakdown: Unraveling the Islamic State's Media Efforts*. Combating Terrorism Center at West Point, https://ctc.usma.edu/app/ uploads/2016/10/ISMedia_Online.pdf.

Mirzoeff, N. (2006) 'Invisible Empire: Visual Culture, Embodied Spectacle, and Abu Ghraib', *Radical History Review*, 95: 21–44.

Mirzoeff, N. (2009) *An Introduction to Visual Culture*, 2nd edition. New York: Routledge.

Mitchell, W.J.T. (2005) *What Do Pictures Want? The Lives and Loves of Images*. Chicago: University of Chicago Press.

Mitchell, W.J.T. (2011) *Cloning Terror: The War of Images, 9/11 to the Present*. Chicago: University of Chicago Press.

al-Mokdad, O. (2017a) 'Bassel Safadi: Killed for Being Two Steps Ahead of the Regime', SyriaUntold, www.syriauntold.com/en/2017/08/bassel-safadi-killed-for-being-two-steps-ahead-of-the-regime.

al-Mokdad, O. (2017b) 'Cinema of Death', Bidayyat, http://bidayyat.org/opinions_ article.php?id=161#.WskBTNVuboA.

Molloy, M. (2016) 'What is the Mannequin Challenge? The Best Videos So Far', *Telegraph*, www.telegraph.co.uk/news/2016/11/05/what-is-the-mannequin-challenge-bizarre-freezing-craze-among-tee.

Morozov, E. (2010) 'The 20th Century Roots of 21st Century Statecraft', *Foreign Policy*, http://foreignpolicy.com/2010/09/07/the-20th-century-roots-of-21st-century-statecraft.

Morrey D. (2005) *Jean-Luc Godard.* Manchester and New York: Manchester University Press.

Moubayed, S. (2011) 'What Will Post-Arab Spring Intellectuals Write About?', Huffington Post, www.huffingtonpost.com/sami-moubayed/what-will-postarab-spring_b_1136621.html.

Moulthrop, S. (2003) '"You Say You Want a Revolution?" Hypertext and the Laws of Media', in Wardrip-Fruin, N. and Montfort, N., eds., *The New Media Reader.* Cambridge, MA: MIT Press, pp. 203–9.

Mroue, B. (2013) 'Syrian War Takes Center Stage on Ramadan TV Series', US News, www.usnews.com/news/world/articles/2013/07/30/syrian-war-takes-center-stage-on-ramadan-tv-series.

Muhanna, N. (2011) 'Behind the Scenes', Syria Today, July.

Naji, A. (2006) *The Management of Savagery: The Most Critical Stage Through Which the Umma Will Pass,* translated by the John M. Olin Institute for Strategic Studies at Harvard University, https://azelin.files.wordpress.com/2010/08/abu-bakr-naji-the-management-of-savagery-the-most-critical-stage-through-which-the-umma-will-pass.pdf.

Nammari, D. (2007) 'Syrian Soap Opera Captivates Arab World', Associated Press, http://web.archive.org/web/20071014045706/http://ap.google.com/article/ALeqM5ipIxVFfDlTQeNIr6tYENcdLWoCKAD8S7J3OGo.

Napoleoni, L. (2015) *L'État islamique: multinationale de la violence.* Paris: Calmann-Lévy.

New York Times (2009) 'Obama's Speech in Cairo', www.nytimes.com/2009/06/04/us/politics/04obama.text.html.

Omareen, Z. (2014) 'A Bedtime Story for Eid', Words without Borders, www.wordswithoutborders.org/article/a-bedtime-story-for-eid.

Omari, M. (2017) 'Syria's Citizen Journalists on the Frontline of Press Freedom', The New Arab, www.alaraby.co.uk/english/comment/2017/5/3/syrias-citizen-journalists-on-the-frontline-of-press-freedom.

Omer, M. (2008) '"Bab al Harra", Gaza's Ramadan Addiction', Washington Report on Middle East Affairs, www.wrmea.org/component/content/article/269/5237-bab-al-harra-gazas-ramadan-addiction.html.

al-Omran, A. (2011) 'Basil Al-Sayed, Who Chronicled the Syrian Uprising, Is Dead', NPR, www.npr.org/sections/thetwo-way/2011/12/29/144448779/basil-al-sayed-who-chronicled-the-syrian-uprising-is-dead.

O'Reilly, T. (2005) *What is Web 2.0: Design Patterns and Business Models for the Next Generation of Software.* O'Reilly Media, www.oreilly.com/pub/a/web2/archive/what-is-web-20.html.

Oweis, K. (2007) 'Syria Blocks Facebook in Internet Crackdown', Reuters, www.reuters.com/article/us-syria-facebook/syria-blocks-facebook-in-internet-crackdown-idUSOWE37285020071123.

Pasolini, P.P. (1975) 'We Are All in Danger: Pier Paolo Pasolini Interviewed by Furio Colombo', http://irenebrination.typepad.com/files/pierpaolopasolini_furiocolombointerview_1975_byabattista.pdf.

Peraica, A. (2017) *Culture of the Selfie: Self-representation in Contemporary Visual Culture*. Amsterdam: Institute of Network Cultures, http://networkcultures.org/wp-content/uploads/2017/05/CultureOfTheSelfie.pdf.

Perthes, V. (1991) 'The Bourgeoisie and the Baath: A Look at Syria's Upper Class', Middle East Research and Information Project, 170, www.merip.org/mer/mer170/bourgeoisie-baath.

Perthes, V. (1992) 'The Syrian Private Industrial and Commercial Sectors and the State', *International Journal of Middle East Studies*, 24(2): 207–30.

Perthes, V. (2004) *Syria Under Bashar al-Asad: Modernization and the Limits of Change*. Oxford: Oxford University Press.

Platt, E. (2014) 'Citizen Journalists Playing a Crucial Role in Syrian War', *Time*, http://time.com/3481790/syria-journalism-kobani.

Power, B. (2016) *ISIS: The Virtual Caliphate. The Behind the Scenes Bloody Propaganda Strategy*. Washington DC: CreateSpace.

Preston, J. (2011) 'Syria Restores Access to Facebook and YouTube', *New York Times*, www.nytimes.com/2011/02/10/world/middleeast/10syria.html.

Qiblawi, T. (2017) 'Missing Syrian Internet Activist Bassel Khartabil Executed in 2015, Wife Says', CNN, https://edition.cnn.com/2017/08/02/middleeast/syrian-internet-activist-executed/index.html.

Rabil, R. (2003) *Embattled Neighbors: Syria, Israel, and Lebanon*. Boulder: Lynne Rienner Publishers.

Rabil, R. (2015) 'Syria's Changing Strategic Landscape', *The National Interest*, http://nationalinterest.org/feature/syrias-changing-strategic-landscape-12807.

Rampen, J. (2016) 'This Sick Selfie Shows Exactly How Twisted the Syrian Conflict Has Become' *Mirror*, www.mirror.co.uk/news/world-news/sick-selfie-shows-exactly-how-7851113.

Rancière, J. (2009) *The Emancipated Spectator*. London and New York: Verso.

Rancière, J. (2013) *The Politics of Aesthetics*. London: Bloomsbury.

Reporters Without Borders (2012) 'Syrian Citizen Journalists and Activists Capture 2012 Netizen Prize', https://rsf.org/en/news/syrian-citizen-journalists-and-activists-capture-2012-netizen-prize.

Rheingold, H. (2000) *The Virtual Community: Homesteading on the Electronic Frontier*. Cambridge, MA: MIT Press.

Rheingold, H. (2002) *Smart Mobs: The Next Social Revolution*. Cambridge, MA: Perseus Books.

Rich, J. (2011) 'The Blood of the Victim: Revolution in Syria and the Birth of the Image-event', e-flux, 26, www.e-flux.com/journal/26/67963/the-blood-of-the-victim-revolution-in-syria-and-the-birth-of-the-image-event.

Roberts, S. (2017) 'Fadwa Suleiman, Actress and Voice of Syrian Opposition in Exile, Dies at 47', *New York Times*, www.nytimes.com/2017/08/17/world/

middleeast/fadwa-suleiman-actress-and-voice-of-syrian-opposition-dies-at-47.html?mtrref=www.google.it.

Roque, R. (2011) 'What is Civic Media', MIT Center for Civic Media, https://civic.mit.edu/blog/ricarose/what-is-civic-media.

Roy, O. (2017) 'Who Are the New Jihadis?' *Guardian*, www.theguardian.com/news/2017/apr/13/who-are-the-new-jihadis.

RT.com (2015) 'CNN Insists ISIS Lures Women ... with Nutella & Kittens. For Real', www.rt.com/usa/233567-cnn-isis-kittens-nutella.

RT.com (2016) 'Syrian Parliament Elects 1st Female Speaker', www.rt.com/news/345576-female-parliament-speaker-syria.

Rudner, M. (2016) '"Electronic Jihad": The Internet as al-Qaeda's Catalyst for Global Terror', in Aly, A., Macdonald, S., Jarvis, L. and Chen, T., eds., *Violent Extremism Online: New Perspectives on Terrorism and the Internet*. Abingdon: Routledge, pp. 8–24.

Said, E. (1978) *Orientalism*. London: Routledge & Kegan Paul Ltd.

Said, J. (2002) *Non-Violence: The Basis of Settling Disputes in Islam*. Damascus and Beirut: Dar al-Fikr.

Said, J. (2017) *Vie Islamiche alla Non-Violenza*, edited by Naser Dumairieh. Marzabotto: Zikkaron.

al-Saied N. (2015) 'Walid al-Ibrahim: Modernising Mogul of MBC', in Della Ratta, D., Sakr, N. and Skovgaard-Petersen, J., eds., *Arab Media Moguls*. London: I.B. Tauris, pp. 97–112.

Sakr, N. (2001) *Satellite Realms. Transnational Television*. London: I.B. Tauris.

Sakr, N. (2007) *Arab Television Today*. London: I.B. Tauris.

Salamandra, C. (2004) *A New Old Damascus: Authenticity and Distinction in Urban Syria*. Bloomington: Indiana University Press.

Salamandra, C. (2010) 'Dramatizing Damascus: The Cultural Politics of Arab Television Production in the Satellite Era', http://islam.ku.dk/lectures/Salamandra140410.pdf.

Salamandra, C. (2011a) 'Arab Television Drama Production in the Satellite Era', in Rios, D.I. and Castaneda, M., eds., *Soap Operas and Telenovelas in the Digital Age: Global Industries and New Audiences*. New York: Peter Lang Publishing, pp. 275–90.

Salamandra, C. (2011b) 'Spotlight on the Bashar al-Asad era: The Television Drama Outpouring', *Middle East Critique*, 20(2): 157–67.

Salamandra, C. (2012) 'Prelude to an Uprising: Syrian Fictional Television and Socio-political Critique', Jadaliyya, www.jadaliyya.com/pages/index/5578/prelude-to-an-uprising_syrian-fictional-television.

Salamandra, C. (2016) 'Ambivalent Islam: Religion in Syrian Television Drama', in van Nieuwkerk, K., Levine, M. and Stokes, M., eds., *Islam and Popular Culture*. Austin: University of Texas Press, pp. 224–41.

Salti, R. (2006) 'Critical Nationals: The Paradoxes of Syrian Cinema', *Kosmorama*, 237, Copenhagen: The Danish Film Institute.

Sana (Syrian Arab News Agency) (2011) 'Al-ra'is al-Asad li-l-fannaniyyn ... 'aks al-waqa' kama huwa fi-l-a'mal al fanniyya li-l-musa'ada fi-hall al-mushkilat wa ihtiram jami'al-ard' taht saqf al-watan wa mustaqbalihi', 15 May.

Sana (Syrian Arab News Agency) (2016) 'President al-Assad to SRF1 TV Channel: Fighting Terrorists is the Way to Protect Civilians in Aleppo', http://sana.sy/en/?p=91031.

Sanchez, R. (2017) 'New Photos Emerge of Omran Daqneesh, the Boy Who Became a Symbol of Aleppo's Suffering', *Telegraph*, www.telegraph.co.uk/news/2017/06/05/new-photos-emerge-omran-daqneesh-boy-became-symbol-aleppos-suffering.

Sands, P. (2011) 'Syrian Soap Operas Sidelined by Protests and Censorship', *The National*, www.thenational.ae/news/world/middle-east/syrian-soap-operas-sidelined-by-protests-and-censorship.

Sauter, M. (2014) *The Coming Swarm: Ddos Actions, Hactivism, and Civil Disobedience on the Internet*. New York and London: Bloomsbury.

Schäfer, M. (2011) *Bastard Culture! How User Participation Transforms Cultural Production*. Amsterdam: Amsterdam University Press.

Schmidt, E. and Cohen, J. (2010) 'The Digital Disruption: Connectivity and the Diffusion of Power', *Foreign Affairs*, www.foreignaffairs.com/articles/2010-10-16/digital-disruption.

Semati, M. and Szpunar, P. (2018) 'Introduction: ISIS Beyond the Spectacle. Communication Media, Networked Publics, Terrorism', *Critical Studies in Media Communication*, 35(1): 1–7.

Shadid, A. (2011) 'Exiles Shaping World's Image of Syria Revolt', *New York Times*, www.nytimes.com/2011/04/24/world/middleeast/24beirut.html?pagewanted=all.

Al-Shami, L. and Yassin-Kassab, R. (2016) *Burning Country: Syrians in Revolution and War*. London: Pluto Press.

Shifman, L. (2014) *Memes in Digital Culture*. Cambridge, MA: MIT Press.

Shirky, C. (2010) *Cognitive Surplus: How Technology Makes Consumers into Collaborators*. New York: Penguin.

Shoaibi, I. (2007) *Min dawla- al-ikrah ila-al-dimuqratiyya*, Damascus: Kan'aan lil-dirasat wal-nashr.

Silver, S. (2010) 'State Department's Cohen on Technology and Freedom', *Dealerscope*, www.dealerscope.com/article/state-departments-cohen-technology-freedom-25006357.

Sinjab, L. (2007) 'Honour Crime Fear of Syria Women', BBC News, http://news.bbc.co.uk/go/pr/fr/-/2/hi/middle_east/7042249.stm.

Sinjab, L. (2013) 'Syria Conflict: From Peaceful Protest to Civil War', BBC News, www.bbc.com/news/world-middle-east-21797661.

de Sola Pool, I. (1983) *Technologies of Freedom: On Free Speech in an Electronic Age*. Cambridge, MA: Harvard University Press.

Solon, O. (2017) 'How Syria's White Helmets Became Victims of an Online Propaganda Machine', *Guardian*, www.theguardian.com/world/2017/dec/18/syria-white-helmets-conspiracy-theories?CMP=share_btn_tw.

Sontag, S. (1977) *On Photography*. New York: Farrar, Straus and Giroux.

Snowdon, P. (2016) 'The Revolution Will be Uploaded: Vernacular Video and Documentary Film Practice After the Arab Spring', PhD thesis, University of Hasselt.

Srnicek, N. (2017) *Platform Capitalism*. Cambridge: Polity Press.

Stanley, B. (2007) 'Crafting the Arab Media for Peace-Building: Donors, Dialogue and Disasters', in Sakr, N., ed., *Arab Media and Political Renewal: Community, Legitimacy and Public Life*. London: I.B. Tauris, pp. 118–34.

Stern, J. and Berger, J. M. (2015) *ISIS: The State of Terror*. New York: Harper Collins.

Steyerl, H. (2009) 'In Defense of the Poor Image', e-flux Journal, 10, www.e-flux. com/journal/10/61362/in-defense-of-the-poor-image.

Syria News (2011) 'Nida' min-muthaqqafiyyn wa fannaniyyn suriyyn ila al-hukuma li-dakhal musa'adat insaniyya ila Dara'a', www.syria-news.com/ readnews.php?sy_seq=132186.

Syriatel (2016) 'Decaying and Vanishing', www.syriatel.sy/m/press/decaying-and-vanishing.

SyriaUntold (2013) 'Syrian Youth Believed in Freedom and Took the World by Force', www.syriauntold.com/en/2013/07/syrian-youth-believed-in-freedom-and-took-the-world-by-force.

al-Tamimi, A. (2016) 'Archive of Islamic State Administrative Documents', www. aymennjawad.org/2016/01/archive-of-islamic-state-administrative-documents-1.

Tarnowski, S. (2017) 'What Have We Been Watching? What Have We Been Watching?', Bidayyat, http://bidayyat.org/opinions_article.php?id=167#. Wsj3udVub0A.

Treske, A. (2015) *Video Theory: Online Video Aesthetics or the Afterlife of Video*. Bielefeld: Transcript.

VvAa (2015) 'Cost of Freedom', http://costoffreedom.cc/presskit.

Wall Street Journal (2011) 'Interview with Syrian President Bashar al-Assad', www. wsj.com/articles/SB10001424052748703833204576114712441122894.

Wark, M. (2013) *The Spectacle of Disintegration: Situationist Passages Out of the Twentieth Century*. London and New York: Verso.

Warner, M. (2002) *Publics and Counterpublics*. New York: Zone Books.

Washington Post (2011) 'Syria's Ramadan Massacre', www.washingtonpost.com/ opinions/syrias-ramadan-massacre/2011/08/01/gIQAZHCKoI_story.html? utm_term=.fed297bfa4f1.

Wedeen, L. (1999) *Ambiguities of Domination: Politics, Rhetoric, and Symbols in Contemporary Syria*. Chicago: University of Chicago Press.

Wedeen, L. (2008) *Peripheral Visions: Publics, Power, and Performance in Yemen*. Chicago: University of Chicago Press.

Wedeen, L. (2013) 'Ideology and Humor in Dark Times: Notes from Syria', *Critical Inquiry*, 39(4): 841–73.

Wedeen, L. (2019) *Authoritarian Apprehensions: Ideology, Judgment, and Mourning in Syria*. Chicago: University of Chicago Press.

Wendt, B. (2014) *The Allure of the Selfie: Instagram and the New Self-Portrait*. Amsterdam: Institute of Network Cultures, http://networkcultures.org/ wp-content/uploads/2014/10/The_Allure_ot_Selfie_los.pdf.

Wessels, J. (2016) 'The Use of YouTube Videos Documenting Human Rights Atrocities in Syria for Future War Crime Tribunals', Paper presented at Third Workshop on Virtual Zones of Peace & Conflict, Lund, Sweden, 3–4 March.

Wessels, J. (2017) 'Video Activists from Aleppo and Raqqa as "Modern-day Kinoks"? An Audiovisual Narrative of the Syrian Revolution', *Middle East Journal of Culture and Communication*, 10(2–3): 159–74.

Wessels, J. (forthcoming) 'Syria: The Role of Grassroots Videos in Conflict Escalation', in Waever, O. and Bramsen, I., eds., *New Theories and Approaches in Peace & Conflict*. London: Routledge.

Wignell, P., Tan, S., O'Halloran, K. and Lange, R. (2017) 'A Mixed Methods Empirical Examination of Changes in Emphasis and Style in the Extremist Magazines *Dabiq* and *Rumiyah*', *Perspectives on Terrorism*, 11(2): 1–20.

Williams, L. (2011) 'Syria Clamps Down on Dissent with Beatings and Arrests', *Guardian*, www.theguardian.com/world/2011/feb/24/syria-crackdown-protest-arrests-beatings.

Wind, E. (2012) 'Dark Humor Facebook Pages of the Syrian Opposition', Jadaliyya, www.jadaliyya.com/pages/index/6950/dark-humor-facebook-pages-of-the-syrian-opposition.

Winter, C. (2017) *Media Jihad: The Islamic State's Doctrine for Information Warfare.* The International Center for the Study of Radicalisation and Political Violence, http://icsr.info/wp-content/uploads/2017/02/Media-jihad_web.pdf.

Worrall, P. (2016) 'Eva Bartlett's Claims About Syrian Children', Channel 4 News, www.channel4.com/news/factcheck/factcheck-eva-bartletts-claims-about-syrian-children.

Yasuda, S. (n.d.) *The Role of Syrian Tourism in Bashar al-Asad's First Decade* (unpublished MS).

Zabunyan, D. (2014) 'Arrêtez le spectacle!', Art Press, www.artpress.com/2014/12/21/arretez-le-spectacle%E2%80%89dork-zabunyan.

Zamanalwsl.net (2011) 'Musallahuna yuhajimuna Sallum Haddad wa yua'tiduna 'alayhi bi-l-darb li-intiqadi al-mukhabarati', www.zamanalwsl.net/news/19855.html.

al-Zawahiri, A. (2005) 'Letter to al-Zarqawi', https://fas.org/irp/news/2005/10/letter_in_english.pdf.

Zelin, A. (2016) 'The Islamic State's Territorial Methodology', The Washington Institute, www.washingtoninstitute.org/uploads/Documents/pubs/ResearchNote29-Zelin.pdf.

Zimmer, C. (2015) *Surveillance Cinema*. New York: New York University Press.

Ziter, E. (2015) *Political Performance in Syria: From the Six-Days War to the Syrian Uprising*. New York: Palgrave Macmillan.

Selected filmography

300 Miles (2016). Film. Syria/Lebanon: Orwa al-Mokdad.

Akhar al-rijal fi Halab ('Last Men in Aleppo', 2016). Film. Syria/Denmark: Feras Fayyad.

al 'Arrab ('The Godfather', 2014–15). TV series. Syria: Hatem Ali.

Bab al-hara ('The Gate of the Neighbourhood', 2006–17). TV series. Syria: Bassam and Mou'min al-Malla.

Buq'at al-daw ('Spotlight', 2001–17). TV series. Syria: various authors.

Chiffon ('Chiffon', 2011). TV series. Syria: Najdat Anzour.

Coma ('Coma', 2015). Film. Syria/Lebanon: Sarah Fattahi.

Faniyya wa tatabadad ('Decaying and vanishing', 2015). Film. Syria: Najdat Anzour.

Fawq al-Saqf ('Above the Ceiling', 2011). TV series. Syria: Samer Baraqawi.

Ghadan Naltaqi ('We Will Meet Tomorrow', 2015). TV series. Syria: Rami Hanna.

Gharabeeb al-sud (Black Crows, 2017). TV series. United Arab Emirates: various authors.

Ghazlan fi Ghabat al-Dha'ab ('Gazelles in a Forest of Wolves', 2006). TV series. Syria: Rasha Shurbatji.

Hawamish ('Margins'), sketch from *Buq'at al-daw* ('Spotlight') 2003 season. TV series. Syria: various authors.

al-Hayat al-tayiba ('The Good Life', 2016). Propaganda video. Daesh.

al-Hurr al-'ayn ('The Beautiful Maidens', 2005). TV series. Syria/United Arab Emirates: Najdat Anzour.

Ici et ailleurs ('Here and Elsewhere', 1976). Film. France: Jean-Luc Godard with Anne-Marie Miéville and Jean-Pierre Gorin.

Id Wahda ('One Hand'), sketch from *Buq'at al-daw* ('Spotlight') 2012 season. TV series. Syria: various authors.

Jellyfish (2015). Film. Syria: Khaled Abdulwahed.

La Dolce Siria (2015). Film. Egypt/United Arab Emirates: Ammar al-Beik.

La'nat al-thin ('The Curse of the Mud', 2010). TV series. Syria: Ahmad Ibrahim.

Laysa Saraban ('It's Not a Mirage', 2008). TV series. Syria: Muthanna Subh.

Ma'a al-fidda ('Silvered Water: Syria's Self-Portrait', 2014). Film. France/Syria: Osama Mohammed and Wiam Simav Bedirxan.

Ma malakat aymanukum ('Those Whom Your Right Hand Possesses', 2010). TV series. Syria: Najdat Anzour.

Manazil bila abuwab ('Houses Without Doors', 2016). Film. Syria/Lebanon: Avo Kaprealian.

al-Mariqun ('The Renegades', 2006). TV series. Syria/Lebanon: Najdat Anzour.

Nawafidh al-ruh ('The Windows of the Soul', 2014). Film. Syria: Ammar Alani and Laith Hajjo.

Nihayat rajul shuja' ('The End of a Brave Man', 1993). TV series. Syria: Najdat Anzour.

'The Pixelated Revolution' (2012). Lecture-performance. Lebanon: Rabih Mroué.

al-Raqib al-khalid ('The Immortal Sergeant', 2014). Film. Syria/Lebanon: Ziad Khaltum.

Saqf al-'alam ('The Roof of the World', 2007). TV series. Syria: Najdat Anzour.

al-Sirr ('The Secret'), sketch from *Buq'at al-daw* ('Spotlight') 2007 season. TV series. Syria: various authors.

Sullam ila Dimashq ('Ladder to Damascus', 2013). Film. Qatar/Lebanon/Syria: Mohammad Malas.

Ta'm al-ismint ('Taste of Cement', 2017). Film. Germany/Lebanon/Syria/United Arab Emirates/Qatar: Ziad Kalthoum.

Top Goon. Diaries of a Little Dictator (2011–12). Web-series. Syria/Lebanon: Masasit Mati collective.

Wara' al-Shams ('Behind the Sun', 2010). TV series. Syria: Samir Hassan.

Wilada min al-khasira ('Birth from the Waist', 2011–13). TV series. Syria: Rasha Shurbatji (seasons 1 and 2), Seif Sbei (season 3).

Index

The Pluto Press Newsletter

Hello friend of Pluto!

Want to stay on top of the best radical books
we publish?

Then sign up to be the first to hear about our
new books, as well as special events,
podcasts and videos.

You'll also get 50% off your first order with us
when you sign up.

Come and join us!

Go to bit.ly/PlutoNewsletter